Praise for

Every Heart Restored

"Fred and Brenda Stoeker deal with the sensitive subject of how couples cope in the wake of sexual sin with wisdom and compassion. Their message offers hope to struggling husbands and wives who desire to rebuild their relationships and have Christ-centered marriages free from sexual impurity."

—JILL PHILLIPS, singer-songwriter and recording artist

"The Every Man series has shed light into the hearts of men and on the temptation and trappings of sexual sin. Now *Every Heart Restored* gives women compassionate spiritual insight into the often misunderstood, confusing, and heart-wrenching area of sexual sin."

—DR. GARY AND BARBARA ROSBERG, America's Family Coaches
and authors of *Divorce-Proof Your Marriage*

"Finally, hope has arrived! On behalf of the hundreds of thousands of women whose dreams and hearts are shattered, I say 'Thank you!' The authors of *Every Heart Restored* give women the permission and the authority to confront and put an end to enabling their husband's inappropriate sexual behavior…and tell us that with hard work, accountability, and a constant guarding of the eyes and mind, a man can retrain his brain and keep lust out of one's being and marriage."

—MARSHA MEANS, counselor and author of *Living with Your
Husband's Secret Wars*

"From the very beginning in the garden to the very consummation of all things, it has always been about two with one heart. *Every Heart Restored* is destined to bring deep and intimate healing to the union of hurting husbands and wives desperate to move from the wounds back to the wonder."

—LISA BEVERE, author of *Kissed the Girls and Made Them Cry*

every heart restored

Stephen Arterburn
Fred & Brenda Stoeker with Mike Yorkey

every heart restored

A Wife's Guide to Healing in the Wake of a Husband's Sexual Sin

WATERBROOK
PRESS

EVERY HEART RESTORED
PUBLISHED BY WATERBROOK PRESS
2375 Telstar Drive, Suite 160
Colorado Springs, Colorado 80920
A division of Random House, Inc.

All Scripture quotations, unless otherwise indicated, are taken from the *Holy Bible, New International Version*®. NIV®. Copyright © 1973, 1978, 1984 by International Bible Society. Used by permission of Zondervan Publishing House. All rights reserved. Scripture quotations marked (AMP) are taken from *The Amplified® Bible.* Copyright © 1954, 1958, 1962, 1964, 1965, 1987 by The Lockman Foundation. All rights reserved. Used by permission. (www.Lockman.org). Scripture quotations marked (KJV) are taken from the *King James Version.* Scripture quotations marked (MSG) are taken from *The Message.* Copyright © 1993, 1994, 1995, 1996, 2000, 2001, 2002. Used by permission of NavPress Publishing Group. Scripture quotations marked (NLT) are taken from the *Holy Bible, New Living Translation,* copyright © 1996. Used by permission of Tyndale House Publishers, Inc., Wheaton, Illinois 60189. All rights reserved. Italics in Scripture quotations reflect the authors' added emphasis.

Details in some anecdotes and stories have been changed to protect the identities of the persons involved.

Grateful acknowledgment is made for the use of the "His/Her Realities" chart in chapter 18, taken from Ted Roberts, *Pure Desire: Helping People Break Free from Sexual Struggles,* page 255, © 1999 Gospel Light/Regal Books, Ventura, California, 93003. Used by permission.

ISBN 1-57856-784-X

Copyright © 2004 Stephen Arterburn, Brenda Stoeker, Fred Stoeker, and Mike Yorkey

Workbook materials and questions compiled by Elsa Kok.

Published in association with the literary agency of Alive Communications, Inc., 7680 Goddard Street, Suite 200, Colorado Springs, CO 80920.

Library of Congress Cataloging-in-Publication Data

Arterburn, Stephen, 1953–
     Every heart restored : a wife's guide to healing in the wake of a husband's sexual sin / Stephen Arterburn and Fred and Brenda Stoeker ; with Mike Yorkey.— 1st ed.
          p. cm.
     ISBN 1-57856-784-X
     1. Wives—Religious life.   2. Husbands—Sexual behavior.   3. Sex addiction—Religious aspects—Christianity.   I. Stoeker, Brenda.   II. Stoeker, Fred.   III. Title.
     BV4527.A75 2004
     248.8'435—dc22
     2004012536

Printed in the United States of America
2004

10 9 8 7 6 5 4 3 2

To my heavenly Father:
You do things simply because I ask. Amazing.

To Brenda:
How precious you are to Him!

contents

Foreword by Steve Arterburn xi

Acknowledgments. xv

Introduction by Brenda Stoeker 1

Part I In the Wake of Betrayal 7
  1 Brenda's Story. 9
  2 Valerie's Story. 14
  3 Crushed and Angry. 21
  4 What Loss?. 29
  5 All About Those Differences 37

Part II The Hardwired Differences of Male Sexuality. 47
  6 The Eyes Have It 49
  7 Sex—His Language of Intimacy 62
  8 How Does He Feel When You Say No? 70
  9 Chilling Sex 76
  10 Mary's Story. 83

Part III The Softwired Differences in Male Sexuality 93
  11 The Church Has Let Us Down 95
  12 Male Wounds. 104
  13 Self-Inflicted Wounds 114
  14 What Now? 124

Part IV A Rebuilder's Reflection 135

  15 Under-the-Radar Mission 137

  16 Helpmate 147

  17 Dressings and Iron 156

Part V What's Normal? 163

  18 Your Lagging Heart 165

  19 A Merle Hay Road Moment 175

  20 Moving Even Closer 187

  21 The Long and Winding Road 201

  22 Lagging Sexuality 210

  23 Normal Sexuality 222

  24 What If Change Never Comes? 234

  25 Our Parting Thoughts 251

I am so glad you found this book. It could change your life and your love forever.

If you are a woman in a relationship with a man who is struggling with sexual sin, this book can help you in ways you never imagined. You will be amazed that there are so many other women who share your experience. These women have been through that same dreadful period of sensing something in a relationship was not right, and at the same time being unable to identify exactly what was wrong or who was at fault. They have felt the same searing anger that arose when you realized you were being betrayed. They have experienced the same feelings of inadequacy and the false belief that, *If I had just been more of a woman, he would have remained faithful and pure.* They have been blamed for his problems and carried the weight of his shame.

If you have been through what these women have been through, this book will help you see yourself, your circumstances, and your husband's problem in a different light.

Every Heart Restored will guide you from dark despair to new hope, from resentful bitterness to emotional freedom, from protective detachment to the possibility of a deep connection with your husband. The transition and transformation won't be instant, nor will they be easy. Restoration is going to take some hard work on your part, at a time when you may feel you have worked hard enough and are ready to give up. But if you follow the path laid out here by Fred and Brenda Stoeker, your heart can be restored—even if your husband is unwilling to make changes. You will be able to live in freedom even if he chooses to remain in bondage to sexual sin.

Not every relationship can be salvaged, and perhaps restoration and freedom seem impossible to you now. But there is hope. God can use this book as a tool to restore your heart.

If you have felt lost and confused through this journey with your husband and his battle with sexual sin, you are not alone. A friend of mine has an extremely bright little boy named Carter. At the age of four, he and his mother were in a discussion about why Jesus came to die on a cross for us. Carter, recalling Christ's last words, "Father, forgive them, for they do not know what they are doing" (Luke 23:34), very confidently told his mom that Jesus died because, "We don't know what we are doing down here." I don't think it has ever been said better. *We don't know what we are doing down here.* And when it comes to sex, that could not be more true.

Part of the problem for men can be traced back to 1953 when Hugh Hefner began saturating the world with his philosophy, which was articulated in his *Playboy* magazine. Hefner talked about a new view of sex without any boundaries or shame attached. He told us men that if we used the pornography he wanted to sell to us, it would make us more sophisticated, more sexual, and much better lovers. Millions of men bought into that philosophy and made Heffner (and other pornographers like him) rich.

The problem was that Hugh Hefner lied. Then later, with the establishment and accessibility of the Internet, we have seen the true result of pornography: It has not made men more sexually capable and competent; it has made them impotent. Pornography has objectified women and turned the hearts of men away from them. All over the world men have failed to perform sexually unless they are stimulated with pornography. And beautiful women have been destroyed when a man has to pull out a *Playboy* or turn on a video and look at it while he has sex with his wife.

Not only has pornography caused men to be weak sexual partners, it has disconnected them from those they love. This disconnection is often the first step toward a painful divorce and the end of what God intended to be great.

We simply don't know what we are doing down here.

But now, men are starting to wake up to the *Playboy*-porn lie and get their acts together, resulting in hope for marriage and hope for discouraged and persevering wives. There is a counter sexual revolution going on, and men are turning away from their sexual sins and back to their wives for all their sexual gratification. Men are aware that their decision to do so does not heal the hurt and resentments that have built up over the years. And that is where this book comes in.

For some time now my team and I have been conducting seminars for men struggling with sexual integrity. (You can find out more about The Every Man's Battle Workshop at NewLife.com.) The results of those seminars have been amazing. Lives have been changed, marriages saved, and hearts restored. Men from all walks of life—pastors, truck drivers, entertainers, single fathers, old and young—have straggled into the sessions, burdened with the guilt and shame of their past misdeeds. They have often come kicking and screaming, not wanting to be there, not wanting to pay for the workshop, and not wanting to change. But even though they have shown up under the worst of circumstances and the weakest of motivations, miraculously we have seen dramatic transformation, repentance, and healing. The last day of each workshop is filled with open confession and relentless tears as men turn from God-defying pasts to become God's men.

As these transformed men have returned home to bruised women like you, we have realized the possibility of a relational disaster—the reunion is usually fraught with difficulties even though he has obtained help for his wandering eyes and heart. He has returned intent on giving his wife full attention and wanting a deeper connection. He has now committed to receive all of his sexual gratification from her. But just when he is wanting her the most, his wife often is starting to resent him the most—as the full reality of his problem becomes evident to her. He wants to confess past sins that are not quickly or easily forgiven. So at the height of her anger, he wants to be with her in a new way and experience intimacy that perhaps the couple has never known before. He wants her to trust him, while her stagnant heart wonders if he can ever be trusted and if she can ever fully love him again. The aftermath of sexual sin is a tough place for both husband and wife.

There is yet another element of despair for many women whose husbands have been involved in sexual sin. After reading *Every Man's Battle* or attending the workshop, his transformation begins and is often noticeable to others. People start to admire him for the changes he has made and the new way of living he has so bravely embraced. Ironically, the husband who betrayed his wife becomes a moral hero and is often sought out for counsel. For years she struggled, persevered, and served through his sin. But now, within weeks, all of that appears forgotten as he becomes the man of the hour. Her frustration with this new role can lead to her abandonment of the relationship at a time when it has the greatest opportunity to thrive.

If you have experienced any of these emotional and spiritual dilemmas, I know your pain is real and deep. Now here is a resource for you or any woman who has sacrificed for a man who has been sexually unfaithful. Whether it was Internet porn, compulsive masturbation, or an actual physical affair, this book will help you understand him. It will help you understand why he did what he did and show you that you were not responsible for it, even though he might have tried to convince you otherwise.

In no way do you have ultimate responsibility for what he did to you and your marriage. But no one is perfect—especially in difficult circumstances such as those you have been through. The tough reality is that you might have contributed to problems in your marriage (not caused them, but made some contribution to them). For numerous reasons, you might not have been available to him in the ways he thought you should be. You might have withheld sex from him altogether. While that did not help the situation, it did not force him to be unfaithful. That was his choice. Now, both of you have choices, and *Every Heart Restored* will help you make the best ones with the greatest likelihood for success.

I close this foreword with the words of Jesus. In John 5 we find the story of Jesus at the pool of Bethesda with a man who had been seeking healing there for thirty-eight years. Jesus asked the man a simple question that all of us must answer as well: "Do you want to get well?" (verse 6). Healing is a choice, a choice we hope you make as you read this wonderful book.

acknowledgments

(from Fred and Brenda)

Thanks to Stephen Arterburn. When you heard of God's vision for these six books, you stepped in to give that vision legs. We're forever grateful, Steve.

Thanks to Mike Yorkey. Like the Scarecrow in the *Wizard of Oz,* you were the first to join us on this winding road, and you were our defender every step of the way. What a friend you are and what a Christian!

Thanks to Bruce Nygren, who is peerless. What grace under fire! Thanks to Steve Cobb, Don Pape, and the whole WaterBrook team…you've blessed our hearts countless times with your ministry-first vision, and we respect you all immensely. We're proud to stand with you.

Thanks to Patrick Middleton, our friend. God has given you insights, Patrick, and they will be treasured by every reader.

Thanks to the many women whose stories anonymously grace these pages. While we've changed the names, God has known you from the foundation of the world and has felt the scars rippling across your souls. You are ever and only beautiful in His eyes.

Thanks to Vicky Cluney and to Pastor Ray and Joyce Henderson, who have prayed and believed. You are great friends and warriors in the truest sense of the word. Thanks to Pastors Rodger Sieh and Joel Budd, who stood as our covering while we wrote. And thanks again to the wonderful intercessors at New Life. You have prayed in tears for the women who will read this book, and you've put the Enemy to flight. God knows that we could never have written any of these books without you, and He will reward you as only the Ancient of Days can.

Thanks to Brenda's mom, Gwen, her brothers, Brent and Barry, and our sister-in-law Camilla, for their wonderful support and friendship. And special thanks to our ever-faithful children: Jasen, Laura, Rebecca, and Michael. Look what God has done in the lives of an average couple, and see what He has created out of nothing through these no-name hands in the middle of nowhere. Never doubt the breadth and scope of the plans He has for you. He can do anything—you've seen it with your own eyes. Seek His face and find His heart that He might do anything in your lives!

And one thanks just from Fred:

Above all, thanks and hugs and kisses to Brenda, the proud owner of my favorite smile. Where would I be without you? I'm frightened to think on that. You have enlightened me, touched me, and captured my heart. My love, my best friend, and now my coauthor. Who would've thought it? Even the suggestion was enough to make me chuckle and to make you run for the hills. But we did it as we've always done everything—together. I love serving at your side, and may it always be so.

I'll never forget the time I received my first shocking taste of male sexuality.

It began the day Fred Stoeker's forceful father, anxious to get "Freddie" settled into marriage and more focused in his budding sales career, set up a blind date between his son and me.

"It'll be a quick lunch at Jumer's after church gets out so that you and Fred can get to know each other," Fred's dad promised.

Those words made my heart leap. *Could this be God's hand at work?* I wondered. I'd not met this Fred Stoeker, and except for a quick glimpse at an old high-school graduation picture a family friend had shown me, I knew nothing about him. Still, something inside whispered that he was "the one" I'd been waiting for.

When I first laid eyes on Fred at church that Sunday, my heart leaped again. *He's a lot better looking in person.* Then, when he stood up to greet me, I squealed inside: *He's taller than I am!* Okay, call me shallow, but I'd always prayed for someone taller than I. This was a *great* sign.

When we arrived at Jumer's, I was thrilled by Fred's gentlemanly manners as he held doors and chairs out for me. He really seemed to value who I was. He was fun and interesting to talk to, and it wasn't long before he felt relaxed enough to tease me. Of course, in my nervousness I made it easy for him, repeatedly knocking croutons and lettuce leaves out of my salad and onto the table.

After lunch we headed to his dad's house. As his father and stepmother settled into the family room to watch a ball game, Fred and I slipped out to the kitchen to talk. I was glad he had already begun to impress me, because it softened the shock of his stories about his former girlfriends. I was learning quickly that Fred was a very open person. In fact, he mentioned that one of the old girlfriends was flying in from California the next week. He assured me he was not looking forward to seeing her, because now that he was a Christian, he wasn't sure how to respond to her.

While that first afternoon he didn't share any intimate details about his previous loves, it seemed disturbingly inappropriate to share so openly about his past relationships on a first date. Such peculiar behavior didn't exactly inspire hope in me.

But that was nothing compared to the revolting letter I received two weeks later. There Fred outlined all the girls he'd ever had *and* what he'd done with them sexually. Maybe Fred wanted to get something off his chest, but I was flabbergasted and horrified. I exclaimed inside, *What woman wants to hear all this?* I didn't, and I was astounded that Fred was so peculiar and weird.

Fred probably thought that I wanted to know all about his life so we could get to know each other quickly. Maybe in some bizarre way he even thought I would be attracted by his exploits. All I know is that this was another eye-opening glimpse of how differently males view their sexuality and their relationships.

Looking back now, I'm amazed that we progressed anywhere as a couple. I still can't imagine why I didn't shut things down with Fred the day I read that shocking letter (and when he got to know me better, Fred couldn't believe it either). I imagine that either God kept me from flipping out, or that I was naive enough to believe that all of Fred's sexual issues were ancient history now that he was a Christian and none could affect our future. I'd bet on naive!

As the years passed, I learned more lessons on male sexuality. Sex seemed to live in a totally separate spot in Fred's life, unfazed by anything else. I learned that men want sex even if they're sick. Or even if they've just had knee surgery. Or even if they've just had the biggest, blackest knockdown fight with a wife. Making love seemed almost disconnected from relational intimacy.

Yet I eventually learned that sex was *the* crucial avenue by which Fred expressed and received intimacy with me. In fact, I learned that sex was vastly more important to men in building marital oneness and intimacy than it was for women.

What does this mean to us women? Male sexuality can be downright befuddling, and the concept of "becoming one" sexually can often seem patently absurd. But true, beautiful oneness is possible. Fred has helped me immeasurably to understand male sexuality, and that is why I'm excited that he'll handle that portion of the book. Male sexuality is something you need to understand, especially if you've been hurt by your husband's sexual sin. (For the sake of simplicity, Fred and I will be writing this book as if all readers are married. If you are single, please read the book with the knowledge that you could one day be married or remarried.)

Why is in-depth knowledge of a man's sexuality so important? It's because we have learned from our own experience—and through the stories of hundreds of others—that rebuilding love and sexual intimacy together can't happen without that foundation of understanding.

You will come to understand—as I have—that your husband's sexual sin has far less to do with you or your relationship than you could possibly imagine. As startling as it may seem, he truly can be in love with you and still be stuck in uncontrolled sexual sin.

You may be thinking, *But he's betrayed me!*

Yes, he has. But that betrayal, as ugly as it is, does not have the same meaning regarding his love for you as it might from the perspective of female sexuality.

Does it make a man's sin any less wrong? Heavens no! The sexual sin must stop because it crushes us. It crushes our prayer lives together as couples. It weakens the spiritual protection our husbands are called to provide for our homes through their spiritual leadership.

But at the same time, if we are to really understand what this sexual sin means for our marriages, it's vital that we understand the roots of such sin in the male psyche and from the perspective of male sexuality. When we know more about those key areas, then we can begin to align our emotions with the truth underlying the sin, helping God to build or restore the relationship He desires—the one we've always dreamed of.

But even if I understand him better, how can I ever forgive him?

That's the key question, isn't it? I write with no illusions, because I understand that forgiving a deep sexual betrayal comes with great difficulty—especially when you aren't sure what repentance ought to look like and there is no guarantee that your husband won't commit the same sins again. He's been lying and hiding. How can you be sure this nightmare is over?

Unforgiveness is a huge issue, and you'll have to face it head on. I've had to do that with several issues in my marriage. Facing the flaws in our husbands (and our-selves) is never easy work. Offering a man forgiveness for sexual betrayal may be the most gut-wrenching process of all. But what I am so thrilled to tell you is that there is hope. Although life has presented you with a real challenge, don't be dis-couraged. God is on your side, and He will see you through. Hearts can be restored.

I can assure you that in this book you will find a rough blueprint for rebuild-ing any marriage that lies in shambles. Fred reduced our marriage to rubble by his harsh temper, and the principles I learned from rebuilding our broken marriage will be very useful in your rebuilding efforts. There *is* life on the other side.

And as for a blueprint for rebuilding *your* wavering marriage, I've witnessed my husband's true and lasting repentance from sexual sin, so I can explain what it looks like. I know what you can and can't expect from your husband in the short term and the long term. I've seen a rebirth of normal sexuality grow out of the cor-ruption of sexual sin. I'm very eager to share all of this with you.

My husband has been awesome in his battle, and I've longed to be as awesome as his helper and cobuilder. We've both found that holiness is the answer to this whole mess—his holiness as well as mine. Jesus said that "the truth will set you free" (John 8:32), but those words alone hold no magic. Obviously, the truth can set you free only if you choose to walk in it. Fred and I will lay out the truth as God has revealed it to us. Our hope is that you will choose to walk in God's truth and that you'll find the same loving freedom in your marriage that we enjoy today.

WHAT LIES AHEAD

The road map for this book is pretty simple. We'll start with where you are and how you feel today, and then we'll have Fred explain male sexuality in greater detail. From there, we'll move on to your role in rebuilding your marriage.

But while our road map is simple, your rebuilding efforts may not be. The rea-son is plain: the beauty of your marriage is not entirely up to you. Your husband's responses will play a role too.

In light of that, we'll endeavor to address all three of a man's common responses to God's call to purity. For instance, your husband may be a true zealot for purity, growing so quickly in his intimacy with God that it looks like he may leave you in the dust. On the other hand, he may be dawdling between right and wrong—and has been for years. Or he may be refusing to repent altogether, forming a mushy foundation in your marriage upon which nothing can be built. Each husband's response presents its own set of issues.

While the first four parts of this book apply to every reader, the fifth part specifically addresses each of these three male responses so that, regardless of your situation, you'll have the principles you'll need to forge ahead. Please be aware, though, that you may find a moment or two during the first four parts where you think, *That won't work for me… My husband hasn't repented yet.* We understand that reality but simply suggest that you keep reading to the end of each part.

One final note: we've discovered through hundreds of e-mails that many women view pornography and masturbation as entirely different issues. In reality, they nearly always occur together—he's looking at porn with masturbation in mind, either right then or later on. So whenever we refer to "your husband's porn habit," we might just as well have written "your husband's porn and masturbation habits."

And with that, may God bless you as you read *Every Heart Restored.*

in the wake
of betrayal

In this part you'll observe that your feelings regarding his sexual sin are natural and normal—and that you aren't alone. You'll also discover the first step necessary to disperse the pain as well as how your perspective on male sexuality must evolve if you're to approach this problem effectively.

When Solomon consecrated the temple, he prayed, "O LORD, God of Israel, there is no God like you in heaven above or on earth below—you who keep your covenant of love with your servants who continue wholeheartedly in your way" (1 Kings 8:23).

There is no God like Him, and He knows exactly who you are and what you're dealing with. As we begin part 1, give your situation over to Him and continue wholeheartedly in His ways. He loves you immeasurably and calls your heart to His.

Brenda's story

After our first blind date at Jumer's restaurant, I looked at Fred like he was my knight in shining armor. He was easily the most handsome guy I'd dated. A blondish, muscular, and one-time athlete of the year in high school, he swept me off my feet in no time.

From a very young age I'd been praying for my future spouse and carefully defending my purity and virginity for this special person. Still, little did I dream how wonderful Fred would seem to me when he finally came into my life, and I could barely believe it when he said he felt the same about me! When he proposed, I willingly replied yes without hesitation. We looked forward to our honeymoon with all our hearts, and when it came, we were not disappointed. I especially loved snuggling into the strong, warm chest of my best friend and drifting off to sleep with him.

A couple of years down the line, we had settled into a comfortable niche of making love about three times a week. I appreciated how Fred wasn't always pushing me toward the bedroom. He seemed to love a romantic walk down silent wintry streets as much as our intimate times, which was nice. We had found a pleasant balance for the both of us—until that seismic shift flipped us over about four years into our marriage. Practically overnight he couldn't keep his hands off me, forever squeezing me or patting my behind. It didn't matter if I was frying burgers, sorting clothes, or drying my hair after a shower.

It wasn't long before he was really getting on my nerves. Questions came screaming into my head—questions that seemed harsh and unfair. In my darker moments, I wondered, *Is he having an affair and covering his tracks with all this new attention?* I couldn't imagine Fred doing something like that, however. Then the nurse in me wondered if he had a physical problem. *Had some gland gone haywire?*

Was this some sort of hormonal jag? Of course, it wouldn't have surprised me if he was simply experiencing some weird "guy thing"—something I'd never understand in a million years.

THE EYES HAVE IT

Weird guy things were certainly aplenty, and I was finding out more about them all the time. For instance, around the same time that Fred was acting, well, a little strange, we happened to read together James Dobson's book, *What Wives Wish Their Husband's Knew About Women.* I was miffed by Dr. Dobson's description of the visual nature of male sexuality. He said that men's eyes could draw sexual gratification at any time, because guys were turned on by female nudity in any way, shape, or form.

> Men are not very discriminating in regard to the person living within an exciting body. A man can walk down a street and be stimulated by a scantily clad female who shimmies past him, even though he knows nothing about her personality or values or mental capabilities. He is attracted by her body itself. Likewise, he can become almost as excited over a photograph of an unknown nude model as he can in a face-to-face encounter with someone he loves.[1]

While I enjoyed our sex life, some strange aspects of male sexuality began to bug me. It seemed shallow and dirty somehow, but I didn't really say much about it until a month later when an evangelist visited our church. He mentioned the same visual differences that Dr. Dobson had described, even suggesting that women must understand these differences if they expected to please their husbands sexually. Regarding the "vision factor," the evangelist said that wives could use that to their advantage in the bedroom. His remark was disdained by at least a few female listeners that night, including me.

---

1. James Dobson, *What Wives Wish Their Husbands Knew about Women* (Wheaton: Ill.: Tyndale, 1975), 115.

Fred and I discussed the message afterward while we were preparing for bed. My irritation finally bubbled over, and my patience snapped. "So I suppose I have to buy one of those cheap teddies and prance around like some saloon girl!" I exclaimed with my hands on my hips.

Fred laughed pretty hard at that one, probably because he knew I was picturing myself in some flimsy thing from Victoria's Secret. Gratefully, Fred always likes me best when I get snippish. He found my remark thoroughly amusing, and it's a good thing, because he was about to get another taste of it regarding this new sex jag that he seemed to be on.

Or at least I hoped it was a jag. It seemed like every night my "shadow" followed me to bed, ready and willing for some fun. Meanwhile, all I could do was sigh and wait anxiously for this little fever to break. But after about three weeks of this, an unsettling foreboding pushed into my consciousness. *What if this is permanent?*

I'll never forget an afternoon when Jasen was napping and Fred and I were putzing around the kitchen. "Honey," Fred purred, "you are just so beautiful these days."

That was it! He had pushed the final button. Spinning hard, I fired in furious desperation, "What am I doing to make myself so attractive so I can *stop* it!" I demanded.

Fred burst out laughing again. But just as suddenly, his merriment faded away, and his mind seemed to go somewhere else. A few minutes later, he told me a whole bunch of thoughts had suddenly come together in that moment. His next words to me were completely unexpected.

"Sweetheart, I don't know how to tell you this, but I've been in sin, and I'm trying to break out of it. Before I was saved, I was really hooked on pornography. I had the dates of the month memorized when my favorite magazines would be delivered to the campus drugstore. I was always there when the store opened so I could be the first one to buy a copy."

I gulped and wondered what he would say next.

"Then I got saved," he continued, "and I have to admit, I still struggled, even after I met you. I'm really embarrassed about that, but I want you to know that even though this may sound weird, I've never purchased a porn magazine since we've been married. I always figure that my money is your money, and I could never justify spending your money on pornography. I couldn't disrespect you that much."

"I don't get it," I commented. "Then what's the problem?"

"Well, even though I haven't been looking at porn, I haven't really been clean, either. I've been looking at other things, like the lingerie ads in the Sunday newspaper. I've even been watching certain R-rated movies when I've been out of town on business."

Fred paused for a response, but I had none to give. I was totally confused, and I only managed a nod for him to continue, wondering what was coming next.

"Maybe you're wondering what's been going on with me the last few weeks. Well, I think I just figured it out. You see, I've been cutting all of these things out of my life and—guess what?—a funny thing has been happening. You have become even more beautiful and sexy to me than ever before. You've always looked great to me, but you're way off the scale now, and I can't really help my feelings for you. That's why you've noticed me chasing you around so much lately. I guess all my sexual desires are being directed straight at you instead of at those other things."

"So that's why…"

"Right. All I know is that things are going really well in my fight, and it won't be long before this battle is over. And I can promise you this: once this battle is over, I'll quit hanging on to you so much. But you've really got to help me out during this time. I'm just so hungry for you, and I've got to figure out how to deal with it."

I didn't know whether to be shocked or relieved. I was relieved to know that there was a reason for all the extra attention in the bedroom. What Fred said certainly had some semblance of plausibility, and I was *really* happy it wouldn't be permanent. I was also impressed with his courage to tell me about this secret war he was waging.

At the same time, though, I was shocked that we could have had such a great sex life and close relationship, yet all the while this sin was hidden in the walls of our relationship, eating away at its strength. I was also shocked that things like lingerie ads and beer commercials could have such impact on men. Those things seemed pretty tame compared to actual pornography, and while I was glad he was cleaning up things, I couldn't make the connection as to how all this was affecting our lives.

But Fred had already made those connections long ago, and he was already in the battle. As his young Christian wife, all I knew was that I loved him and that I wanted to help him break free. So I told him with a wink and a smile, "Honey, I'll do whatever I can to put up with you until then." Some might look at my reaction to Fred as kind and gentle and see my character as resplendent with the fruit of the Holy Spirit. *What a loving, patient wife and Christian you were!* I can assure you, that wasn't the reason for my patient answer.

Others might think, *Of course your reaction was calm! He was at least halfway to victory already.* I'm sure that was part of it. After all, I didn't catch him gazing at glossy centerfolds. Still, that wasn't even close to the main root of my calm reaction. The real reason? I was naive (again!). I was ignorant of the seriousness of this sin. The Bible says ignorance will cost us dearly:

My people are destroyed from lack of knowledge. (Hosea 4:6)

And Fred's sin *was* costing me dearly. I just didn't understand it at the time. Had I truly understood the cost of his sin, I'm sure my reaction would have been much different. A little later I'll outline those costs.

Gratefully, my ignorance didn't hurt our relationship as much as it might have, because Fred was attacking the problem with all his heart. He did the right thing by confronting this sin and turning all his sexual energy in my direction.

Not all men are like that, of course, and not all women have experienced the happy ending that I've enjoyed. That's why you have to read Valerie's story in the next chapter. I'm afraid that many more women will identify with her story rather than mine.

Valerie's story

Note from Brenda Stoeker: I've asked Valerie, a friend of mine, to share her perspective. Her story is difficult to read, and while it may seem extreme, I think stories like hers are more prevalent than rare.

Brad and I had been married just over ten years when he asked me to watch a movie with him. He mentioned nonchalantly that it was a good show and I'd probably learn some things that I'd really like. I wasn't listening too carefully, though, because I was straightening up the kitchen after a long day. But a quiet evening on the couch, relaxing with a movie, sounded like a good idea, so I told him I would be there in a few minutes.

I quickly popped some corn and plopped down next to him with the bowl and a couple of Dr Peppers. At first I thought Brad was fast-forwarding through the ads and credits, but when he stopped and pressed Play on the remote, it was all there in full color—full-bore, hard-core pornographic sex. What I witnessed shocked me and sickened my stomach.

"Brad, I can't watch this!" I said sharply. I leaped up from the couch and ran into the bedroom.

That angered Brad, and he rushed in after me, barking, "Valerie, you are making it harder and harder for me to love you because you won't do the things I ask for in bed! This was a good chance for you to see what I'm talking about, and you aren't even willing to learn!"

"Brad, those kinds of movies make me feel dirty. I don't want to learn anything from them. It feels so evil."

Now he was *really* mad because I was questioning what type of Christian he was. Brad stormed out of the bedroom while I sat there crying alone for a long time, torn up by what was happening to our marriage.

DOWNWARD SPIRAL

A few months later I was home alone when I received a collect call one evening from a woman. I accepted the charges. When the operator put her through and she heard my voice, however, she hung up immediately. I thought that was odd, but on a hunch, I went up to Brad's desk to look around. That's where I found copies of e-mails they had exchanged.

All I could do was stare at them, as if my brain had been snatched out of my head. I just couldn't believe what he had done; it just didn't compute. It wasn't possible for him to be unfaithful to me. I trusted Brad. I trusted him so much that he must have felt secure enough to leave these things lying on top of his desk, because he knew I never bothered his things.

To see what I saw was just shattering. I don't remember how long I sat there trying to take it in. As my mind began to clear, I searched for other evidence that would exonerate him, knowing that I had to be wrong. It had to be a mistake.

But as my brain kicked into gear, the troubling connections began racing through my mind, like all his strange behavior over the previous few months. The distance between us had grown wider. After that episode with the porn video, he continually harped at me about my lack of sexiness. He complained that I was too childlike for him in bed, and nothing I did to sexually please him worked. I didn't dress sexy enough, and besides, he said I was too fat, even though I only weighed 125 pounds. He told me I was incredibly stupid, far too naive to be able to satisfy a man. If I had been a garment, he said, Goodwill would have thrown me out. I wasn't even fit for the five-cent table. Under that barrage of criticism, I had to start all over again, trying to figure out who I was.

Then one night, after he had been surfing the Internet, he came into my sewing room fully aroused. Without foreplay, he raped me—if that can happen when you're married. It grieves me to say that I got pregnant that night in this brutal, ugly way.

All of these happenings were hitting me like blows to my head and stomach. I stumbled around the house crying, unable to deal with all the conflicting emotions tearing at my heart.

Oddly, what seemed worst was that I did not feel like I could tell anyone—not one soul. My family hated Brad, and so did my friends, who all thought he was far too domineering. I couldn't afford to tell any of them, or they would like him even less. Exposing that I knew he had some mistress stashed somewhere wasn't going to be a good thing, because that would mean more conflict between us all—conflict that I did not know how to deal with.

As time passed, I became so afraid. I was afraid that he was lying to me about where he was and what he was doing. I was afraid he would never stop or that he would never be able to be free from that other woman or from lust itself.

The fear was terrible! It pushed me to demand and control things in a wild effort to prevent even further loss. In retrospect, I know that this was the wrong way to react. I couldn't make Brad stop sinning, no matter how much he hurt me. I couldn't control his will, no matter how much I wanted to.

But fear wasn't my only problem. The pain became crushing when he just continued to sin, either unable or unwilling to give it up, and the anger was overwhelming whenever I saw more evidence of his lying. I'd open a drawer or closet and find a strange woman's coat or scarf or the magazines and tapes he would sneak home. As the pain and anger piled higher and higher, I felt I was losing my mind.

STILL IN DENIAL

From the beginning Brad and I never had a real relationship. He would never talk to me about what he thought or felt inside, and yet, in my desperation, I kept hoping this crisis might bring us closer and that he might finally open up to me. I would *try* to draw him out by asking him lots of questions. I was curious to know what was driving his actions. But the more I asked, the worse it got... He just withdrew further into his shell. Sometimes I wondered if he loved me at all. He would *tell* me that he loved me, but his actions told a different story. It got so confusing.

Eventually, I went to Plan B and simply settled for the fact that there never would be any closeness. By now I was convinced that marriage was just a fairy tale and that the "happily ever after" stuff was a big, fat devastating lie. I honestly thought all marriages were like mine.

I felt guilty for having these thoughts, because marriage had been so sacred to me. I had taken a solemn vow before God and my friends and family to be Brad's lawfully wedded wife until death do we part. But since our marriage was so lousy, I had to settle for living on the surface, talking about inconsequential stuff, and never, ever letting him see me cry.

Of course, this made our sex mechanical, merely a function to be performed on occasion to keep up appearances to ourselves, almost to convince ourselves that we were actually married. After I found out about his unfaithfulness, our sex became even worse than mechanical. For me, being touched by him made me feel dirty, because in my mind *he* was dirty. I began to despise sex, because now I knew he was not even thinking about me while he held me; he was thinking about something he'd seen on a tape or fantasizing about some other woman. For me, this was emotional trauma at its worst. To think about his penis being inside another woman and then coming home and asking me to let him put it into me was so shaming—and wrong. I don't have words to explain the unbelievable repulsion I felt. It literally made me want to vomit.

In time, I had no choice but to put myself on autopilot to get through the act. How else could I bear it? Yet this only compounded the problem. Brad said he wanted to satisfy me, but I really couldn't respond while on autopilot, which hurt his ego. This drove him further away, which hurt me more, which spun our cycle of pain deeper.

In the end, Plan B didn't work any better, so I just gave up. My self-image had been annihilated. I felt inadequate as a woman in every way. Worst of all, my faith was shattered, especially when the news of his philandering got out, and his whole family blamed me entirely for the affair. I felt my mental state beginning to break free from its moorings when his mother told me that I needed to shape up and become a "normal" Christian.

"Come on, Valerie! Everyone knows it's your fault! What's wrong with the porn? Brad's girlfriend watches those videos with him, and she sees nothing wrong with doing that. Face it! You've driven him away yourself, because you won't watch the movies that he needs in order to be fulfilled. Whatever happened to all those vows to love him that you made on your wedding day? How can you have the nerve to call yourself a Christian? You're a nut, that's what you are."

Was I a nut? My head was spinning. Was I out of line to desire to be clean before my Lord? Not unsexual, but sexual in a way that was pleasing to the Lord—clean and righteous? Right or wrong, pure sexuality wasn't nearly enough to carry the day for me in my marriage, and divorce seemed like my only path back to sanity.

Looking back now, after all these years, I still don't think I was asking too much to expect my husband to be pure. Was it too much to ask Brad to allow himself to be aroused only by thoughts of me, while rejecting the lusts wrapped up in the tapes and magazines? I don't think it was too much to ask my husband to guard his eyes and to protect his affections for me this way. I think any husband should refuse to share himself emotionally with another woman or become dependent on her affection. Shouldn't a husband even refuse to place himself in a situation where his integrity or intent could be questioned in regard to relationships with other women?

Because my marriage and my life were in shambles, I've come to believe that men are a sorry lot in general. They are undisciplined, unholy, unkind, and untrustworthy. They are selfish, self-centered, egotistical, and greedy liars who lust for power and sex. To me, they are loathsome and repulsive most of the time. They only want to feel good, regardless of how it makes anyone else feel. They are without honor.

I feel disgusted by men and don't trust any of them. After what I've been through, I couldn't feel any other way.

FROM FRED

Valerie is gripped by anger and bitterness, but who can blame her? It doesn't surprise me that she doesn't trust any man as far she could throw one these days. And I feel horrible that her supposedly Christian mother-in-law justified pornography *and* adultery in their marriage and castigated Valerie regarding her stand for righteousness.

But that only goes to show you how pervasive the problem of pornography is these days. Surveys regularly reveal little difference between the rates of pornographic addictions in Christian and non-Christian men. The Hart Report, a confidential survey taken by Dr. Archibald Hart, disclosed that 61 percent of all married Christian men masturbate regularly. Research also reveals that somewhere between 30 and 40 percent of the pastors standing in our pulpits visit pornographic Web sites each year, depending upon which sources you choose. *Leadership* magazine, for instance, found that not only had more than one-third of the pastors surveyed clicked on an adult Web site, but 75 percent of pastors still hadn't made themselves accountable to anyone for their Internet use.

FROM BRENDA

As a young single Christian woman growing up in a quiet, rural community, I had no idea that such broad, heaving swells of sexual sin bubbled and churned beneath the surface of Christianity. But I can't miss it now. My heart aches and my mind is appalled by what I've seen in my lifetime. During the past twenty years, I've witnessed five pastors dismissed for sexual sin from my church alone.

Frankly, my thoughts about men parallel Valerie's to some extent, although to a much less bitter degree. I don't want to sound mean, but it sometimes seems like men are uncontrolled perverts who think about nothing but sex. Logically, I know that this can't be true, but the breadth of the problem is so overwhelming that it colors my perceptions. Like Valerie, it has affected my trust in men to know that even pastors and deacons are harboring this secret sin. And since I personally know many church leaders who have this kind of problem, it's difficult for me to trust them in other spiritual areas, too.

I remember reading the *Every Man's Battle* manuscript for the first time and being horrified when I learned about the sexual games men play in their minds. I wrote Fred a note in the margin, saying, *I hate this chapter. Men seem like untrustworthy pigs whose minds and thoughts just go wherever they want. Is nothing sacred to them? Even the title "pastor" means little when it comes to sexual purity. Fred, if anything ever happened to you, I doubt I'd ever remarry because I would never trust men enough a second time around.*

I hate the fact that many men lustfully take advantage of women in their thoughts, and I would especially hate being married to such a man. Jesus must have known how a wife would feel when He said that if a man so much as looks lustfully at a woman, he's committed adultery in his heart. That's exactly how I would feel, no question.

It is crucial for men to get control of these areas. How can oneness thrive in the shadows of such darkness? Answer: it can't. Even thinking about lingerie ads, old girlfriends, and women at work feels 99 percent as unfaithful as an actual affair. It is devastating to us as wives, and the hurt never completely goes away.

FROM FRED

Are you struggling with *your* thoughts toward men these days? It's awfully easy for us guys to smugly judge you for your harsh feelings toward us, but as I said, I don't think Valerie's feelings are that far off-base, and I certainly don't think men have a right to cast stones. Our sexual sin is too widespread. As a group, we are failing you quite miserably.

But even if you aren't struggling in your feelings toward *all* men, I know that you are struggling emotionally toward at least *one* man if you've caught your husband in sexual sin. Whichever the case, you don't have to apologize for your feelings. Your trust has been shattered, and being a Christian doesn't deaden the sound and pain of your shattering hopes and dreams.

When your trust is in shambles, there is only one person you can rely on—Jesus Christ. He understands pain all too well, and He's well acquainted with grief. He's here to comfort you and to build an intimate relationship with you, the only one that lasts for eternity.

He's also here to comfort and restore your relationships on Earth as well, and there are certain things you can do to work with Him toward that end. But before we get to that, let's take some time in the next chapter to explore your feelings just a little bit further. After all, as we found with Valerie, the mishmash of emotions sloshing around inside you and your sisters goes far beyond shock and grief.

crushed and angry

FROM BRENDA

Like Valerie, the average woman often feels that she can't talk to her friends about her husband's sexual sin, partly because she isn't sure they'll understand the depth of her pain. She may not fully understand the depth of her pain herself, but when that agony reaches the point where she simply *has* to talk to someone, she'll often approach her pastor. Sadly, we've found that even pastors may struggle to fully understand the effects of sexual sin upon a wife's emotions, and even they can inadvertently make a woman feel a bit silly for even bringing the matter up. That's exactly what happened to Nancy, who sent us this letter:

> I've been married to my husband, Alex, for nine years. He has a lust problem that I've known about from day one, but I thought it would go away once we were married. I guess the joke's on me, huh?
>
> We went to our pastor, but his advice was that Alex should be accountable to someone else, not me, and that I should *not* worry about it. I tried that approach, but after eighteen months of seeing no changes in my husband, I find myself in exactly the same spot.

How could the pastor tell Nancy not to worry about her husband's wandering eyes and masturbation? That's simply ludicrous, especially when her heart was crushed to her toes! How could she not think about that?

After all, what if her husband was actually sleeping with another woman? Would her pastor have told her not to worry about that either? Of course not. But didn't Christ teach that lust is *also* adultery? Shouldn't advice to a woman like Nancy reflect that?

Unfortunately, some leaders in the church can have a peculiar blind spot when it comes to the sexual sins of porn and visual lust. When pastors counsel thieves, they don't suggest seeking out an accountability partner. Instead, they expect the guilty party to knock it off. They may even quote Ephesians 4:28, which says, "He who has been stealing must steal no longer." And just in case the thief wasn't a good listener, the pastor might say for good measure, "Do you hear that buddy? Stop stealing!"

When pastors counsel liars, they don't lean back and say, "Let's just agree together in prayer about your lying, and sometime during the next week I'll tell your wife to quit getting her britches in a knot over all this." Sure, pastors will offer to pray with liars, but they'll also say, "Knock off your lying, and I mean now, friend! It's killing your marriage!"

The double standard born of this blind spot baffles me, and it deeply bruises the wives who have just stumbled over their husband's sexual sin for the first time. Instead of receiving support in confronting both the sin and the sinner, they may actually hear a pastor say, "That's simply the way men are, so don't worry about it."

Why aren't such pastors more "in your face" with sexually impure men? My cynical side suspects that many pastors are stuck in this sin themselves, so they don't know what else to say. Since they've lost the battle for purity themselves, they have no real advice to offer other men on getting free.

But my nicer side suggests that some pastors are simply letting their mercy get the better of their reasoning. After all, if they *have* won their own battles to avoid sexual sin, they know firsthand the fierce struggles these guys are grappling with, which means they may not have the heart to pile on to the husbands too hard.

I must admit that Fred and I don't always see eye to eye on this issue. Sure, we both agree that men need to face their sin and knock it off, no question. But Fred has been through the battle and understands the Enemy's treachery well. He believes that wives should exhibit grace both inside and outside the bedroom to help their husbands win the battle.

Fred makes a great point, and I agree, but—and this is a big *but*—most of my mercy still runs toward the wives. All I want is for men to stop crushing their sisters in Christ. Read more of Nancy's letter:

Alex says that he does not *want* to desire other women, but he knows what he likes, and he can't help that. I am obviously not what he likes. My spirit feels crushed, and yet he still questions whether it's wrong for him to look at these other women. How can it be right to crush me? Why can't he see that?

He says he loves me, but I feel he only says it because his head tells him that's what he *should* say. I can see in his eyes that his heart has changed toward me. I don't remember the last time he looked at me and I felt loved. I feel that God has given me some assurances that He will work this all out, but there are times like today that seem so dark that I can't possibly see how He'll pull it off.

I know that after bearing four children, I am not what I used to be. Alex always counters that there is more to loving me than just liking the way I look. I realize this, but it hurts so much when I see him giving other women second and third looks. How do I get it across to him that it is wrong for him to keep this ideal woman in his head, a woman to which I'll never compare?

I'm sorry, but I can't scratch up much mercy for Alex. Maybe Fred can, but his mercy for men has been enhanced by having lived *through* the battle. My mercy for women has been enhanced by living *on the other side* of that battle. I understand just how wonderful Fred's purity is to me, and every Christian wife deserves exactly that.

The security I feel in knowing that I'm not married to a man who is always looking at other women is incredible. It is like a gift that Fred gives me every day. Knowing that Fred is sexually pure allows me to easily give myself completely to him sexually. If he was giving long looks at other women—along the street, on billboards, in television commercials, or in magazines—I'd be reluctant to have anything at all to do with him sexually. To do so would be very hard on my self-esteem, and if I knew he was looking elsewhere, I'd surely feel as though I was unattractive to him.

But now that I know much more about how men are wired sexually, Fred's courageous fight to control and restrict his natural sexual tendencies for *my* sake has become the most priceless gift he'll ever give me. Since men are built by nature to look, it takes a loving, daily commitment to keep that part of his nature pure. I can assure you that this is a gift I don't take lightly. I cherish knowing that when he looks at me, I'm everything to him, though I tease him that he's definitely wearing rose-colored glasses. As time goes by, this gift only grows in value. I feel an incredible security knowing that I'm still the only woman that Fred allows his eyes to feast upon, and that he's fully satisfied with what he sees.

Come now! Is that really possible? As we've seen earlier, Nancy's husband certainly doesn't think so. He claims that while he doesn't want to desire other women, he can't help what he likes.

But we disagree totally with this guy. Fred claims that although I can never look like I'm twenty again, his passion for my body *can* remain the same. The Bible says so, and he's taken the following scripture to heart:

Let your fountain [of human life] be blessed [with the rewards of fidelity],
and rejoice in the wife of your youth. Let her be as the loving hind and
pleasant doe [tender, gentle, attractive]—let her bosom satisfy you at all
times, and always be transported with delight in her love. Why should you,
my son, be infatuated with a loose woman, embrace the bosom *(physically
or visually)* of an outsider, and go astray?

For the ways of man are directly before the eyes of the Lord, and He
[Who would have us live soberly, chastely, and godly] carefully weighs all
man's goings.

His own iniquities shall ensnare the wicked man, and he shall be held
with the cords of his sin. He will die for lack of discipline and instruction,
and in the greatness of his folly he will go astray and be lost. (Proverbs 5:18-
23, AMP)

Obviously, it *is* possible for a man to take joy in the wife of his youth and to be always and only ravished by her beauty alone…*if* he exhibits the discipline to do so. What's more, since it's God's Word that defines what normal behavior is for Christians, we're also forced to conclude that the discipline of guarding the eyes and the heart is not only possible but that God considers such discipline to be normal among His sons.

Then why do more men think like Alex than like Fred? Well, look again at the passage above. It clearly stands to reason that when a man like Alex *doesn't* discipline himself, he will be ensnared by other passions and his logic will be led astray. Instead of thinking normally and logically like Christ, he'll be duped into thinking things like, *I can't really help what I like to see.* He won't even see that his logic is warped.

Since so many men have not disciplined themselves, most have weak logic when it comes to their sexuality. The irrational often seems rational. One man we know actually justifies his actions by telling his wife that since none of the nude women he looks at on the Internet are engaging in sex acts, these pictures aren't pornography. Not only is such thinking abnormal, it also buckles a marriage.

Is it right, then, to ask women not to worry about their husbands' roving eyes and hearts? Of course not! We have every right to expect normal Christian behavior from our husbands, and when we don't get it, it's normal for us to feel hurt and disappointment. Each Christian wife deserves the same gift that Fred has given me, and no argument can dissuade me from believing that. If your husband is not leading a disciplined life, he is robbing you, so you naturally feel crushed.

What other feelings will surge over you in the wake of his porn and the masturbation that follows? Anger, for one. When Fred's business office was robbed a few years ago, we were both furious. Why not? It's normal to be angry when you've been robbed, and so it's normal to be angry at your husband's sexual sin. You needn't apologize for that.

"I was angry, hurt, and humiliated when I found his stash of porn," Linda wrote us. "I had so treasured the thought that he had no one to compare me to. I'm short and fat, so I can never compare to those bodies he's looking at. Worse yet, after I made my discovery, I started eating to medicate my life-is-so-unfair depression.

I gained even more weight doing that, which made me even *more* depressed. What a vicious cycle!"

Don't be surprised if you're feeling like an outright fool too. What could be more normal? When you find out that your husband has been secretly looking at another's bare body and masturbating, you'll feel utterly blindsided. You may even be kicking yourself for not having seen it coming, especially if your female intuition sent out early warning signals…signals that you, in your faithfulness to him, laughed off as paranoid or even out-and-out silly.

Don't be too hard on yourself. Patrick Middleton, who counsels those bound up in sexual addiction, told us, "It is not uncommon for wives to know for some time that something is wrong with their sexual relationship, but they dismiss their feelings of disconnection and shame as being crazy. For some reason, they refuse to trust their own intuition, which is plainly telling them something is wrong.

"I cannot tell you how many times a wife has said to me, 'Patrick, I knew it. I knew there was something wrong. When we made love, it was like there was no one home. His eyes were lost in some blank stare, like his thoughts were on someone or something else. When we finished, I did not feel closer to him. I just felt used and dirty. But I never said anything.'"

If you've ignored such clues, you feel like a fool, another common emotion swamping wives in the wake. But that feeling becomes an overwhelming flood if you've beat yourself up over his lack of sexual desire over the past few years, figuring that your "home cooking" should have kept him coming back for more if it tasted any good.

Out of guilt you may have shouldered the whole load of responsibility for his lack of desire—maybe dieting hard to lose weight and pouring out sweat in heavy workouts to draw out the desires of your one and only. Perhaps you've stopped by Victoria's Secret in order to drape yourself in something visually tantalizing to spark his attentions, even though wearing it made you feel uncomfortable. And often, when you bravely initiated a passionate encounter, your vulnerability was flung back in your face.

And now? You've found out it was never your fault at all. While you were sacrificing juicy burgers for limp salads and running treadmills like a gerbil on a wheel, he was masturbating away his sex drive on others. On your darker days you now even suspect that he conveniently led you to believe that you were to blame, intentionally and artfully using your guilt, fear, and disciplined regimens to cover the tracks of his undisciplined life. How stupid you feel! How conned!

Kelsey wrote to say this: "I don't fit the mold of the wives in your stories. I'm the wife with the strong sex drive who was unfulfilled by my husband, because he was finding his own pleasure and orgasmic release through hard-core pornography."

Mandy said that she always believed her husband when he told her that he simply didn't have much sexual desire—until the day she happened to open a package that came in the mail. Inside were two DVDs of naked women, a *Sports Illustrated* swimsuit issue, a Fredrick's of Hollywood catalog, a Victoria's Secret catalog, and a Howard Stern tape.

She was devastated, saying, "Most men want to have sex all the time. Mine now says he totally hates sex, but that he likes to look at nude women and fantasize, and he's been masturbating two or three times a day and has nothing left for me! I feel completely rejected by my own husband. Do you understand that? Do you understand that I love my husband and I want him to love me? I have no one to talk to about this. I know I should pour myself out before the Lord, but I hurt too much. Is there any earthly help for me?"

The Current State of the Union

You've been crushed by your husband's behavior, and rightly so. Where do you go from here? Do you stay with him? Punish him? Dump him? All you know is that you cannot and will not compete with the stuff he's filling his mind with.

And what of the emotions? These feelings are plain awful, and you know you will have to do something about them if you're ever to begin rebuilding your life with him. But what do you do with them? You may be wishing you could just forget the mess and let these feelings go, passing them off as overreactions. So would he.

But even if you *could* manage that, something tells you that this would be the worst thing you could possibly do. You can't put your finger on it, but you sense that the effects of his sin range far beyond the emotional chaos of your wounded heart. To let it go seems not only foolish but very perilous to everyone involved.

Don't ignore your intuition this time. You are right on target, and you must recognize the very real and treacherous spiritual dangers lying beneath the stormy emotions swirling on the surface. I didn't realize just how much Fred's sexual sin was rocking the foundations of our home until much later. You can't afford to wait that long.

If you ever expect to rebuild a stable life with your husband, you need to understand this clearly now, up front, as we'll demonstrate in the next chapter. As we do, you'll clearly see what the actual state of your marriage was before the revelation of his sin, and this dose of reality should help you to stabilize your emotions and refocus your heart on what God envisions for your future.

what loss?

FROM BRENDA

My response to Fred's admission of his sin was a willingness to help out. I meant it when I said, "Honey, I'll do whatever I can to put up with you until then."

Gratefully, Fred went on to win his battle over sexual sin, although it would be a few more years before God revealed just what a mirage my marriage had been.

My revelation began when Fred was invited to teach a four-week series on sexual purity to a Sunday-school class for married couples. As he poured out his heart through his tears during each session, I saw for the first time just how tortured he'd been and just how savagely our little home had been assaulted by the Enemy. Let me try to re-create the scene over the next few pages.

I'll never forget how Fred began his message. "It happened every Sunday morning during our church worship service," he said. "I'd look around and see other men with their eyes closed, freely and intensely worshiping the God of the universe. Myself? I sensed only a wall of separation between the Lord and me, and it was getting worse over time. I just wasn't right with God."

As Fred recalled his feelings during those dark days, tortured tears flowed from his eyes. Most of us in the class, including myself, were hearing this kind of honesty about sexual sin for the first time, and we were deeply moved. I had no idea he'd been suffering so, though I'd been standing right next to him in church Sunday after Sunday.

As he continued, Fred explained that there was a monster lurking about, and it surfaced each Sunday morning when he settled into his comfy recliner and opened the newspaper. He'd quickly find the department store inserts and begin paging through the colored newsprint filled with models posing in bras and panties.

"They were always smiling, always available," Fred said. "I loved lingering over each ad insert. It was wrong, I admitted, but it seemed like such a small thing. It was a far cry from *Playboy,* I told myself, and I'd given that up long ago."

Fred confessed that he was tricked by the seeming innocence of "small things"…glancing at joggers, looking at billboards, and peeking at scantily dressed women in various advertisements. "The addictiveness of these little things shocked me. Every week I said I wouldn't look at those ad inserts, but every Sunday morning the pictures compelled me. Every week I'd vow to avoid watching sexy R-rated movies when I traveled, but every week I'd fail, sweating out tough battles and always losing. Every time I gazed at some glistening jogger, I'd promise to never do it again. But I always did.

"A couple of months slipped by, and then a couple of years. The distance from God grew wider while my impurity still ruled me. My faith waned further with each failure, and each horrible loss caused more desperation. While I could always say no, I could never mean it. It felt like something was gripping me, something really relentless and mean."

He Couldn't Look God in the Eye

Growing up as a young Christian farm girl, I'd never experienced anything close to addiction. Well, maybe I have a thing for chocolate. But I could tell that my love for chocolate was nothing compared to the choking bondage Fred was describing during our Sunday-school class. I was mesmerized by his words, and my heart ached for him. When Fred began to describe the "bills" piling up in his life because of his sin, I finally began to understand how this "mild" form of sexual sin can really destroy a marriage and a family.

"After a few years of trying," Fred went on to say to the class, "I still couldn't look God in the eye. I knew I was a hypocrite, so my prayer life was feeble. Once my son Jasen was very sick and had to be rushed to the emergency room. Did I rush into prayer? No, I could only ask Brenda if she could call others to pray for Jasen. 'Have you called our pastor to pray?' I asked her. 'Have you called Ron?

Have you called Red to pray?' I had no faith in my own prayers because of my sin. I just couldn't connect with God."

As Fred spoke, my mind flashed back to that frightening event. He was right—we *didn't* pray together about Jasen's sickness, even though his little life was at stake. At the time, it didn't really strike me as strange because I just assumed that Fred was too emotional about Jasen's sickness to settle himself to pray. Now I knew the *rest* of the story.

And Fred's stories continued: "But if the truth were known, I always felt uncomfortable the few times I did pray with Brenda. I felt so guilty. Here was my pure wife kneeling before her God, and here was her perverted husband trying to pray with her when I'd just been lusting over movies in my hotel room the night before. For those who doubt the Word, let me assure you that Peter was right in 1 Peter 3:7 when he said that sinning against your wife hinders your prayers.

"My marriage was suffering in other ways, as well," Fred said. "Out of fear of what she would think of me if she learned of my sin, I couldn't commit 100 percent to Brenda. I was scared that she might dump me. But that's not all. Brenda told me she was experiencing frightening dreams in which she was being chased by Satan. Sometimes she'd come running downstairs in terror on a Sunday morning while I was in the very act of lusting over ad inserts."

Fred broke into tears again. "My immorality had destroyed my spiritual protection over her, and she was paying a huge price for my sin."

Our Sunday-school class was very quiet after these revelations. Maybe some wives were wondering whether sexual sin was at the root of their own miserable prayer lives as couples, or maybe some husbands were worried that their wives might soon be asking some very uncomfortable questions. All I knew was what I was thinking. Satan had been chasing me in my dreams regularly at that time, but I never made the connection between these dreams and Fred's sin until he mentioned it during his Sunday-school talk. I sat amazed, lost in my thoughts.

But Fred's voice soon recaptured my attention that morning as he recalled a sermon in which our pastor spoke about "generational sin" in Exodus 34:7 and how we can pass patterns of sin from father to son. Crying, Fred said, "Sitting in my pew, I recalled that my grandfather had run off from his wife in the middle of the Great Depression, leaving her with six kids to raise. My father abandoned his family to pursue multiple sexual affairs, and he was hooked on pornography. That same pattern had been passed to me, proven by my multiple girlfriends in college and my slavery to porn. And now that I was married, I found that I still didn't have this purity issue settled in my own life, and I was scared by the thought of passing this pattern on to my kids.

"Sometimes when I'd be watching my firstborn son, Jasen, toddle around on his little legs, I'd see him grinning and drooling up at me, but instead of smiling back, my heart would break because I thought about his future," Fred said.

"I'd beg, *O God, isn't there anything I can do for my son? Isn't there any way to keep him out of this pit I'm in? Please, Lord, don't let him grow up to be like me!* I just ached and groaned at the thought of my precious son trapped by the same addictive porn habits that had gripped my grandpa, my dad, and finally me. I didn't ever want him to feel what I felt when I looked in the mirror. My distorted sexual desires owned me, and I knew it. I didn't want Jasen paying those same prices."

Those four weeks of Sunday-school lessons—in which Fred shared much of the story you just read—were quite an eyeopener to me and to others. Believe me, Fred and I had some interesting conversations at home during that time! What a mirage I'd been living! Never before had I sensed such urgency in my call as Fred's helpmate, or helper. Clearly, we were in this marriage together in things seen and unseen, and if I failed to be a good helper with his legitimate sexual desires, it could easily boomerang back onto my head. I finally realized just how ignorant I'd been to naively think, when first I learned of his issues, *His sexual sin is his problem to deal with!*

And if you're caught in a similar situation, know that your husband's sin is also your problem, and like it or not, you're his helper! The word *helper* in Genesis comes from a Hebrew word that means "a help as his counterpart." So what does a helper do? Fred and I agree that as a helper, one of a wife's key roles is to encourage her husband's growth and maturity as a follower of Christ, whatever that may entail.

Granted, if Fred was to answer God's call to holiness and seek Christian greatness by walking closely to Christ, he had the first responsibility to commit to sexual purity on his own. But my job as his counterpart was to help him deal responsibly with his sexual impurity—or other sins for that matter—in any way that I could—in spite of the pain.

Which brings me back to the question I asked you earlier: what are you going to do with your feelings? If you're to get past the pain and catch the vision for your role as helper, you might begin with a few penetrating questions.

For instance, what have you genuinely lost through the revelation of your husband's sexual sin? Think hard about what your marriage was like before you discovered his sin. I suggest that you haven't lost as much as you think, because the foundation you thought you had was never there in the first place.

Was your marriage a mirage, like mine? That's not to say I didn't love Fred or that we didn't have a lot of connection and fun times. Our marriage was good in many ways. But something was definitely missing behind the scenes, and my marriage wasn't what it appeared.

Was something hiding behind *your* healthy-looking, marital facade? Did you and your husband ever experience spiritual intimacy? You might have *believed* you did, but you couldn't have, could you? Your husband was harboring sexual sin. By his very silence, he was lying to you regularly. He was a fraud, presenting a false image of himself to you continually. True spiritual intimacy could not exist in this environment.

Did you ever have genuine, ongoing intimacy in prayer? Maybe you *thought* so, but according to Scripture, it wasn't there. After all, when a husband sins against his wife, his prayers are hindered. Looking back on my own marriage, it's clear that Fred's sexual sin had placed a spiritual wall between us, though I didn't know it. That same wall stands between you and your husband whether you've sensed it or not:

> Husbands, in the same way be considerate as you live with your wives, and
> treat them with respect as the weaker partner and as heirs with you of the
> gracious gift of life, so that nothing will hinder your prayers. (1 Peter 3:7)

Fantasizing over some buxom actress during *Baywatch* reruns is adultery. Do you suppose his adultery is an act of being considerate to you as a wife? There are no secrets in God's realm—your husband's sexual sin wrecked your intimacy together in prayer many times over.

What about oneness together? Think back. Can you honestly state that your marriage was all you had ever dreamed it would be? At the time, you might have sworn on a stack of Bibles that you were living your dream, but in truth, you weren't. Your dream began to die with the birth of his secret sin.

Face it. Because of his sexual sin, your marriage was compromised. Sure, you're hurt and very angry. You've lost that warm, cozy image of your marriage, and that naturally wounds you deeply. But in another sense, you haven't lost as much as you think, because your marriage wasn't what it appeared to be. My point? There is a bright silver lining to this dark, billowing cloud. Think about it: you have been living in a false world, and had it not been for this revelation of your husband's sin, you might have blindly and tragically gone through your whole life without ever experiencing the richness God intends for your marriage. But God is faithful, and He loves you too much to leave you where you are now. Of course, it's my odds-on guess that this hasn't felt much like love to you, and perhaps you've been as mad at God as you have been at your husband. But that anger is misplaced. Though the revelation hurt, the Lord has proven His undying love for you by exposing your husband's sexual sin, and He stands ready to help you get through this.

While you may not feel good about what has happened, this event could bring about one of the most hopeful times of your life. The discovery of your husband's secret sin has revealed the true state of your marital union, and now you have the opportunity to experience something real with him. Marriage doesn't have to be a big fat lie, as Valerie suggested in chapter 2. Whatever it's been up until now, it doesn't have to stay there.

It will be helpful if you view the discovery of your husband's sin as God's grace in your life. His sexual impropriety has been like a huge life-sucking tumor silently attacking your marriage. But now that you've found the cancer, there's hope. Now you can pray for healing, begin treatment, and seek a marital life restored and brimming with health. Best of all, this is your chance to live out the truth that all things work together for the good of those who love Him.

God has set you free to pursue your personal healing. And He aches to see the same thing for your marriage. Here's your chance to live like a real Christian, to truly sacrifice, and to truly align your thinking with Christ regarding your marriage.

Moving On

You now have a choice. So what will you focus on—the pain or the hope? Probably both at first, and I don't blame you. There will be days when the pain of your husband's betrayal will overwhelm you, and your anger will drive hope far away. That's okay. God understands, and He won't bop you over the head for your lack of faith. He'd rather hug you and draw you near, if you'll let him. You're His child, remember?

Still, thanking God for the revelation and choosing hope for the future is the first step to your freedom. Yes, even if your husband hasn't fully repented yet. Sure, your first faltering steps in this direction will be like crossing a stream by jumping from rock to slippery rock, which means it won't be easy. Being thankful in the midst of chaos is always a challenge. Sometimes it'll feel as if you're thanking Him for your pain, which may seem comical and even hypocritical in your eyes. And it may take daily discipline, even moment-by-moment discipline, to maintain a grateful outlook.

But as you discipline your heart to the truth and choose to be thankful for what He has done in opening your eyes, your obedience will kick up a breeze of the Spirit's breath in your life that'll begin to dissipate your pain. That's what we're after.

Not that "thank you, Lord" is some magical phrase that will instantly make everything better. Until your husband commits his whole heart to winning the battle, until God can get your husband's full attention, things will still go roughly for you.

But even in that case, a thankful heart is your best first step, a step that begins to give you your sanity back as you wait for God's work to be done in your husband's life. Everything is in the light now. You're no longer guessing what's going on, and you know the score regarding your marriage. Sure, you may have to wait awhile for victory, but even so, all is not lost. This time can serve you well, as you still have plenty of work to do in your *own* life if you expect to answer God's call as your husband's helpmate, a work that'll serve to focus your husband's attention on God, as we'll see later.

As part of this work, let's step back and take first things first by asking a pair of questions:

- How is it that so many Christian men succumb to sexual sin?
- What is it about their nature that greases their slide down the hill?

We'll discuss the answers at length in the next two parts of the book, but before we can do that, we must ask a third question that turns the spotlight back on you. What is your current attitude about the differences between female and male sexuality?

Sour? The differences between men and women are the fragile fault lines that can crack a marriage asunder, and you must treat these differences with care and honor if you expect to build your new marriage upon a firm foundation. Now that you can see the hope in what God is trying to do in your marriage, let's take a look in the next chapter at how He expects you to approach these differences.

all about those differences

FROM FRED

When Brenda and I taught Wednesday night premarriage classes for those marching toward Matrimony Lane, our motto was simple: Prepare for Potholes. That message resonated in Iowa, where springtime potholes bloom across the streets and avenues of Des Moines like the tulips and jonquils that push up through the last traces of snow.

Couples take a pounding from the cavernous potholes born of the freeze-thaw cycles of early marriage. As they clunk crazily in and out of these axle busters, young spouses cry out, "Auugh! I married the wrong person!"

Brenda and I sought to vaporize this pothole panic by being so honest about early marriage that marital idealism vanished before any of our couples ever walked the aisle. We joked that if our bluntness didn't cause at least one couple to break off their engagement during our seven-week session, we'd suspect we'd been too soft on the truth and weren't doing our jobs. Having warned our students about these potholes during our premarriage classes, we always hoped to help them navigate *through* them during our young-marrieds class on Sundays.

Our class discussions always got very raw and real, which didn't surprise those who knew me well. Once, after reading the six chapters on masturbation in my book *Every Young Man's Battle,* a friend blurted out, "What's with you, Fred? What do you do—go to the drawer labeled THE THINGS NO ONE WANTS TO WRITE ABOUT and pull out the most difficult topics you can find?"

Okay, so maybe I *do* ask for trouble sometimes. That's probably why I agreed to talk about menstruation and PMS when a few wives in the class asked me to. I knew the topic would be like juggling flaming torches. Still, we'd been talking about the brain differences between men and women, and the wives were hoping I'd teach their husbands to be compassionate regarding their physiological differences too.

I actually thought our first Sunday morning session on PMS went well—until that Sunday afternoon. That's when I received a phone call from Becky, and she was all over me like a duck on a June bug. Was she ever hot! "Who do you think you are even talking about PMS!" she blasted. "You aren't even a woman! You have no idea what it's like, so you have no business telling me how I should act during my period!" I held the phone a foot from my ear so that Brenda could hear what Becky was saying. Her arched eyebrows said, *I told you so.* I received several other phone calls that matched Becky's blasting tone note for note.

Recently, Brenda and I recalled that weekend of misfortune. "Remember what happened after Becky called?" I said. "My stomach was tied up in so many knots that I couldn't eat!"

"Oh, you always find a way to manage," Brenda teased.

We both chuckled at the memory. After pausing to think, I admitted, "Their rage still shocks me to this day, but you know what? I still don't understand why they were so angry. You heard what I said in class. You know I didn't say anything controversial."

"But you remember what got to them, don't you?" said Brenda. I could sense her loyalties to the sisterhood rising a bit.

"What?" I replied, my defensiveness rising along with them.

"It was when you said, 'Women, let's be honest. You can control how you treat people at work and at church during your period. I've seen you do it, so let's face it. If you can control it there, you can control it at home.'"

I shrugged my shoulders. "What's wrong with that? Isn't that the truth?"

"Well…," she wavered and then stopped. She wasn't going to comment any further. Divided loyalties, I reckon.

"Now hold it, Brenda. I wasn't picking on the women. I believe men need to control themselves too. You know I've always been consistent. Take Dad, for instance. Remember when I drove over to his place and asked him to start controlling his temper and his swearing whenever I brought you and the kids over? I told him, 'Dad, I've never once heard you yell or swear in front of your business clients. You know it would hurt your business if you did, so you control it. Well, you're hurting your relationships with us now, so I'm just asking you to control it when I bring my family over in the same way you control yourself on business calls.' Brenda, you never saw anything wrong with *that* argument."

"Well, yes, it *is* similar," she conceded, but I could tell my wife was holding back her full approval.

"No, it is the *same*," I stated. "All of us can control ourselves if it's in our best interests to do so. And since we should be one flesh with our spouses and treat them in the way we want to be treated, how can it *not* be in our best interests to control ourselves around our spouses, even during these cycles?"

Brenda thought for a moment. "I know what you are saying. But you were also telling them that their struggle wasn't real and that PMS was all in their heads."

Time-out! I couldn't believe what I was hearing. Was she in the same room that day?

"Hold on, dear. I *never* said that, and you know it. I clearly acknowledged that PMS is real. After all, I grew up with two sisters. If anyone knows it's real, it's me. But that doesn't mean we don't have control over how we act to some degree."

"But it's *very* real," Brenda said, sliding in more tightly with the sisterhood and suggesting by her tone that my position was wrong and that I would never get it right because I was a man.

"So let me see if I understand," I said, applying logic to my defense. "You are saying that the power and the fruit of the Holy Spirit, like kindness and self-control, are not as strong as hormones. Because of this, Christian women are help-less before the onslaught of their hormones, and they are free to act any way they want during their period. You are saying that the Holy Spirit leaves for Bermuda once a month and stays there for a week while the fruit of the Spirit rots away like bruised pears. Come now, Brenda."

Backpedaling like an all-pro safety, Brenda said, "No, no. I know you're right, and you were right that Sunday when you said it. But you know what the problem really was? It was *who* said it. You're a man. It's even hard for *me* to keep that out of the equation, and I'm your wife!"

That dumbfounds me on one level, but I'm not surprised in the least on another. After all, judging by the phone calls I received that afternoon, *many* wives in our Sunday-school class "heard" me say that PMS was not real, even though I never said it, I don't believe it, and my class notes (which I still have as evidence) proved that I was clearly careful to teach that PMS was very real and that we men should have compassion. It was simply that I was a guy weighing in on a woman's issue that had them going.

What about you? Maybe you're thinking, *The sisters were right! You couldn't possibly understand this or speak to the heart of this issue.*

I hate to say it, but the roots of this attitude could become the same roots that will prevent you from ever rebuilding oneness with your husband, because they'll keep you from believing that your husband can ever tenderly understand your sexuality. Even worse, they'll keep you from accepting male sexuality as equal and as valid as your own, worthy of *your* tender care.

The truth is, your husband *can* understand PMS enough to be compassionate, just as *you* can understand his male sexuality even if you have no firsthand experience as a man.

An Air of Expectation

I'd like to prove my case through this story. Not long ago I was up at daybreak and sitting on our basement couch while organizing a lapful of papers and e-mails for this manuscript. The footsteps that had been pattering across the ceiling for the past hour finally fell silent... The kids were off to school. Brenda wandered down the stairs to say hello and start her day in the laundry room. She was still wearing her Cuddl Duds, a brand of silky long underwear. Brenda wears them as a second skin all winter so she can stay warm during the day. At night she wears them as pajamas.

Now, I can assure you that Cuddl Duds aren't particularly sexy. There's not enough lace, I suppose, and there's certainly not enough skin, since they run from the neck to the ankles.

But as she bent over the couch to give me a kiss, the shirt fluffed open and I could see everything. When she straightened up, I said, "Hey, beautiful, how about another kiss? I like the view! I normally don't kiss with my eyes open, but I'll make an exception in this case."

She bent over and laced her arms around my neck and kissed me again, and then, with bright eyes and my favorite grin, she teased, "Maybe you would like to see a little more than that later tonight."

Well, well. My day suddenly looked a whole lot brighter and, if you know anything about men, you can be sure that my engines stayed revved all day long as my mind floated back to those words fourteen-hundred times during my wait for nightfall.

Before long, however, Brenda's day took a hard turn for the worse. The holidays were right at the door, and the whole family was coming our way this time. Time was seeping away, and there was so much to do! After getting the first load in the washer, Brenda planted herself in the kitchen, where she began baking items that could be frozen for the many holiday meals to come. Brenda prides herself on being a flawless roll maker, but on this day, her butter horns flopped. An even better cookie baker, she baked countless batches of a new cookie recipe only to find out later that no one in the family liked this new recipe at all.

I suspect our older son, Jasen, had thrown her concentration off. We had rushed up to Ames to bring him home from Iowa State University the night before. It was just days before finals, and he was so sick with the flu that he couldn't study or get the proper rest that he needed in the dorms. Brenda was worn out with concern for him. To add insult to injury, Brenda's period was right at the door, hormones churning with a vengeance.

By five o'clock she was mumbling, "This day just never seems to end." She managed to get a nice meal cooked, but after the last pot was scrubbed, I heard her moan, "I'm at the end of my ability to cope." As bedtime neared and the kids got annoying, she gritted her teeth and whispered to me, "I'm about to get angry if I don't hurry upstairs to bed."

"I'm right behind you," I said quickly with a hug and a grin.

As for myself, her early morning words weren't the only thing on my mind. Because of the rushing, crushing week, I also yearned for worship and prayer with Brenda. I needed the peace that our worship times bring, and I hoped it would settle her heart, too.

After saying good-night to the kids, I turned on a worship CD in our bedroom, and we both sang along. Eventually, we came together for prayer, which was wonderful. Still, I could tell she hadn't quite connected with the Lord in the same way I had. *Her PMS must be really terrible,* I thought.

Putting my arm around her, I asked, "How are you feeling, sweetheart?"

"Still stressed, still tense. But I sure love this CD, don't you? I like every single song on it."

She then went to check on the kids before bedtime while I stayed behind and fluffed up the pillows. In my heart, I decided that sex would have to wait that night, in spite of her words that morning. Making love had to be the last thing on her mind. It was time to sacrifice.

But in spite of her long day, she came back into our bedroom and, after locking the door, managed a wink and a little smile. She had not forgotten her promise of this morning. "I'll be right back," she said, popping into the bathroom to brush her teeth. While I waited for her return, I laid back and stared at the ceiling. *She is so amazing,* I thought. *She really knows male sexuality. She knows I've been thinking about it all day, even though I've never mentioned it again. She knows how important it is to keep her promises, even though her day has fallen apart. She wants me to have that connection, even though she's hurting.*

But I knew the timing wasn't right. When she climbed into bed, I said, "Sweetheart, why don't we just lay here with that CD playing and listen to the music for a while? Maybe it'll take the stress away and settle your heart."

I gave her a big hug, and she laid her head on my chest while I stroked her back and shoulders. It was nearing eleven o'clock, and soon her head got heavier and her breathing a bit deeper. She'd soon be fast asleep, and I knew what that meant for my hopes from that morning. But I didn't care.

Then she whispered, "I hope the Lord gives us a lot of years alone together after the kids move on. I love you so."

"Me too, sweetheart." I felt my passions bubble like crazy for her, but I chose to let her rest on. As we lay quietly listening to the music, I fought the urge to reach out and fire her up sexually, though I knew full well how to do it. I chose instead to miss out, for her sake, not because I'd experienced PMS or because I really understood it all in some personal way. Instead I simply trusted what she'd said about it, and I reached out in the way I figured she needed it most.

As the last song of the CD faded off in the darkness, Brenda stretched long and hard and murmured, "Wasn't that a great worship CD?"

"I loved it, sweetheart," I said, patting her shoulder and rolling over to go to sleep. You'll never guess what happened next. It turns out I didn't miss out after all when Brenda pulled me back over to keep her promise from the morning.

Why did Brenda do this though she was this tired, stressed out, and racked by hormones? Did she do it because she personally understands male sexuality? Of course not—she's a woman.

Still, she's heard enough to respond lovingly as if she *does* understand. For instance, she's learned that the comments she made that morning would have had me thinking about it all day, and she knew that my desires couldn't be shaken off easily later in the evening if she changed her mind.

That night Brenda *willingly* put my sexual needs into play equally with her own needs when making her decisions. That is what oneness means, after all. She chose to honor my essence equally with her own.

A Conversation

Why was I willing to forgo sex that evening, even though my engines had been idling all day long? Because I understood PMS? Not really. I've never experienced the gut-wrenching cramps or the black cloud of hormones that wash inexplicable waves of discouragement over a woman and make her feel ugly and unattractive.

But I've felt unattractive before, and I've felt discouraged before, and I understood enough from those experiences to understand what Brenda needed in that moment. So I poured worship music into her heart that night, and I held her and stroked her hair and told her how much I loved being married to her. I responded as if I *had* experienced PMS, taking at face value what she'd shared about it through the years and responding accordingly, respectfully putting that knowledge into play in my decisions and my interactions with her.

As you can see, if you want to build a strong marriage, it is vital that you treat your differences with great respect. Any arrogant attitudes have got to go. Clearly, Brenda is doing a great job, and surprise of surprises, even men can learn a thing or two in this regard, as you can see from my half of the story.

Let me emphasize the word *learn,* because this doesn't come naturally to most of us. Brenda didn't always accept these differences gracefully. In fact, she once had trouble putting up with them at all.

I remember early in our marriage hearing a good sermon that encouraged me to make a concerted effort to verbally praise Brenda more often. In an argument a couple of months later, she challenged me to prove how deeply I loved her, so I responded, "What do you mean? For the past two months I've been working hard to praise you and build you up every chance I get. Isn't that love?"

With a roll of the eyes, Brenda wanly replied, "That would be fine if only you would do it other times too…not just when you have sex on the brain."

That stung, primarily because it wasn't true. But it also felt like a jab below the belt because it revealed a hard attitude toward my sexuality, implying that it's impossible for a guy to say anything nice to his wife unless he's dying for an orgasm.

I have acquired some understanding of how our sexuality appears from a woman's angle. When I told one husband that Brenda and I were planning to write a book for women, he replied, "That's wonderful, but I hope your wife plays a significant role in writing it. My wife has a difficult time accepting some of the things men say regarding our sexual issues because she thinks it's just talk and that men are perverts. If she would hear these things from a woman, it would make a big difference."

Did you catch the double standard here? Too often, women won't allow guys to speak on tender female issues, but they'll only listen to women when discussing ours. Why?

Perhaps some women view female sexuality as superior because it is tied to relationship and touch, while male sexuality seems baser, vulgar, and far too prone to sin.

In fact I agree that male sexuality *is* more prone to sin. But while our maleness may be *our* worst enemy in this battle for sexual purity, any superior attitudes you might have toward male sexuality may be *your* worst enemy.

I understand why you want to hear from Brenda on this topic, and you will. But you also need to hear the guy's side. I want to help in any way I can. I earnestly believe that the better you understand male sexuality, the more quickly and effectively your pain will dissipate.

Male sexuality is complex stuff. Perhaps by the time I'm done explaining it, you'll sigh deeply and say, "Fred, after reading this book, I don't think there's ever been a time that I've been more happy to be a woman. I'm glad I don't have your issues."

Go ahead and be happy! But you absolutely must learn to view the marriage bed from the perspective of our male sexual hardwiring as well as your own. To do that, you must root out any negative attitudes and accept your husband's sexuality as worthy of your tender care. If you don't, oneness won't thrive.

Now, before we move on, let's look back on where you've been. We've explored the crushing pain born of a husband's sexual sin and the emotional quagmires that waste a wife's heart and soul in its wake. We've seen God's hand in revealing the mirage of your marriage, and we've felt a faint, fresh breeze of hope as you've obediently offered a tentative thanks to your Lord for His grace. We've pondered what to do with your pain.

The first step in defusing your pain is to honestly and humbly study the roots of male sexuality until you recognize that his sin hasn't been about you in the first place. Toward that end, I will share as much as I've learned about male sexuality and how it works.

Let's get started!

the hardwired differences of male sexuality

FROM FRED

Men are just plain different from women. I know, that's fairly obvious, like telling you the laundry basket will be full come Saturday morning. But as you read the following five chapters, you'll discover how these differences hinder our sexual purity as husbands.

Since there are three main hardwiring differences between men and women, we'll devote space to each one. Chapter 6 portrays the strong visual nature of male sexuality. Chapters 7 and 8 list the brain differences between men and women, which can complicate your effort toward rebuilding your marriage in the wake of sexual sin. Finally, in chapters 9 and 10, we point out how sexual intercourse is a man's primary language for sharing interpersonal intimacy and describe why your saying no affects his heart.

At first glance, this may seem like a lot of chapters on the topic, but trust me: there is nothing more critical to your healing than a clear understanding of male sexuality.

the eyes have it

FROM FRED

Brenda and I recently visited our friends Kim and Stew, and as the kids chased Mario and Luigi through the hills and dales of Nintendo, we parents sat together talking and laughing into the night. Brenda looked great to me. Four or five times I looked at her and thought, *I can't wait to get her into my arms later.*

Look, I'm a guy. I'll be visual until the day I die. Whenever I step out of the master bathroom in the morning and catch her in lingerie as she's dressing, I'll murmur breathlessly, "Is NASCAR running this early, or is that the racing of my heart?"

Yes, seeing Brenda like this gets my motor revved up, and that's fairly universal. Guys can get turned on by a long look, and this aspect of our nature isn't always easy for women to understand. Young Amber wrote, "It's honestly inconceivable to me that just by looking at something sensual, a guy can get so turned on that he has to masturbate! I can't comprehend that at all."

But guys can. We're made that way. We come hardwired with certain qualities that make it very tough to remain sexually pure. We don't need a date or a mistress—our male eyes give us the ability to sin just about any time we want. All we need is a long, lingering look at a partially clothed or unclothed female body to receive a jolt of sexual pleasure.

We aren't picky, either. The jolt can come just as easily from staring at the tight sweater on the girl on the bus to work as it can from a romantic interlude with our wife. In short, we have a visual ignition switch when it comes to the female anatomy, and it takes very little to flip it on.

Women seldom understand this, because they aren't naturally stimulated in the same way. Think back to your high-school days. Did you get turned on when the guys' swim team paraded around in their skimpy bright blue Speedos—the ones with the telltale bulge? The answer is likely a resounding no! In fact, if you're anything like Brenda, you were probably grossed out. Why? The ignition switch for women is tied to touch and relationship—not to the guy's body.

It's just the opposite for us as guys. Our eyes hug all the curves, and given the fact that it's pretty easy to see a lot of skin and tight tops in America these days, it's no surprise that there's a natural desire to take a good look. It's no wonder that men's eyes resist control without conscious effort.

Visual Foreplay

Allow me to restate this characteristic of male eyes in different words. For guys, impurity of the eyes is a type of sexual foreplay. That's right. It can create the same sexual buildup as stroking an inner thigh or rubbing a breast.

Isn't that a little strong use of the word foreplay *here?* Not in the least. When we see a hot movie scene, there's a twitch below our belts, and our mouths go a bit dry. When we're walking along the beach and suddenly pass a lady lying on her stomach with a hitched-up thong bikini, we get weak in the knees. We gasp while our internal mission control drones, "We have ignition!" We can have her in bed on the spot, although only in our minds. Or we can file away that remarkable image and fantasize about her later when we're alone in a hot shower.

We can page through the morning newspaper and stare at demure young women wearing push-up bras and tight panties, looking at us with their pouty lips. We stare back and lust, and then we stare some more and lust some more. Before long, the sexual pressure builds so high and our motor revs so far into the red zone that we must have some type of sexual release—or else the engine's going to blow.

Although it may seem so, there's actually nothing inherently dirty or detestable in this at all. My wife *wants* me to look at her and desire her. She knows she's beautiful to me, and she's mildly amused that I'm turned on by gazing at her and daydreaming about our night ahead. In its proper place, maleness is wonderful.

But let's face it: without conscious discipline, our visual foreplay is rarely confined to the marriage bed, and that's when it becomes detestable. Sam remembers the time he was watching television with his sister-in-law. The rest of the family was at the mall. "She was lying flat on her stomach on the floor in front of me, wearing tight shorts, and she'd fallen asleep. I was in the chair behind her, and I happened to look down and see her upper thigh and a trace of her underwear. I tried to ignore it, but my heart started racing a little, and my eyes kept looking at the back of her upper thigh. It got me so excited that I began to stare and really lust. I had to release it somehow. I masturbated while she slept, right out in the open."

A story like that makes it easier to understand why so many otherwise godly men fall into sexual sin. With abundant sensual images so close at hand, men naturally and easily engage in this visual foreplay and fall to sexual temptation—simply by being male. That's why God gave us an unusual command when it comes to sexual sin and lust of the eyes:

Flee from sexual immorality. All other sins a man commits are outside
his body, but he who sins sexually sins against his own body. (1 Corinthians
6:18)

Men needed an unusual command because this particular sin is unique. I told Jasen the same thing back when he was eleven. "Jasen, it's hard to describe the effects of pornography, but it is like taking drugs," I said one evening. "You know how your teachers warn you about drugs?"

Jasen nodded his assent that evening. He had heard some DARE cops talk about drugs in his classroom, so he understood the comparison.

"When we look at women without clothes on, there is a chemical reaction that happens in our brains that some say is much like the reaction the brain has to taking cocaine. There were studies showing this way back when I was in college. I'll never forget watching some of my rich Stanford friends blow thousands and thousands of dollars on cocaine in just a few days over spring break. They just couldn't get enough."

"Wow," my son exclaimed.

"You got that right, Jace. But listen. I've never done cocaine, but I *have* viewed pornography, and once I did, I was hooked and wanted to see more and more, just like those guys with their drugs. It was a brutal habit to break, Son, and I just don't want you to make the same mistake that I did."

This is another reason why pornography habits are so tough to break: men receive a natural chemical high from looking at pictures of nude women. When our eyes lock onto images of nude women, pleasure chemicals bathe the limbic pleasure centers in the brain, and because it feels good, we want to come back for another hit (look). Quite often then, our addictive behaviors are not rooted in some lack of love for our wives. Rather, they're linked to the pleasure highs triggered by the images entering the eyes.

Jesus understood how these natural male inclinations would open the door so easily to sexual temptations. That's why He said:

> You have heard that it was said, "Do not commit adultery." But I tell you
> that anyone who looks at a woman lustfully has already committed adultery
> with her in his heart. (Matthew 5:27-28)

Jesus clearly equated a man's lustful thoughts over a woman with actually making love to her. And when you think about how our eyes work, looking at women and thinking about sex really *is* the same as doing it. The strong wash of chemical pleasure men get when they lust with their eyes is similar to the wash of pleasure they receive when they do the real thing with a woman.

I believe that when the apostle Paul said that those who sexually sin are actually sinning against their own bodies, he was referring to how the male body craves this chemical high more and more once we start down this path of sin. The eyes have it—they keep searching and hunting and lurking for more nudity and more highs.

That's why it's so hard to say no to porn. It's addictive. It's like athlete's foot of the mind, as one person described it. It's always asking to be scratched, but when guys scratch, they cause more pain and intensify the itch.

Answers and Effects

So the ability of male eyes and mind to draw sexual gratification from the world around them helps explain why sexual sin is so common. It also explains why so many young men experiment with masturbation early in life. With all this foreplay of the eyes going on, and with no guidance on what to do with the feelings, the overwhelming desire to feel pleasure is understandable, and the orgasmic highs explain why they keep coming back for more and more.

Young men aren't perverts. Without an adult's training in a young man's life, obsessing over a girl's looks is simply the predictable result of a guy's makeup, because there are natural tendencies built within him that will make him *very* interested in looking at the female body. (That's why we wrote *Preparing Your Son for Every Man's Battle.*)

But why doesn't marriage stop this habit? A man must train his eyes to flee. If he doesn't, they'll just keep doing what comes naturally.

Maybe you had a sixth sense about your husband's roving eye during those exciting days of courtship, or maybe you even knew about the porn, but you weren't all that concerned about it, figuring God would forgive him and it would all be over once he could see *your* body every day after marriage. God will forgive your husband, all right, but it's not over. The Bible is clear that what we sow we will reap. Sin comes with inescapable consequences that follow a husband into marriage.

Victory wasn't granted with your husband's signature on the marriage license. He must fight his battle for purity, and if he doesn't, he will have to pay the price at the same toll bridge as the rest of us did. Tim, a married graduate student, told us this:

> When I was eleven, my best friend and I found someone's hidden stash of
> old pornographic magazines. We then spent the next fourteen years of our
> lives hiding our sins and growing progressively worse in our addictions. We
> constantly sought the thrills that lust brings to a man. I must say that my
> darkest hours were dark ones indeed. I spent many hours in porno arcades,
> adult theaters, strip clubs, and even resorted to massage parlors several times.

I've spent hundreds of hours looking at online pornography, and I've seen myself do things that I thought I'd never do. I've been praying constantly for a way out, but I haven't even the slightest ray of hope.

You may be thinking, *This guy is a pervert!* Yes, his behavior is sinful, but I wouldn't call him a pervert. He could easily be someone you know—your next-door neighbor, your friend's father—maybe even your father. He could be your Sunday-school teacher, deacon, or even your pastor.

And so, in spite of marriage, don't be surprised when your husband's sexual sins keep spilling over everywhere just like they did when he was single. Marriage alone won't free your husband. Sooner or later, he'll have to commit to purity if he wants a true relationship with Christ and with the woman in his life—you.

But my husband is a Christian! Why can't he simply pray about this and stop it? We can go to the altar of prayer and be freed, but if we stop short and never fully close the gates of our eyes to sensual pollution, the sewage seeps right back in, day in and day out. When the chemical highs return, we're captured again.

After I spoke on Long Island, New York, one night Paul cornered me and said, "I'm thankful for your practical message tonight. My story really backs you up."

"I'd love to hear about it," I said, intrigued.

"Though I have a wonderful wife who really takes care of me in bed, I've always had eyes for women and Internet porn, which led to a problem with masturbation for years. I cried and prayed long and hard for God to deliver me. One night as I slept, I believe He did."

"Really?"

"Yes, really. I had a dream where I was standing cold and lonely in a vast dark room, frightened and unable to get out. Suddenly, a spotlight showed straight down on me from above, and a pure, white raiment floated down and settled over me, covering me in His grace.

"The next day I noticed that the pull toward porn had vanished. The desire was simply gone. I praised God all day, and I continued praising him as the days and weeks passed without making any late-night visits to the computer."

"Wow, that's great!" I exclaimed. "What a story!"

"Unfortunately, that's not the end of my story," he said.

"Really?"

"Yup. While God had delivered me miraculously, I never really dealt with my character or my looking-around habits. Last summer, I was still staring way too long at the girls walking by with their breasts half hanging out. Before long, one gal with particularly large breasts got me pretty excited, which tripped a memory of someone who looked exactly like her at some porn site on the Internet. The next time I got online, I thought, *It wouldn't hurt to take a quick peek. I'm delivered, after all. It can't hurt me.*"

I knew what was coming.

"Well, that one look led to many more looks over the next few weeks, and today I'm as stuck as I ever was."

I felt sorry for Paul, and I encouraged him to flee from the computer *again,* because it was evident to both of us that looking at pictures of naked women resulted in his wanting to look at *more* pictures of women. You either train your eyes to flee or you fall right back into your old addictions, in spite of your prayer. That's just the way it is.

What does fleeing look like in practice? Simple: it is cutting off those sensual images that create that mental pop. Bouncing the eyes is one form of fleeing. Starving the mind of new images and taking lustful thoughts captive are two more. Fleeing into a deeper relationship with God and drawing on His power through regular worship, prayer, and Bible reading is another. Going partway doesn't cut it, because little peeks and other such concessions keep the sewage floating into a man's life.

That Little Chemical Pop

Let's step back a moment. Since women have no firsthand experience looking through a set of male eyes, I find that they can feel a bit of trepidation about all this. I'd like to clarify some things so that you don't go overboard with your husband regarding his visual side.

We all agree that sexual perversion is rife across the land, but does that mean all men are always looking at you like a piece of meat? Of course not. While every man has the visual hardwiring, not all men choose the path of lust every time they see an attractive woman. Perhaps they were protected from perverted, unhealthy views of sexuality while growing up and never began to objectify women as sex objects. Perhaps they've been delivered by God's grace, like myself. Pure men can notice a woman's beauty and still see her as a sister, moving from thinking *She is beautiful!* right back to their previous line of thought.

But even for these men there are things happening inside them that they don't always consciously recognize, which explains why men appreciate beauty so intensely and why they are so curious about the female body. I'll explain with this story about my son Michael.

One evening when Michael was eleven years old, he traipsed into the kitchen where Brenda was puttering around. "Mom, how do I get pictures of women in their underwear out of my head?" he asked innocently. "They've been there all day!"

Brenda brought all her mental power to bear to hide her shock. As calmly as possible, she replied, "I'll bet your dad can help you out with that. But tell me…what pictures are you talking about?"

"From that Secret store at the mall," he replied. Suddenly, it all came together. Brenda had taken the kids to the mall earlier that day and strolled by the Victoria's Secret window displays a couple of times. Clearly, Michael had experienced that little chemical pop that older guys know only too well. When the epinephrine and other pleasure chemicals hit the bloodstream, they lock into the memory whatever stimulus is present at the time of the excitement. That's what happened to Michael, though at his age he couldn't understand what was happening.

I want you to notice a couple of things about this. First, the chemical hit to the pleasure centers was natural and immediate. Michael wasn't looking for trouble—he was merely walking through an indoor mall, so it wasn't like he set out to stop, stare, and lust. Chemical pops are not the same thing as conscious lust.

Second, it didn't take pornography on a screen (computer or television) to create this chemical reaction in Michael's limbic pleasure centers. For Michael, it was a Victoria's Secret window display. When I was Michael's age, there was something about my classmate Marianne's denim-clad curves that nearly caused me to drool on myself during French class in middle school. Sure, she was fully clothed, but the mere sight of her punched every button, and her image returned to my dreams on many nights.

Again, notice that the original chemical pop is not a choice and may not always be conscious. What happens is that the beauty of a woman's body simply hits the eyes and then the pleasure centers of the brain. The choice is whether to take that image to the next level of lust.

Most guys will admit they understand the little pop quite well. It's just a quick little hit, and it can come from watching a glistening Anna Kournikova strolling slowly back to the service line or Michelle Kwan bent at the waist and smiling broadly as she glides over the ice. The chemical connection from a woman's body to a man's pleasure center in the brain is quick and strong, bringing a natural curiosity about women.

But when that curiosity is allowed to run where it will, either through porn and masturbation or through fantasizing over the girls at school, it leads to the objectification of women (an attitude of rating women by size, shape, and harmony of body parts), an obsession with looking at women as much as interacting with them. When we do interact with them, there is generally a subconscious, low hum of their sexuality buzzing through our heads. While it's hard to say what percentage of men are in this group, it is easy to say that the vast majority of the husbands of the wives reading this book are in this category.

Getting back to our discussion of the eyes, seeing an attractive female doesn't always lead to a sexual pop. In my business, which is heavy in sales calls, I have contact with pretty women all the time. As I work with them across a conference room table or conduct business in their offices, I obviously see them and talk with them and laugh with them. That's natural and normal, but now that I've trained my eyes, there is no sexualizing of these interactions as long as I keep my eyes from straying below the woman's neck, lingering to "appreciate" her beauty, or savoring her allure.

Which brings us to an important question: when do looks become lust? I think we know that a glance is different from an open-mouthed stare that results in a pool of drool at your feet. We can easily tell which of these is wrong. But if a lingering glance gives us guys enough "eye juice" to trigger that little chemical hit, what do we do with that? It may not reach the classical definition of lust, but we are clearly getting some sexual gratification from it, and it is costing us something in our relationships.

Before I made the decision to train my eyes, I would have told you that looking at female joggers, sexy billboards, and pretty drivers in passing cars was harmless and had no effect on me. There were no "yeah, baby" reactions from me. Like most guys, I would have argued that since I detected none of that stuff, I was fine. No big deal.

But as it turns out, I was wrong. After I'd gone cold turkey on lingering glances at women for about three weeks, Brenda noticed a vivid, geometric rise in my desire for her. Perhaps you remember. She blurted, "What am I doing to make myself so attractive so I can stop it!"

Those days revealed to me just how much sexual gratification I'd been getting, not only from the lingerie ads, but also from the lingering glances at the joggers and passersby.

Which brings us to another critical question: does that sexual pop really matter in the battle for purity if it falls short of conscious drooling-at-the-feet lust? Should we try to eliminate it, too?

Those who were raised without perverted views of sexuality or who have never entered that objectification stage often argue no. Sure, they are getting a little pop of sexual gratification, but it isn't always conscious, and since they've always been relatively free of sexual sin, it isn't as big a deal. Why go to that degree of discipline? They're apt to think, *I can accept a woman's beauty and my attraction to it as something from God, something healthy and wholesome. I can choose to stop there and not take this sensual pop deeper into lust.*

Fair enough. That is one level of freedom—a place where men notice a woman's beauty and don't automatically take it to sex, possession, or lust. No doubt many wives would be satisfied with this level of freedom for their husbands.

On the other hand, the battle for sexual purity never really ends at this level because of a regular choice that must be made: *What do I do with this pop—should I take it to lust or not?* These men are often fighting skirmishes on the boundaries to avoid that road to lust, a path harder to avoid if a woman is dressed in a certain way or a man is in a more compromised state—like watching a sensuous R-rated movie in a hotel room while on a business trip.

Men at this first level of freedom will say, "All men—even the godly ones— occasionally give that long look." Or, like the pastor who put his arm around me and pulled me aside with a knowing smile, they say, "We all slip up from time to time." At this lower level of freedom, men can't even envision complete victory over sexual sin because of always having to make that difficult decision about what to do with those sexual pops.

But what if a man eliminates all the sexual pops in the first place and so doesn't have to make that decision anymore? What if he gives up that right to linger, to "appreciate" the beauty of women? After all, if I don't watch Anna Kournikova play tennis, I don't have to decide whether to take her image to lust or not. It's here we'll find a second level of freedom that we can choose to go to. It's the level of freedom that cuts off visual sexual gratification from outside your marriage completely and transforms the visual circuits back toward innocence.

For a husband who is in the objectification stage, this second level is the one he must go to if he's to escape sexual sin completely. Without going there, he can't break the addictive cycles and return to normal. Your husband will need to not only get rid of the conscious lust but also those images that bring a subconscious sensual pop to his brain. Only then can he be freed to relate with you and other women in healthy ways. For instance, today I can talk to a beautiful woman without feeling that hum of sexuality that was once a constant in my life. I love this freedom.

How did I get to this deeper level? I had to engage the battle fully. To me it no longer mattered what it would cost me—it only mattered that I would win and win decisively. In short, I moved from the "How far can I go and still be considered a Christian?" mode to the "How holy can I be?" mode.

That first mode is the mind-set at the first level of freedom, which poses questions like, *Can such discipline really be healthy?* or *Would God really cramp our style this way? After all, He created us to be visual!* Such men are focused primarily on the costs, making decisions about what they'll look at based upon the visible, detectable damage that might come of it, and project the costs based upon their own wisdom, insight…and desires.

But that mind-set doesn't protect against the addictive nature of the chemical pops, nor does it take into consideration that their detectors are often so seared they're of little use in judging the spiritual costs of the sensuality around us.

When the wife of a good friend had an affair, he turned off the television for two months and began reading Christian books every night to cope with the chaos. When he finally came back to watching a little television again, he was shocked by the sexual vulgarity and even more dismayed that he hadn't noticed it before. Our detectors can be off-line without our being aware of it.

But what about that second level of freedom? In the "How holy can I be?" mode, guys don't care about what they're missing or whether others think they're taking things a bit too far. They're focused primarily on the gains and upon how much closer they might get to God. It doesn't matter what it'll cost—they're on a mission.

I understand that there is male pride surrounding this area, and your husband may demand, "Back off! How do you know what is happening inside me?" You don't, and I don't, either. That's why I'm not issuing any commandments like "Thou shalt not watch *Stars on Ice*" or "Thou shalt not watch beach volleyball." Each man is different, and it gets a bit fuzzy defining the boundaries on this middle ground.

On the other hand, men who say there are *no* costs to living in that middle area are simply making an arbitrary declaration with no facts or experience to back it up. How could they really know? First, their detectors may not be sensitive enough to pick up on these costs if they *were* there, and second, they've never lived without the chemical hits of that middle ground, so they haven't experienced the difference it can make in a marital relationship or in a relationship with God.

But I've lived both ways, and I'm not guessing on the costs of stopping short. It is well worth throwing caution to the wind and blitzing right past that first level of freedom into the deeper level of discipline, and I urge every husband to reassess the question he's asking at the root of the issue.

At the first level of freedom, men accept the hits of sexual gratification as long as they can stop short of lust. To them, the only important question at this level is this: *Am I lusting?* But perhaps men should be asking themselves a better question that would cover both the lust *and* the pops: *Is what I'm doing with my eyes costing me anything with my relationship with God and my wife?*

Asking the right question can be transforming. And if you ask your husband to read *Every Man's Battle*, he will understand how to practically apply these principles to his life. Once your man goes to the second level of visual freedom, he'll look at you a whole lot differently—and you'll be pleased with those looks being directed at *you.*

FROM BRENDA

Wow. This whole thing with the eyes is jarring to my senses. Probably the most surprising and most valuable thing I've learned about a husband's sexual impurity is that it works more like a habit than a choice. Before Fred helped me understand this, I just assumed that men always chose what they looked at. I didn't know that their eyes are naturally drawn toward anything sensual around them.

More than anything else, this has helped me understand why sexual sin is such a difficult sin to break. I used to think, *If a guy loves his wife enough, he'll simply stop.* Clearly, it's not that simple. Unless they train their eyes and minds, men will be naturally prone to consume everything sensual that comes their way during the course of their day, not just the lustful things they actively seek out. This helps me have mercy on men regarding the false starts they make in their effort to win their personal battles.

As a mother, I'm glad to have this information so I can watch my sons a little more diligently. If you are a single mom, this will give you some idea about what you should discuss with your son. Not that *this* will be a very easy conversation!

In any event, the male eyes give us our first hint as to why men so easily fall into this trap of sexual sin: their own hardwiring can easily do them in, as naturally as stepping through a thin sheet of ice on a frozen lake. In light of this, we obviously need a humbler, less harsh attitude toward the husband who is really trying to win this battle. We also need to seriously study the other hardwiring differences between men and women if we expect to rebuild a marriage that lasts. Let's take a look at a few more in the next chapter.

sex—his language of intimacy

FROM FRED

When young, muscular Brett returned home after another session of weightlifting, he found his lovely wife, Jenna, tucked softly into bed, reading a novel. His passions percolating at the sight, he hurried into the bathroom to clean up and consider his next move. As he stepped out of the shower and caught a glimpse of his muscular frame still pumped up from his workout, he concocted the perfect plan. *I know. I'll just walk out and "accidentally" let my towel slip off. That'll get her going!*

Turning the doorknob, he confidently made his approach, and just as he neared the bed, he let the towel slip to the floor. "Oops," he said with a big grin.

Jenna merely glanced up briefly from her reading, then returned to her book. *Nothing.*

Snatching up the towel and scurrying into the walk-in closet for some boxers and a T-shirt, Brett grinned for another reason. "I should have known! Her eyes are sure pretty, but they certainly don't work the same as mine!"

Like me, you may find Jenna's reaction to Brett's scheme quite amusing. *Been there, done that.*

But when it comes to the differences in the sexual hardwiring between spouses, little is funny, and few of us are laughing. We discussed our first set of differences in the last chapter. Let's take a peek at another one that will help you understand why men fall into sexual sin so easily.

The difference? Men get their intimacy tanks filled primarily from what they do prior to and during intercourse. It is their native language of intimacy. Have you ever wondered why guys push so hard against the sexual boundaries when dating? It's not because they are godless pigs; it's because they're longing to express their hearts in their own innate language of love.

It's no different in marriage. Because of this natural desire to express and receive intimacy *sexually*, and because of hormonal factors related to sperm production, men generally desire sexual intercourse every few days or so, especially in the early years of marriage. (For single guys without regular sexual release, this consistent, short cycle of desire "goes to sleep" or "dries up," in the words of two of my single friends.)

FROM BRENDA

Women, on the other hand, share their intimacy in talking, sharing, hugging, and touching, and a woman's hormones are of little help in keeping her at his speed. However, since her sexual triggers are relational, positive relationship factors can easily draw her alongside him in her level of sexual desire. Clearly, then, these differences don't have to create problems.

But they often do. Let's face it, differences bug us. And many of us, out of pride, assume that our spouses are *choosing* to be different because they are stupid, mean, insensitive—even defective. If they cared or weren't so obtuse, they'd naturally think exactly like us. How could they not? After all, if I weren't right, I wouldn't think the way I do!

Blinded by pride, our attitudes are poor, which then leaves our responses very questionable. In the end, we either respond impatiently, as we would with a child who just won't shape up and act right, or ineptly, as we might in dealing with a stranger from another country and culture.

So it's not hard to understand why it is difficult for women to understand men and vice versa. We experience our sexuality differently than our husbands, and it's very easy to respond impatiently and ineptly by developing a prideful attitude.

In fact, from our sexual perspective, guys can seem not only wrongheaded but morally defective, leaving us with an inflated claim to the moral high ground.

FROM FRED

For instance, in our marriage class, one young wife scornfully blustered, "Men are no better than dogs in heat." Another blurted, "Oh, what a cross to bear!" I'll admit I laughed out loud at both comments. I'll also admit our sexuality may at times be a cross to bear, especially if a wife doesn't have a matching desire for regular intercourse, and yet she is expected by God to follow through as if she does.

Because wives don't experience sexuality like men do, our whole sexual gig can really stretch our credibility with them at times. "Oh, so you really feel love for me tonight, and you really want to make love, huh? Well, what do you know? It's been seventy-two hours since our last go at it. Hmmm? It doesn't sound much like love to me. Sounds more like some kind of hormone bath! Go fly a kite!"

On the surface, it's hard for wives to see our desires as having even a whiff of relationship to them. Since, to them, sex is inseparably swirled with relationship, and since mutual desire is the only kind of sex that seems right to a woman, therein stands the moral high ground upon which wives plant their flags. On this hill righteous pride makes its stand, and much too often, women sharpen the blades of belittling attitudes.

Raymond said his wife had a huge blind spot way up there:

I'm wondering if you have any advice for me, as my wife, Kara, isn't interested in fulfilling my needs. I believe the sexual needs of a man are very real,
but Kara disagrees. She sort of thinks men are perverts.

This situation makes it more difficult to resist sexual temptation. With
God's help, I have managed to avoid much sexual sin up to this point, but
as the situation between us continues to deteriorate, it becomes increasingly
more difficult.

We are both active and involved in church. I play the guitar on the
worship team and am a member of the church board. I feel God's presence
in my life daily and depend on Him for everything. Kara is involved in children's ministry, and she's a wonderful mother and has really dedicated her
life to our children.

What a tough spot Raymond is in. He can't just shrug it off, because his sexuality is at the center of his being, and his wife controls it. When Raymond chose to marry Kara, he knew he was limiting his sexual options to her alone, and he entrusted the most emotionally vulnerable part of his being into her arms. But Kara is not treating his vulnerability tenderly. Instead, she's forcing Raymond to think and live like her, sexually speaking. This can be catastrophic to the relationship.

FROM BRENDA

When we're standing on such moral high ground, we can even stop thinking Christianly. As part of the research for an upcoming writing project, Fred sent copies of a secularized version of *Every Man's Marriage* to some non-Christian readers to get their take on the message. If you've read it, you know that there are several chapters outlining various aspects of servant leadership and how it looks to honor wives in day-to-day life.

Fred asked each reader to score the message of each chapter on the Olympic gymnastics scoring system, with a grade of one being the lowest and a grade of ten being the highest approval possible. Fred's marks in the early chapters were well within medal range—nines and tens. The female judges loved what he was saying, which was basically that men ought to honor the inner essence of their wives and should allow them to blossom fully in their homes.

But when the chapters on sexual relationship came into play, Fred took a few hard tumbles off the beam. Fred's suggestion that wives should sexually honor their husband's inner essence earned him ones and twos on the female judges' scorecards, and one rifled this dissenting view in this way:

> I think your opinions about women and male sexuality are way off base. I'm forty and have been married twenty years, and I no longer care to have sex at all. That forces my husband to masturbate? Really, now! Ha! Ha! Ha! I'd never let my husband read this BS.

Both Kara and this reader see sexuality solely through a narrow female perspective, though one is a churchgoer and the other isn't, and any suggestion that there are differences in male sexuality that are equally valid or that wives should meet these with sacrifice and tenderness is met with disdain by both of them.

Believers and nonbelievers shouldn't think alike here, and if you've taken a broad brush and painted all men as perverts, that's a red flag marking a serious blind spot in your character. We cannot afford such attitudes, because it is far too damaging to our relationships. Instead, we must try to put ourselves in their shoes and open our ears to their hearts and perspectives, and I don't think it's so hard to do.

Read what Gary recently said to his wife, trying to help her understand his heart:

> Honey, I think you understand that I need some kind of release fairly often, but I don't think you understand that it goes much deeper than that. My drives and hormones don't have a brain and therefore can't think for themselves. They simply cause me to realize I have a need for intimacy. When I seek you out to make love, I am not just looking for a release of some pent-up sexual frustrations. I have a deep desire to connect with you.
>
> When you consistently ignore my advances and put me off, I get frustrated. I miss you.

Can you relate to Gary? I sure can. When I had four kids at home between ten and eighteen, how often did I say, "Honey, with all the taxiing and running around with the kids, it seems like I haven't seen you or talked to you for days. I know we talk at night before bed, but it just doesn't seem enough. I miss you."

And what about the drives and hormones? We needn't look far to get the glimpse we need of the male perspective, because, if we're honest, our hormones and drives aren't all that different from the guys. There are certain days in our cycles when we have a much stronger sexual desire for our husbands. When that desire comes, do we minimize it or disdainfully dismiss it as some hormone bath? Of course not, because it doesn't feel that way to us at all. We simply feel a desire for sexual intimacy, pure and simple—feelings that are close enough to the ones Gary's describing above that we can understand what he's saying, if we're honest about it. Any of us would be fighting mad if our husband sniffed away our advances by snorting, "Honey, you're like a dog in heat!"

Our husbands don't just ache for orgasms. They ache for us. But our hard attitudes can make us blind to this. We think that if we sacrifice for their need, that is enough. But it isn't.

One night when Fred wanted to make love, I moaned inside, *Not again already!* I felt put out, so I managed to say, "Okay, I can put up with a quickie for your sake, but let's hurry. I'm tired and want to go to sleep."

Fred took a deep bow and said, "Thank you, oh great and noble martyr!" Obviously, I was offering little of myself, and as I recall, things slid downhill quickly from there.

That week I wondered if those halfhearted, short experiences with me were fulfilling for him. While women draw intimacy from their mates primarily through sharing, hugging, and talking, men draw theirs from the sex acts themselves.

Mulling this over, I reversed the scene in my mind. What if Fred reacted to my need for sharing and hugging in the way I'd reacted to him? What if he said, "I'm only in the mood once or twice a month to give you a hug and talk to you in any meaningful way, but I can give you a quickie talk before I fall asleep."

The light popped on in my head. Factoring out the hardwiring differences, these two situations are exactly the same, but because of those gender differences, men aren't nearly as concerned about hugs as they are about sex, and women aren't nearly as concerned about sex as they are about hugs.

When I offered Fred that quickie, I honestly thought I was doing an enormously nice thing. But let's analyze this a little closer. If a man gets his intimacy from the sex acts themselves, will a halfhearted, "Are you done yet?" experience be fulfilling? While I thought I was going the extra mile to help him release some sexual tension, in terms of his *actual* need and desire for intimacy, I was miles away. It is easy for a wife to forget this part because her intimacy is not tied so tightly to sex, and she doesn't experience it that way.

While it's hard for me to grasp that sexual intimacy with me does the same thing for Fred as his "talking times" do for me, I must give the marriage bed my full attention as if I do. This is what wives need to understand. It's that simple. Life isn't a big game of chess. It's all about telling the truth about your needs and responding in love to the other. That is what marriage is made of.

Sadly, Gary's wife never even went *that* far:

Even after telling Therese my feelings, to this day she refuses to get it. She once told me she prayed to God and asked Him to reveal all areas of pride in her life. This is surely her biggest bastion of pride. Either she is ignoring my needs or she is blind, but either way, the root is pride.

Why can't Therese hear me? I can hear her! I understand *her* top emotional needs, and I understand what listening, sharing, talking, and encouraging does for her. I've fully given myself to these.

Why is sex in a class all by itself to women? Why shouldn't women be expected to develop a genuine interest in sex for themselves so that they can really connect with us when we need it? Why is it accepted that women will always "really" only be doing it for their husbands? Am I being clear? Something in that really grinds on my sensitivity.

Forgive me for belaboring the point, but I am trying to understand why it's okay for women to just "service" us, like that is enough. I want a full investment of my wife in the act of lovemaking and in our sexual life as a whole. I want Therese to care deeply about it herself.

I had some hope when the counselor suggested we schedule sex once a week for eight weeks and each take turns initiating it. That never happened. I think Therese will still do it if I bring it up, but I just haven't brought it back up. It just enrages me that she hasn't initiated the schedule in light of our sessions. I don't get it.

Scheduled sex would help because it would no longer be a shell game. And she'll probably go for that, but I've been waiting on *her* to make the schedule. I want *her* to care. When Therese asked, "Why can't people like you just chill on this sex thing," I replied, "It's really quite simple for me: make love with me once a week, and I'll be a very happy man."

This conversation was Tuesday, but we'll see. It's been three weeks again since our last time, and five weeks between that one and the one before. Ugh! What a life, huh?

Can you hear the longing and the emotional need beneath the raw physical desire in Gary's plaintive letter? This empathy holds the key that can bring a husband and wife together in a way that feels good and right to both of them.

So here's a pop-quiz question for you: do you agree that Gary has a right to be angry? If not, you may have a blind spot in need of an attitude change. If you can see his point, however, then you are positioned to move toward a strong marriage because you've begun to understand how men actually experience their sexual lives.

But for those who failed this quiz, let me be blunt. As I was finishing up this manuscript, a *Newsweek* cover story hailed America's newest cultural wave: a tsunami of women engaging in extramarital affairs. The primary cause? Inattentive husbands are failing to provide oneness in marriage by ignoring their wives' native language of intimacy—time, deep conversation, hugging—and stuffing their freedom to blossom as women.

As Christian women, we despise this new wave for the sake of our Lord. But if we're honest, outside of His Word we would find it pretty tough to condemn these women. *Why throw stones at her when it's mostly his fault?* We understand her need all too well. We're women.

But what if you are the one failing to provide oneness in marriage by ignoring your *husband's* native language of intimacy? Outside of God's Word, I won't condemn him, either. How can I throw stones? The parallel is exact, and I don't have to be a man to understand that. A wife's inattentiveness in providing regular sexually intimacy may not literally force her husband into the arms of cyberspace, but until she removes this log from her own eye, she is the last woman on earth who should be tossing stones his way. From God's viewpoint, her sin is showing.

In Gary's most recent e-mail, he pleaded, "I need your help. I know that you have prayed for Therese and me before, but I want you to pray specifically for me this time. Today it's been three weeks since our last time together in bed. What if I were to talk deeply with her only once every three weeks? Pray that she would *hear* me and *listen* and *feel* me—empathize with who I am. I don't want to create a bad relationship between us by talking about all this, because that's what always seems to always happen. I probably deserve a good lecture at this point, huh?"

Not as badly as she does. Not even close.

Granted, this is not easy to hear when you're hurting, but it's a foundational truth critical to the rebuilding process. In light of this, we should take a deeper look at the issue, which we will do in our next chapter.

how does he feel
when you say no?

FROM FRED

Just to be sure I'm clear on where I'm coming from, I did *not* say in the last chapter that wives must give their husbands sex anytime they're asked. I never have said that and hope I never will. To prove my contention, let me quote myself from *Every Man's Battle:*

> Does that mean your husband should have sex anytime he wants? Of course not. The Bible says you should not withhold sex for long periods of time, but men love to interpret that scripture incorrectly by saying they have a right to intercourse as often as they want. We've heard stories about some husbands who coerced their wives into sexual intercourse one, two, and sometimes three times a day!... If your husband is demanding sex more than once a day, he likely has a lust problem that needs to be dealt with.

I've been consistent in calling men to honor their wives sexually from the beginning. I'm firmly on a wife's side in this, but I also can't help it that Scripture commands us to make ourselves available to each other sexually:

> The husband should fulfill his marital duty to his wife, and likewise the wife to her husband.... Do not deprive each other except by mutual consent and for a time. (1 Corinthians 7:3,5)

I have to stand by that truth—after all, God is God, and man is man. But I also know that this is not the only text in the Bible. This verse was never intended to trump the rest of Scripture and let husbands off the hook for boorish, sinful behavior in bed or anywhere else around the house.

Sure, men are promised regular sexual release by Scripture. But by the same token, women are promised that their husbands will treat them with honor and tenderness:

> Husbands, in the same way be considerate as you live with your wives, and
> treat them with respect as the weaker partner and as heirs with you of the
> gracious gift of life, so that nothing will hinder your prayers. (1 Peter 3:7)

I once heard that the Greek term for "weaker partner" can also be translated "fine china," which I think is a better translation within the context of marriage. How do you handle fine china? With respect, as you tenderly appreciate and display its finest points. You don't slam fine china around or put it through the blast of a dishwasher.

Brenda is a piece of God's finest china, lovely in His sight. How can I treat her like an old tin plate, trampling her soul's beauty, a soul that's been honed by years of obedience and generations of Christian heritage? If she pulls away because I abuse her sexually—selfishly using her for my own greedy pleasures—how can I possibly expect God to take my side?

After all, who is more wrong: the woman who deprives her husband or the husband who disrespects his wife? The husband, of course. He is the leader of the home. He must lead by example and show others how to walk like Christ.

And how would Christ walk? Given His words below, He'd start here, I suspect:

> Why do you look at the speck of sawdust in your [wife's] eye and pay no
> attention to the plank in your own eye? How can you say to your [wife],
> "[Wife], let me take the speck out of your eye," when you yourself fail to see
> the plank in your own eye? You hypocrite, first take the plank out of your
> eye, and then you will see clearly to remove the speck from your [wife's] eye.
> (Luke 6:41-42, bracketed words added)

The bottom line is this: if a husband isn't willing to submit to oneness (intimacy and tenderness) outside the bedroom, how can he expect his wife to submit sexually *inside* the bedroom? He needs to take care of the log in his own eye first, and then he'll be able to see clearly to help her.

FROM BRENDA

When we wives disobey God and do not make ourselves sexually available to our husbands, we block off their main, natural route for expressing intimacy.

Of course, in the wake of his sexual sin or his addiction, it may be necessary to mutually agree to a sexual moratorium to allow the healing process to begin. I understand that well enough.

But before you cavalierly cut him off, consider exactly what you are doing. You aren't just depriving him of one of his favorite recreational pursuits because he's been a bad boy with computer porn and needs to be punished, as you might cut off television privileges for a child who crossed the street when you told him not to.

No, cutting him off sexually is more the equivalent of telling your wandering little boy, "Because you crossed the street, I'm not going to touch you, hug you, tuck you into bed at night, or even speak to you for the next month. Eat static!"

It's serious. Let's flip the tables in an effort to understand our husband's sexuality a little more. When Fred turns me down sexually, it's usually not that big of a deal for me. I figure he's got a good reason, and besides, I get more sleep before morning, so why complain? And, of course, there's always tomorrow night.

But what happens in a man's heart when a wife says no to him? Far more, I can assure you. First, it reflects on her respect for him:

> However, each one of you also must love his wife as he loves himself, and
> the wife must respect her husband. (Ephesians 5:33)

Respecting Fred is my highest calling as a wife. No, he hasn't always made it easy, but it is still my calling, and Christ still expects me to do it for Him, even when I can't do it for Fred.

Respecting Fred takes on many forms, but I know that respecting him sexually means trying my best to make sure he's fulfilled, putting my whole self into it each time we're together, and making sure by my actions that Fred knows that I like sex with him. I know intellectually that a wife's respect in the sexual arena is very important to her husband's self-esteem, and I know personally that Fred is happier and more contented—and more able to handle a heavy load of stress with a wife, four kids, and his careers—if he knows he has my respect.

The well-being of a married man's psyche is tied inextricably to the quality of his sex life. If he feels good about his sex life, that sense of satisfaction spills over into every other part of his experience. And conversely, if his sex life is floundering, then in his mind, other disasters cannot be too far behind.

Every day a man walks into a world that says essentially, "Prove yourself. Prove that as a man you have something worthwhile to offer." In ways both blatant and subtle, a man is evaluated and measured and stacked up against the next guy all day long. The big question in his mind, conscious or not, is whether he is man enough. Does he have what it takes to win the golf tournament, get the promotion, or woo the woman? Successful, adequate sex certainly isn't the only route to affirmation, but it surely is the quickest and most direct one for a man.

Fred may be great at marketing, and his peers may see him as a great role model in business, but if he's not too desirable to me in the bedroom, in his mind it's only a matter of time until everyone else discovers that he's not as competent as everyone thought he was.

As women, we often struggle to understand this. One wife asked me, "Why does sex have to be such a big deal? Why can't he just go with the flow and be happy?"

Because he's a man. And he shouldn't have to apologize for that, whether I get it or not. All I have to know is this: if I show no interest sexually and don't meet his sexual needs, he feels hurt and wonders just how much I really love and respect him. Life will always feel pretty meaningless to a husband without regular sexual intimacy. Whether I understand this or not is irrelevant. That is how men are made.

And while we're at it, respect is not the only thing involved when we say no to our husbands—it goes even deeper than that. Counselor Patrick Middleton says it also has to do with abandonment and rejection:

I think sex is also about risk, dependency, and shame. When I am interested and excited enough to risk reaching out sexually, only to get turned down, I think shame gets activated because of the wall of rejection erected when my wife says no. I react in anger to cover the empty, weak feeling that this brings.

I talked with a couple of men in counseling about their reactions when they get turned down. One said this: "I really connect with my wife through sex. When she says no, it's like she doesn't care about me. I'm not important to her."

You *could* label the whole thing disrespect, but the emotional reaction is deep for men, and it probably feels more personal than it should. I think it triggers a whole bunch of old hurt, and the hurt turns to anger.

In light of this, perhaps the best way to understand our men is to remember how it feels when they're trampling *us* and wrecking oneness. I long for Fred to truly hear me and understand what I'm up against. If I bare my soul to him, and he just stares at me blankly or even starts to inch out of the room, the pain is crushing. You and I both know how that feels. Your husband feels the same pain just as poignantly—only his sense of being overlooked, unwanted, and ignored is *sexual.*

The most crushing difference between the sexes is not felt in the short term but the long term. We women have healthy alternatives while we wait for our husbands to turn their hearts back to us. We have our children to raise. We can create a new web of friendships. We can bury ourselves in hobbies and church work. Our main pathway of giving and getting intimacy can be used with others in godly, healthy ways, no matter how bad it gets with our husbands. In fact these relationships and activities can become so meaningful personally that they can replace the thing you really want and make it harder to reconnect intimately with him later.

Tragically, married men have no alternative in the long term, which means we have them in a much more treacherous spot. Their language of intimacy is sex. Where do they go to build an alternative intimacy if you pull away from them? All their alternatives are sinful: Internet porn, masturbation, sexual involvement with coworkers. When a man chooses a woman to marry, he knows he is limiting his sexual options to her alone. In the arms of this one woman, he rests the most emotionally vulnerable aspect of his being.

Consider what this husband must be feeling after his wife wrote us this note:

> In sorrow, he asked if I was committed to working this marriage out. I couldn't honestly answer that from my heart, but I did commit to walking along his side and to try to be patient as he grew. But I could not even *think* of being sexually intimate with him right now, no matter how much he needs it. I know this sounds harsh, but that's how I feel.

I know it was the husband who messed things up in this marriage. The wife need not apologize for her feelings. She's been crushed. But she does need to understand the final goal and push toward it quickly, because full intimacy will never occur until sexual oneness is established.

In some sense, her commitment to be patient is about all he can currently ask for as her husband. But God can ask a little more of us than that, and He sometimes does.

Jesus Christ didn't dawdle when the time came to obey His Father's words and reclaim the world. Christ set His jaw and headed toward Jerusalem, ignoring His fear of what He knew His destiny would be—Calvary.

As His daughters, our Father is asking us to rise above our feelings and to obey His Word in the marriage bed, because therein lies *our* destiny…a God-honoring marriage based on His principles.

chilling sex

From Brenda

There will come a time when future generations will laugh at us for our "modern" thinking that men and women are the same, because the truth is—we're not. For instance, medical scientists have identified the part of the brain that drives sexual desire. The nerve bundle that trips sexual desire is usually twice the size in a man's brain as compared to a woman's.

Other structures of the brain are different as well. Years ago Fred and I heard an accomplished linguist describe the differences between the brain structures of men and women and why men have difficulty accessing their emotions and expressing them verbally. His explanation, which I found fascinating, described how the mother's androgens naturally break down many of the communication links between the two hemispheres of the male brain between the sixteenth to twenty-sixth weeks of fetal development. During that time, the left hemisphere of the male brain shrinks and changes color while the right hemisphere flourishes. At the same time, the brain's corpus callosum is damaged, so to speak, and the number of communication points between the two hemispheres is reduced greatly.

This development explains why male brains work quite differently from female brains. The two halves of the male brain cannot talk to each other very well, but the two halves of the female brain communicate with each other just fine.

Men, then, are less able to express emotions and feelings verbally than women, generally speaking. A recent study at the Indiana University School of Medicine revealed that women use both hemispheres of the brain when listening, while men use only one. This means that men, to paraphrase a popular radio talk-show host, are communicating with half their brains tied behind their backs.

Hmmm. And we always thought that men were just lazy and insensitive to our needs. What a relief to know it's only brain damage!

While I'm teasing a little, in truth this specialized male brain is actually advantageous to women and offers a lot to the marriage relationship. Guys can be single-minded and focused, which helps on the job front, and setbacks don't phase them as much. The problem is that this focus-oriented drive also creates obstacles to intimacy in a marriage relationship.

In *Every Man's Marriage* we called such obstacles the Top Ten Love Chillers because they tend to induce a cooling effect on the flow of warmth and affection in the relationship. In *Every Man's Challenge* we called them Prayer Chillers because of their frosty effects upon a couple's prayer life.

Well, these obstacles can ice over the marriage bed, too. That's why here we're going to call them Sex Chillers. See if you recognize any Sex Chillers in your husband's nature.

FROM FRED

Here's my list of Sex Chillers:

1. Men are rebellious by nature. Eve was deceived in the Garden of Eden, but Adam wasn't. He *knew* it was wrong but ate fruit from the Tree of the Knowledge of Good and Evil anyway. Through the millenniums, Adam's sons—including your husband—have been just as rebellious. The last time I checked, males were starting and fighting wars in various places around the world, committing far more crimes than women, and driving crazier on the roads.

Why are guys like this? We get bored fast with the straight life. Said another way, we quickly tire of submitting our rights to Christ. We'd rather have things our own interesting way.

The desire to control our standards and chart our own moral course is overwhelming. We give God a say on a few things while retaining our veto power in case the road gets too narrow. No wonder I get e-mails like this so often:

> I also began to see all the reasons why my attempts for "sexual sobriety" had failed in the past. I had said to myself many times, *I'll give*

up pornography, but not masturbation or *I'll give up everything but checking out women.*

Note his exercise of his line-item veto.

2. The male ego is bigger but more fragile than the female ego. If you think we want control of our morality, you should see the control we want in our sex lives. Our sexuality is tightly tied to our male ego, so controlling our sex life makes us feel more like a man. Dean justified his stash of porn this way:

> I feel my wife is the most beautiful woman in the world. Still, I guess she doesn't provide what I get from porn and masturbation, which I know is awful to say in light of how much I love her.
>
> What do I get with porn? I like how naked women look in the pictures. They look so seductive, so sexy, and they are willing to show you all they got. They are there to please me, and I don't have to give anything in return. I can take whatever I want, when I want, and how I want, through masturbation.

In reality, porn and masturbation are really the coward's way. In real life, most guys would *never* approach the hottest-looking girl on the beach; they'd be totally intimidated. But online, a man can find hundreds just like her, and every one of them has already taken her clothes off without even being asked to. Porn and masturbation are a seductively powerful substitute for reality, because an orgasm produces a strong sense of manhood in a guy. He feels dominant and strong at the moment of release, even though the sensation is fleeting. What a guy can't get through a real sexual encounter, he thinks he can get through looking at porn and ejaculating, because it feels good and provides many of the same feelings experienced from the real thing. Because our native language of intimacy is sexual, masturbation feels like intimacy to us.

The trouble with masturbation is that because of this false sense of intimacy and manhood, it can become an easily obtained feel-good drug. If life is going badly and we're depressed, we masturbate to feel better. If life is going good, we masturbate to have a good time. If we're stressed heavily for time, we masturbate to relax and to reassert control of our lives.

Because of this, we can get emotionally hooked on that orgasmic surge of power and virility, and our addiction may have nothing to do with our wives or our passion for them at all. It simply soothes our fragile egos.

3. *Men are relatively less sensitive to the needs of others.* In a perfect world the head of the home would be the most sensitive one in the house. Well, you already know this, but we don't live in a perfect world! Mary told us:

> I read once that a strong sexual bond can strengthen a man's attachment to his wife, and that is why I have submitted to Tommy's sexual desire on every occasion but one. I can accept that Tommy may never be a good lover, and I'm not terribly disturbed that intercourse may never last longer than fifteen to twenty seconds for us. Given my busy life, I certainly have more on my mind than achieving orgasms.
>
> What upsets me is that he really doesn't do much of anything to help make sex with him tolerable, and I'm not sure how much longer I can or should take the kind of treatment I am getting from my "godly" husband (publicly, anyway). I don't feel loved or cherished in our marriage bed; instead, I feel that I have been trapped and assaulted. Though I desperately want to be a good and godly wife, how can I live with a man who will use my body almost nightly for as long as his virility holds out? I am seriously thinking of giving up this battle. Tommy has, in some measure, stripped my heart to a wasteland.

For most men, sensitivity does not come naturally. Believe it or not, this husband probably doesn't realize that he is being sexually insensitive at all. Guys just naturally assume that if they are happy and satisfied, then their wives are happy and satisfied. So, while she thinks this selfish behavior should be obvious to him, it really isn't. Our wiring doesn't pick up signals like this very well, and this is critical for you to understand if you desire to rebuild your marriage.

If a wife doesn't quietly and rationally explain to her husband that this type of lovemaking is more about making it good for him than about making it good for both of them, he may not get it. While it may seem unromantic to have to do so, you should explain how and what makes it good for you and explain why your desire is much lower now because of his behavior. Don't be afraid to be a mentor in this area. After all, if it isn't you, who's it going to be?

4. *Before marriage, males initiate the love relationship.* After marriage, he sees the bride as someone to look after him. Having conquered this frontier called love, he kicks back, thinking more about himself than the relationship, as Jeannine described it to us:

Up until our engagement, Trent treated me with great consideration. We had long conversations, and the thing I liked the most is that we laughed together. As we dated longer and longer, there were many expressions of affection, both verbally and through hugs and kisses.

But once Trent had that ring on my finger, it was as if he no longer had to woo me to get what he wanted, so why bother? He started doing whatever he wanted, whether I liked it or not. That attitude pretty well defines our sexual relationship since the wedding.

Husbands don't naturally understand the work necessary to hold intimacy together, so our insensitivity is not necessarily a reflection of our love for our wives. As bizarre as it may seem from your relational perspective, we're blind as bats and we often just don't know it.

5. *Men need less romance than women.* Once the coals of love are burning bright, we tend to forget to stoke the fires of the relationship. We say to ourselves, "Okay, now I've got a wife, and it feels pretty good. What's next on the agenda?" But romance lies at the heart of a woman's sexuality. Every wife is an incurable romantic since romantic love is the fuel that runs the female engine.

By nature, romance draws less of a man's focus after the wedding. The wife may see this as cold and heartless and take it personally. The husband may not even realize how his behavior is being interpreted.

Chrissie said this:

I have now been married for almost a year to the only guy I ever dated, and I love him very much; he is my brother in Christ and my best friend. But my romantic feelings for him have pretty much flat-lined because he ignores me romantically.

I love the intimacy of a hug and extra attention, but the most fulfilling aspects of our relationship have pretty well disappeared. Calling out, "Hey, you're a babe" when I pass through the room as he channel surfs endlessly hardly measures up to actually taking the time with me after a hard day at work. Yet he seems to expect me to be turned on every time we touch.

Low on romantic fuel, a wife may run on the fumes of memories from days gone by, when her man initiated the love relationship. Left to natural male thinking, sadly and often tragically, this crucial area of female sexuality is forgotten.

6. Men can compartmentalize their sex lives. Somehow the split-brain hemispheres allow a guy to compartmentalize his life. Since sex is a guy's primary means of giving and receiving intimacy, you might think that this would be impossible.

Ah, but it is. Men who are ignoring the Holy Spirit's nudgings can manage to place pornography into a separate silo from their deep love for their wives, no matter how incredible that may seem. Since sex and relationship are normally inseparable to a woman, it is hard to see that this sin on a man's part is anything but a breach of the relationship and perhaps evidence that his wife just must not have what it takes as a woman.

I love Brenda with all my heart, and she is my one and only. I honestly could never imagine loving another woman, but because of my ability to compartmentalize, my moderate level of sexual sin didn't trump my love and emotions for her at the time. Really.

Unfortunately, that's how we're wired. I'm not making this up, and I'm not even stretching the truth—your husband's sexual sin doesn't necessarily mean he doesn't love you.

That being said, I'm glad that I don't have to live in compartments anymore, and your husband doesn't have to either. No man can fully serve Christ until he flattens these silos holding these sins.

FROM BRENDA

Although that list of chillers is sobering, understanding and adjusting to them will take us far toward realizing the kind of sexual relationship we want in marriage. Besides, our husbands needn't stay like this. According to 2 Peter 1:3-4, God's divine power has given our husbands everything they need for life and godliness so they can participate in the *divine* nature rather than their evil ones.

And I've also found that once husbands understand our needs and their weaknesses, then the frustrating, specialized male brain can be *very* advantageous to us. Once guys turn that single-minded focus onto us and the marriage, vast improvements can happen rapidly. Fred has been remarkable that way.

So while it may be a discouraging list to read now, remember what we've said: you absolutely *must* learn how your husband is sexually wired if you ever want to escape your pain and rebuild a satisfying marriage. It will be very beneficial if you can understand how to look at this whole situation through male eyes and with an awareness of how a man's sexual hardware and software work.

If you have any negative attitudes toward your husband's sexuality, with God's help, work on rooting them out. Although it may hurt to even consider such a thing now, male sexuality is worthy of your tender care. It won't always be easy, but it can happen if you open your heart. Believe us, it's for your ultimate good because this is the quickest way to face and relieve your pain.

Mary's story

Authors' note: The following story comes from Mary, a reader of *Every Man's Marriage* (formerly titled *Every Woman's Desire*), and we use it to demonstrate how easily a woman can mislabel her husband's intentions and decisions through biased female perspectives. After much passionate discussion, we've decided to leave her vivid and edgy language as she wrote it so you can better catch her emotions:

As a wife struggling to find intimacy and oneness for years, I have never found a book that so clearly described my feelings as *Every Man's Marriage*. I have been married for fifteen years. While the sex was great early on, it didn't take long for me to feel like a commodity and that Greg was only interested in me when I was in bed.

I manage a Christian bookstore, so I've probably read every book out there on marriage and sex. Most of the books on these topics are terribly disappointing, however. The vast majority use the passage from 1 Corinthians 7:1-10 to declare that a wife is always obligated to have sex with her husband, regardless of the state of their marriage. She must just do it whenever he wants it if she wants to be a godly wife, even if part of her dies every time because she feels like a prostitute.

One author, whose parenting books I've enjoyed in the past, recently wrote that unless a woman is willing to have sex at least three times a week for the rest of her life, she has no business getting married. That was a very difficult thing for me to read, especially since I'm struggling about feeling used by my husband. Another author suggested that her readers increase their sex drives by taking certain hormones, which just happened to be available for purchase on her Web site at rather steep prices.

But the most damaging book I have ever read destroyed my sexuality completely.

Up until I read it, I struggled with the fact that my husband had plenty of time for his work, hobbies, and friends, but no time at all for me. I was horribly lonely in my marriage and desperate to try anything. This writer assured me that if I had sex with my husband whenever he wanted, he would absolutely desire to spend more time with me.

That notion sounded plausible enough, so I decided to put her words to a test, taking a New Year's Day vow to have sex with Greg whenever he wanted. I didn't mention this vow to Greg, but he quickly discovered my nonstop availability on his own.

It was the worst, most degrading year of my life. We had sex nearly every day, and often more than once in a day. My husband kept telling me that this was the closest he had ever felt to me during our marriage, but I kept feeling more and more distant and used. I told myself that if I just kept it up, he would soon start spending more time with me. He never did.

Things deteriorated until eventually he was awaking me every morning at 5:00 to roll me over and screw me. Sorry for the vulgar term, but that's what it was. Afterward, he'd leave to go fishing or golfing, only to duck back into the house later in the morning with just enough time to clean up and rush off to work. Under this constant assault, I became the master of "out of body" intercourse, shipping my mind far away during sex so that I could bear it. After a year of letting him thrust away, my self-worth had been scorched to the ground.

Mercifully, New Year's Day rolled around again, and my vow was complete. I told Greg about my experiment and mentioned that I would be unable to keep it up anymore. He was enraged that I'd kept my plan to myself, which essentially set him up to, in his words, "rape me" daily for a whole year. He demanded why I didn't tell him it was against my will.

But his anger was the least of my concerns.

I was so confused that I no longer knew how to set reasonable boundaries. I was sick of what I call Greg's "testosterone temper tantrums"—how angry and mean he got if we went four or five days without sex. I wanted to be a godly wife, but at that point, I hated sex so much that I didn't care whether I ever did it again, although we did keep it up two to three times per week.

Sexually, I felt like nothing more than a hole. I tearfully screamed at God in anger and frustration, "If my purpose in this life is to be nothing but an orifice, why didn't You have the compassion to make me a dog instead of a woman so that I could be loved and appreciated?"

I also felt like a human toilet for semen. I apologize if this seems rude and gross, but that's exactly how I felt. You know how most people have to go to the bathroom when they first get up in the morning? Greg felt he needed sex every morning, and I was the receptacle for his ejaculation.

I hated morning sex. I am not a morning person, and I like to squeeze every last bit of sleep in before starting a busy day with four children. Even when I initiated sex at night so he could be satisfied, he *still* wanted it at the crack of dawn, even if I was completely asleep. So I felt like a toilet, and the dripping semen he left in me each morning after his "constitutional" made me think that a toilet was all I was worth.

Greg was so selfish. My husband habitually took three showers a day to relax. With my busy schedule with the kids, I could only fit in one shower per day, and I liked to relax under the hot water, as well. But that rarely happened for me, because turning on the shower was like the bell and Pavlov's dog. Moments after the first droplets hit the floor, my husband came scurrying in with me, salivating for me to soap him up for a hand job. So, instead of relaxing, I was even put to demeaning work in the shower—it was about as romantic as milking a cow.

I've begged Greg to go to counseling about this with me, but he's refused, partly out of pride. Gratefully, he is very open to talk about relational issues, and we've come a long way in our relationship over the last several years. Greg has already improved so much, and this improvement has increased our oneness and intimacy. Part of that is due to *Every Man's Marriage,* which I think has accomplished a lot of what we could have achieved in counseling sessions.

But as of now, I still feel mortally wounded sexually. Sex has now been separated from love in my mind, and now that I know that men can separate sex from love so easily in their minds, it is hard for me to bring them back together in my mind. It's also hard to ignore that while sometimes a guy does it to show love for his wife, at other times it seems little more than a chance to have an orgasm. That leaves me very cynical.

I feel the weight of the whole world when I think how women are mistreated in the marriage bed. If we could survey every woman at the end of their lives, I would like to know how many women in history would say that sex was something that enhanced their lives. Odds are that a huge, huge majority would admit that it damaged them.

This is the one area where I cannot understand God. I know He created sex to be a wonderful thing, but so many Christian marriages are not experiencing it this way. Why did He create something that has so much potential for misuse and damage in women?

FROM FRED

When I first read Mary's e-mail, I cried. How anyone could treat another human being in this way—and she *was* the love of his life—was beyond words for me. What a horribly crushing year she spent, and what a devastatingly slow growth curve she is on with her husband. And yet, from the perspective of my own male hardwiring, I can understand how this happened.

Mary posed a great question: why did God create something that has so much potential for misuse and damage in women?

Why *would* God do this to us? The answer: He didn't. We've done it to ourselves. Or, more accurately, men have done this by ignoring the apostle Peter's message to treat our wives with understanding and like precious china. I don't care what philosophy you care to study, none honors women more than Christ's way.

Now the fact that Christian men aren't following in Christ's footsteps is tragic. Some have heard the truth—or sense the truth deep within—but they aren't practicing the truth inside and outside the bedroom.

God created sex because of its awesome potential to draw hearts together as one and for its potency in picturing Christ's relationship with His bride, the church. You see, God never talks about sex in the context of one person, and He did not give us our sexuality for ourselves. He gave us our sexuality for our partner:

> The husband should fulfill his marital duty to his wife, and likewise the wife
> to her husband. The wife's body does not belong to her alone but also to her

husband. In the same way, the husband's body does not belong to him alone but also to his wife. (1 Corinthians 7:3-4)

Sex is not about our individual needs. My role is to give Brenda sexual pleasure. She is to do the same for me. Your sexuality exists in the relationship for your husband's pleasure, and his sexuality exists in the relationship for yours. While sexual self-focus is normal everywhere else, it is not normal in the Christian marriage bed.

Of course, because of male hardwiring, men don't naturally have that Christian view of sex. As we've discussed in detail, a man's sexual triggers lead him to sexual blind spots, especially within our vividly sexualized culture. So, as men, we must be taught and led toward this pure focus by Christ, and we must be helped along in that direction by our wives. Surely one reason God gave us wives was to encourage us to take part in the divine nature rather than to stagnate in our natural sexual bents.

FROM BRENDA

Perhaps you have a problem with Mary's story—especially the part about her year-long experiment. We have received numerous e-mails that tell stories like Mary's. I think there are several ways to explain them.

First, because of the lopsided teaching on female submission in the church, we hear from wives who make unilateral, behind-the-scenes decisions in hopes of improving their marriages because they don't know they have a right to bring up these issues with their husbands. That's really all Mary did here, though admittedly to an extreme.

Second, it's true that Mary and Greg have sexual issues. But because both are now communicating better and growing as a couple, they are showing more health than many supposedly normal Christian couples who are not able to even talk to each other about their sex life.

And while this year-long experiment was horrific in its effects, Mary's plan was only the logical extrapolation of the common "give men all the sex they want and they'll be good husbands" teaching. To her credit, Mary was trying to be a responsible Christian woman and do everything she could to be a good wife—she didn't know that her secret plan was unwise until she applied it to its logical end.

Don't be put off by the unusual nature of the story—there is much to be learned here about how we can judge the motives and actions of our husbands too harshly, especially in light of the natural differences between men and women that we discussed in the last chapter. If we expect to rebuild normal intimacy together, it is critical to understand that our biases as women can chill the marriage bed as quickly as the Sex Chillers themselves.

Take a look inside. Any woman's heart is stirred deeply with sympathy for Mary, and doubtless you felt what I felt when you read her letter. But also check carefully your heart for Greg. What was your reaction to him? Did you feel any sympathy for him?

Sympathy? He perpetrated this mess and acted like a sexual pig! True. But I believe your heart can stretch further now that you've read these chapters on how men are wired. Male sexuality is complex. Greg didn't ask for this hardwiring, and he probably doesn't understand it as well as he should. Yet his sexual makeup contributed to his fall, and look especially at how Mary mislabeled his missteps.

I'll choose some passages from Mary's letter, and Fred will comment on them from a man's point of view. Perhaps some of Fred's comments will seem like a stretch to you—they occasionally did to me! But maybe that's to be expected when we are talking about such vast differences between men and women, and these insights have really broadened my understanding of men through the years and have made me a better wife and Christian.

Mary wrote: *I struggled with the fact that my husband had plenty of time for his work, hobbies, and friends, but no time at all for me. I was horribly lonely in my marriage and desperate to try anything.*

Comment: Because of the hardwiring of men, if they don't watch it, they can be so into their own desires that they won't even know they are ignoring their wives. While it may seem bizarre and shallow to women, we men can honestly think that if we're happy, our wives are happy, and we won't know otherwise unless you say something. Without Brenda's patient guidance through the years, I'd be some variation of Greg, I'm sure.

My husband kept telling me that this was the closest he had ever felt to me during our marriage, but I kept feeling more and more distant and used. I told myself that if I just kept it up, he would soon start spending more time with me. He never did.

Comment: Although Mary justifiably was not happy with Greg's words and behavior, more than likely Greg was being sincere when he said he really felt close. Sex does that for a man. Based on his hardwiring, his response was predictable. His primary language of intimacy is sex. Of *course* he felt closer to her than ever before. She was allowing him to "know her" intimately two or three times a day.

The trouble is that Greg didn't recognize that Mary's language for intimacy was different from his. Although he certainly could have done better, it isn't really fair for her to just dismiss everything he did as blatant insensitivity. Given his hardwiring, he was naturally blind to the fact that she has a different language and, to his credit, he *did* start working on it once she'd explained it.

Things deteriorated until eventually he was awaking me every single morning at 5:00 to roll me over.

Comment: Again, Greg's hardwiring at work. The orgasmic pleasure chemicals are exhilarating and relaxing. Any normal husband loves how he feels during and after ejaculation. I can understand why—from a female perspective—Greg's unabated enthusiasm for frequent, almost mechanical sex makes him look like a selfish pig. But his behavior must be carefully and correctly labeled. When Mary set up her experiment and started offering sex "on demand," it became very predictable that the result would be a year of frequent sex late at night and early in the morning.

To put it bluntly, Greg pretty much lived out every married man's dream. Granted, the fact that he never questioned why Mary was doing this, and more important, whether this sexual feast was pleasing to her, is reprehensible. Still, to label him "ignorant" is a much more apt description than "heartless."

He was enraged that I'd kept my plan to myself, which essentially set him up to, in his words, "rape me" daily for a whole year. He demanded why I didn't tell him it was against my will.

Comment: Maybe you're appalled that this "insensitive brute" would appear to shift the blame to his wife. But what if he's not being insensitive?

What if he's just been duped by his hardwiring and has stumbled blindly into this stupidity, as suggested by his fuming response? If so, he has every right to be angry—after all, she *did* hide the truth for a year. Of course, that doesn't excuse sexually abusing his wife, but it *does* help to explain how it could happen pretty naturally without an insensitive, conscious choice on his part.

I was sick of what I call Greg's testosterone temper tantrums—how angry and mean he got if we went four or five days without sex.

Comment: Mary is right to condemn Greg's anger and meanness. But I will offer some defense on his behalf: if a man has that much sex that often, even a small break in the action is going to turn him into Mr. Grump. I know that rationally we might think that abundant sex would satisfy and fill up a guy like a mountain reservoir fills up when the snow melts in spring. But it just doesn't work that way. When you consider Greg's hardwiring, and remember that he was addicted to natural chemical highs after one, two, to three hits of sex a day for a year, his crabbiness and bizarre behavior should be expected—similar to the withdrawal symptoms seen with a drug addiction.

I know that men can separate sex from love so easily in their minds… It's also hard to ignore that while sometimes a guy does it to show love for his wife, at other times it seems little more than a chance to have an orgasm. That leaves me very cynical.

Comment: If males were wired like females, cynicism would be a reasonable response. But considering what we've discussed about the brain differences between men and women, the ability of a man to separate sex from love makes sense and will happen. To be cynical is to simply ignore the truth of our makeup. And the extreme sensuality of our culture makes it even easier to separate the two in a guy's brain. Does that make it right? Heavens no! As men, we can stop doing this, and we must. But not every separation of sex from love in a man's behavior is the result of a purposeful, conscious, selfish choice. Also, Mary needs to acknowledge the perfectly normal and satisfying role of the "quickie" in marital sex—something that both men and women are known to initiate and enjoy.

Healing Relationships

Did you notice how easy it is to negatively mislabel things when you don't consider a man's hardwiring? Mislabeling is the most dangerous act we can perpetrate against our relationships.

When we were first married, Brenda was late everywhere we went. I hated this, and I used to berate her insensitivity to me and to everyone waiting on us. I chided her mercilessly, saying it was time to grow up.

Similarly, when the stress level rose too high in our home, she used to withdraw to the couch with a book or watch television. I berated her for this, too, as well as for being weak and not facing her problems like a "real Christian."

When I considered these and other such traits, I honestly thought I'd married a lemon—until I read some books by Tim LaHaye about our temperaments. Then I realized that *I'd* been the lemon for mislabeling her so.

People of Brenda's temperament are always "late people." They are wired that way. The revelation of such truths surely saved my marriage.

Imagine. All that time I'd been viewing Brenda as defective, childish, and irresponsible. But she wasn't. She was simply different. I stopped mislabeling, and I never yelled at her again for being late. (That's not to say we can't eventually rise above our hardwiring through Christ, of course. Today, Brenda is always on time.)

LaHaye also mentioned that people of Brenda's temperament are wired to retreat to the couch and television under stress. Imagine how *that* truth changed my perspective toward Brenda, especially since my *own* temperament is wired to attack and conquer when under duress. Today I never belittle Brenda when she retreats to the couch. In fact, I often chuckle.

From Brenda

Can we wives do the same and stop labeling *sexual* differences so harshly? Regarding Mary's letter, it would be easy but far too simplistic to paint Greg as totally insensitive to his wife. But in light of his hardwiring, might we be mislabeling Greg to some degree? I think so, and that's detrimental to any relationship, as you can see from our early marriage.

Greg didn't consciously make the decision to use his wife the way he did and, in many ways, his sexuality is confusing to him, too. He deserves grace regarding these differences. And it wouldn't surprise me if your own husband deserves grace for many of the same reasons.

That was the whole purpose of these five chapters explaining our husbands' hardwiring—to keep us from mislabeling their actions and to allow us to move in with grace. When Fred mislabeled my actions, it continually sabotaged God's plan for us. We can't afford to do that in the marriage bed.

Hopefully, these chapters have given you much to consider and will keep you from mislabeling your husband and sabotaging God's intentions for your marriage.

In most cases, your husband probably does not consciously choose cold, mechanical orgasms over relationship and oneness. Consider the possibility that with the assistance of his wiring, he's slipped into this sexual self-focus somewhat effortlessly—aided and abetted by our immoral culture and the barrage of sensual messages that clog our media.

Should you give him a pass? Not on your life. Too much is riding on it, and he is responsible to lead your family into full truth and purity. Still, don't dismiss the rest of the truth: because of nature's hardwiring, your husband will need time and the opportunity to mature spiritually so he can lead your family in this direction. Blind spots will be prevalent. But he can learn, just as so many other men have learned and made their marriages better.

So will you help him? In an effort to help you do that, we've taken a look at male hardwiring in this part, and next we'll explore their sexual softwiring. Staggering spiritual and emotional wounds are pounded into our husbands and sons by the church and our culture, warping their sexuality and feeding their sin. We need to see what these wounds look like before we can help bind them up and encourage our husbands to claim full sexual purity for the health of our marriages and the glory of God.

the softwired differences in male sexuality

As we've just seen, male hardwiring sets men up to fall after they reach adolescence, but the wounds that come later explain why men can't always escape as quickly as you'd hope for or expect.

Who inflicts these wounds? The church, the family, and men themselves through their own lack of discipline. In this part, we'll devote one chapter to each of these.

You may be wondering why, after spending five chapters on male sexuality, we are spending three more on this issue. The answer is quite simple. The most common e-mails we receive from wives contain this haunting cry: "My heart is shattered and the pain is unbearable.... Please, please convince me that this is not about me. If I could only believe that, I know I could make it."

We believe that the most important part of your healing process is helping you understand that his sin is not about you. It is our hope that the next three chapters will finish this job in your heart.

the church has let us down

FROM FRED

For guys, this is the era of masturbation. There's more masturbation today and more things to masturbate over than ever before. There are entire industries whose sole intention is to get men to masturbate every day of the week and twice on Sunday.

The porn-film industry rents out seven hundred million videos a year. To keep up with the insatiable demand for new product, porn filmmakers produce eleven thousand movies each year so that men can succumb to this evil filth in the privacy of their homes.

Porn-related Web sites have been an amazing success story in the Internet world. While the dotcom industry crashed several years ago and investors lost billions of dollars, seventy thousand pay-for-porn sites found business to be quite good on the World Wide Web.

How in the world has this happened? I pondered this after a close Christian friend phoned me after Super Bowl XXXVIII in early 2004. My friend was all worked up. "Fred, did you see Janet Jackson's halftime show?" he exclaimed.

Certain he was joking, I laughed. "Of course not! We turned the channel during halftime because I know Janet Jackson has always been about sex. Plus I heard that MTV was producing the halftime show, so it doesn't surprise me what happened."

"Well, I watched it!" my friend blurted out. "What a shocking show! Justin Timberlake ripped off part of her top just before the lights went out, and her breast popped out in plain sight of everyone! You should have seen it. It was amazing!"

Though it was already quite late on Super Bowl Sunday when I answered his call, it would be some time before I'd drop off to sleep after hanging up the phone.

Anger flooded over me, and the more I thought about this conversation, the angrier I got. Why didn't my friend turn the channel when he saw the dancers sexually gyrating or Janet Jackson grinding with Justin Timberlake early in the song? As Christians, we all should have done that, because that's what God's Word counsels us to do:

> But among you *there must not be even a hint of sexual immorality,* or of any
> kind of impurity, or of greed, because these are improper for God's holy
> people. (Ephesians 5:3)

> Finally, brothers, whatever is true, whatever is noble, whatever is right,
> whatever is pure, whatever is lovely, whatever is admirable—if anything
> is excellent or praiseworthy—think about such things. (Philippians 4:8)

Do these scriptures mean anything to most Christian men? I wonder, just as I wonder how many Christian men *did* change the channel upon seeing early bumping and grinding on that Super Bowl halftime stage. If these men were still watching by the time Janet's breast popped out, then these scriptures mean nothing to them.

And this begins to answer my original question: how in the world did our culture sink so quickly into this sexual stew? The answer: we've dumped Scripture and lost our saltiness.

> Let me tell you why you are here. You're here to be salt-seasoning that brings
> out the God-flavors of this earth. If you lose your saltiness, how will people
> taste godliness? You've lost your usefulness and will end up in the garbage.
> (Matthew 5:13, MSG)

As Christians we have little preservative effect upon our culture anymore. We wouldn't be useless if we feared God more than we feared men. After all, what if Christians stopped watching sensual halftime shows and refused to buy tickets to the latest R-rated releases and stopped purchasing videos that titillate our genitals? Things would change pretty quickly around here.

Be realistic, Fred! That's not possible anymore. The very fact that you can't imagine this reveals that we've lost our saltiness, and it also begs another penetrating question: what exactly has the church been up to during this era of masturbation? Has she been calling back the strays and setting the captives free? Hardly. The words of author and evangelist Leonard Ravenhill haunt me:

> This present day is like an arena whose terraces are filled with the militant godless, the brilliant and belligerent skeptics, plus the blank-faced heathen millions, all looking into the empty ring to see what the Church of the living God can do. How I burn at this point! What are we Christians doing?

Sitting around silently mostly. In our quest to remain hip and relevant, our churches have become irrelevant to the greatest issue of our day, playing right into the hands of the Enemy whose clever temptations reveal a deadly understanding of male sexual hardwiring.

This type of stuff goes on even in church settings, and we barely notice anymore. One recent Wednesday night, my daughters were visiting another youth group when the youth pastor asked everyone to pay attention to a little promotion for the upcoming spiritual retreat weekend, which was to feature a disco dance on Saturday night. The lights were turned down, and three deacons' daughters bounced out in tight, low-cut black dresses and began dancing and thrusting to a strong disco beat. My daughters were stunned by what they saw.

When they told me what happened, I inquired, "What kind of dance was it?"

"I can't name the dance, but it was plenty vulgar," Laura replied.

"You can say that again," Rebecca replied with disgust.

They said the guys were clapping, whistling, hooting, and begging for more. As they spoke, I pondered if this evening's theme for youth group was "Wounding Your Purity Night."

On another Wednesday the youth leader asked the group how many had seen the movie *Dead Poet's Society,* a film probably ten years old, starring Robin Williams. More than 90 percent of the teens raised their hands. At this he proceeded to spend the rest of the evening preaching the truths he'd mined from that movie, yet he failed to mention the biggest-busted truth of all…that a *Playboy* centerfold flips wide open, front and center, for at least a whole minute during the film's early scenes. Having just given tacit approval to watch the film, what about the boys who hadn't seen the film yet? A single viewing of such films can set a boy up for years of masturbation and guilt, as this letter attests:

> I was eleven when I first masturbated. It just kind of happened while watching a strip scene in a TV movie. For about two, three years, I didn't even know it was masturbation. It just felt good. Then in middle school, my Sunday-school teacher separated the genders for some "adolescent teaching."
>
> Fortunately, I was taught a lot about puberty and lust. Unfortunately, my teacher was not too clear on masturbation and took a very neutral standpoint so as not to offend anyone by saying that masturbation was wrong. I took that as a green light, and from there it started to become a daily habit. But a funny thing happened. Though no one had spoken against it, I started to feel guilty about the practice. I guess that even though my Sunday-school teacher didn't make it clear, my Teacher inside me did! But by then I was hooked, and I was locked into masturbation for years.

You already know that our male hardwiring is prone to addictive lusts of the eyes. Now you can see how our own churches wound us with their desire to be "relevant," promoting and approving the very things that rev a guy's sexual engine into the red zone. Once there, however, masturbation eats our spirituality alive.

It would be one thing if we could do nothing about it. The truth is, many guys think we can't because of the teachings of the church. For instance, one old train of thought still riding the rails today declares that masturbation is a certainty and that virile teenagers and single males cannot stop masturbating, no matter how hard they try. Calling masturbation "forbidden fruit" only makes the practice more attractive, which means we should deemphasize the embarrassment since that only pours needless shame onto young males' heads.

Why fight it, when masturbation is physically and emotionally harmless? goes the claim. *Trying to stop young men from masturbating will fail anyway, because nothing works as a cure—cold showers and lots of exercise are foolish and ineffective.*

My response? Cold showers and exercise don't work because they never address the root issues in our hardwiring or our need for intimacy. Besides, just because these particular measures don't work doesn't mean *every* campaign is destined to fail, and it certainly doesn't mean silence is our best bet.

In defense of those who give masturbation a free pass, they make the assumption that young males' sex drives are fixed as high as a kite and can never drop nearer to earth. Given that assumption, they feel they *must* declare masturbation kosher, and in that light, the only humane, reasonable thing to do is to lift the burden of shame and guilt from their helpless young shoulders altogether, leaving them alone to masturbate in peace.

But their assumptions are false. The sex drive *isn't* fixed, and masturbation *isn't* as physically and emotionally harmless as many think. No, masturbation won't grow hair on your palms, but it *is* an addictive practice, and there's no doubt that the false intimacy of masturbation turns men inward as they struggle with loneliness rather than turning them outward to God and to others for their intimacy. And as for the shame, given that we know so much more about the issue these days, discussions with our young men about masturbation needn't be shaming anymore.

After all, the ability of the male eyes and mind to draw sexual gratification from the world is simply a fact of life for guys. With all this foreplay of the eyes going on, and with no guidance on what to do with these feelings, the result is understandable. There's nothing defective in them, so why be ashamed? They're just normal guys who need to learn to manage their sex drives. That's just part of becoming a man.

Obviously, we need to be careful how we communicate about masturbation. Young men react negatively to harsh preaching about sexual sin, and we all know that the shaming approach often adds fuel to the fire. But at the same time, we must make sure the pendulum doesn't swing too far in the other direction. We must never, ever see masturbation as just guys being guys, helpless before their monstrous sex drive. They aren't, as this letter states:

> I have struggled off and on with my purity, and pictures and fantasies have
> plagued my relationships with people and my intimacy with God. My life
> used to be an endless cycle of sin, sorrow, redemption, over and over again. I

hated the torturous grasp of pornography and desperately desired the freedom to live in complete integrity before God and man.

Since I read *Every Young Man's Battle* during Christmas break, I have been totally clean. The time I spend with God is so full now, and I can worship Him without barrier, pretense, or hypocrisy. Most Christian guys can only dream about this freedom. I am gorging on it every day!

Silence is no longer the most humane, reasonable way for the church to handle the discussion. The battle's landscape has changed dramatically, and our guys are getting blasted off the spiritual battlefield.

Today's overwhelming blitzkrieg of visual stimulation has our engines running at high idle at all times, and if our youth pastors and pastors are longing to be relevant, they might formulate some relevant defense strategies for this fast new world. Granted, cold showers and exercise never worked very well, but to assert that *nothing* works in this battle is ridiculous and irresponsible, especially considering the era we're living in. Just ask Jake:

I've tried to stop masturbating many times on my own and failed miserably, pathetically and embarrassingly. But not after reading your book. Now I'm free!

When I tell the other guys at our campus ministry about how I'm doing, they are astounded. They didn't know that a twenty-two-year-old Christian guy doesn't have to be a victim of lust and masturbation. Thanks so much for encouraging me toward total sexual purity. Honestly, I didn't think it was realistic, either.

Stunning. What an indictment against the shepherds of the church that these men were so astounded! Because their shepherds had been silent and they hadn't been told they could be free, they had never even considered the possibility:

Son of man, prophesy against the shepherds of Israel; prophesy and say to them, even to the [spiritual] shepherds, Thus says the Lord God: Woe to the [spiritual] shepherds of Israel who feed themselves! Should not the shepherds feed the sheep?… The diseased and weak you have not strengthened, the sick you have not healed, the hurt and crippled you have not bandaged, those gone astray you have not brought back, the lost you have not sought to find. (Ezekiel 34:2,4, AMP)

This is God's eternal, chilling warning to His shepherds, and too many are not only failing to bandage the crippled with the truth, they're compounding the fractures by tacitly approving things that make purity tougher.

For instance, one pastor used illustrations from the movie *Titanic* to make his sermon relevant to his congregation. Look, I'm all for relevance, but let's talk specifics about this movie. How did *Titanic* ever pull a PG-13 rating? The raw sexuality of the sketching scene alone should have qualified this film for an R rating. Frankly, that nude scene was reminiscent of some of the 1970s "soft-core" flicks that I watched in the dorms back when I didn't give a fig about Christ's laws.

How many young men have popped *Titanic* into the VCR and masturbated over this sketching scene? How many Christian parents have unwittingly purchased this video so their sons can have mental sex with actress Kate Winslett anytime they choose, day or night? Yet the pastor never once cautioned his people about the sensuality in that movie. This isn't relevance—this is irresponsibility! Mainstream feature films can pollute as surely as pornographic Web pages, but we ignore the truth because everyone else is watching them too. These films damage our oneness with Christ as surely as cyberporn.

Husbands and sons simply stumble on in their warped sexual behavior, wondering why they can't get control of themselves, trapped by the church's silence. Meanwhile the sheep bray foolishly on, saying, "I'm glad our pastor is finally talking about movies in his sermons. Now I don't have to feel guilty about watching them."

What are we thinking? Oh, we begin innocently enough, hoping to soften things up to make things comfortable for the seekers sitting in the pews. But we've forgotten that the primary call of the local church is to equip the saints, and by approving practices that play against our natural wiring as men, we've not only failed to equip them, we've emasculated them as leaders. No wonder our men are slipping so easily into sin. Kenny explains:

I have been dealing with lust, masturbation, and pornography since I was twelve. Now I'm eighteen and a leader in my youth group harboring this huge secret sin. Don't get me wrong, I have loved God with all my heart for the last four years or so, but I never knew it was possible to be free.

And to think that I've spent all of my high-school years being heavily depressed! Yeah, there were multiple reasons, but the biggest one was never being able to conquer masturbation. It was hell, and it didn't have to be. I could have been free long ago.

Why be silent? Why not counsel freedom? Too often, our shepherds are still fighting yesterday's war:

I have decided to use your book for all of the young men's Bible studies in our ministry this spring, and the guys are stoked. My question is this: My immediate pastor does not see things the way I do. At his seminary, he was taught that if you can masturbate without visualizing a woman, then it's all right. So he has perfected the art of masturbating without visualizing a woman. I probably exaggerate in my description of his thinking, but I think you get the picture.

This makes it very difficult for me, a lay leader within the ministry, to talk with guys trying to overcome their lustful addictions, which includes the act of masturbation. When they tell my pastor what I've taught them, he responds that I am being a little too radical or even legalistic and that there is no biblical basis for eliminating this act. If they feel a need, then masturbation is natural and they just need to make sure they aren't being lustful while committing the act.

This drives me nuts. What do I say to this? I have forty young men who have been developing in-depth accountability over the last year, and they are finally at a point where they are ready to take a bold and radical step together to eliminate the sexual and lustful patterns of sin in their lives. But I need my immediate pastor to be on board.

It doesn't have to be this way. In fact, with forty committed young men, things could be a *lot* different. I'm reminded of another campus where students began discussion groups around *Every Young Man's Battle* and formed accountability groups so they could stand together.

One group of guys developed a plan to help one another to stop masturbating. Each person picked out one day of the week to masturbate, and that was the only day it was acceptable to do it. If you missed your day, you had to wait until the next week. Once you had developed this measure of control, you moved it up a notch and picked one day every two weeks as your day of masturbation.

As it turned out, by the time the group was ready to notch it up to once every three weeks, they all agreed that the whole exercise had become silly and unnecessary. The guys each had formed so much control over their sexuality that they no longer needed a day of masturbation.

Professors have told us of young men who had been trapped in compulsive masturbation for years and then found complete freedom as the openness and accountability robbed the habit of its power to dominate their lives. Guys who had been quite reserved came out of their shells and began to connect with others in new ways. And as word of this group's victory spread, more groups grew, and more young men who had felt alienated from God began to experience a connection with Him they had never known.

Why settle for masturbation without lust? Why stop short? That's yesterday's tactics, and we've been wounding our sons this way for too long.

FROM BRENDA

Note how the male hardwiring sets up our men to fall, but that the church's silence can push them over the edge. This is one more clue that your husband's sexual sin may not be about you at all, but about other things, like the unfortunate silence surrounding sexuality in our churches. In our next chapter, we'll look at how families can inflict their own set of wounds.

male wounds

FROM BRENDA

I love maleness. I don't always understand it, but I love it in my boys, and I cherish it in Fred. The other morning, Fred bounced downstairs wearing the same medium-weight navy jacket he had worn the day before. On this particular day he'd looked outside and seen the sky was as blue and sunny as the day before without realizing that the January sun had pulled a typical Iowa ruse on him: it was actually forty degrees colder this morning.

"Honey, you're going to need a warmer coat today," I commented. "It's cold out there." That's when the fun began.

First, a nearly imperceptible hitch in his stride revealed his pride was on the line. *Real men don't need heavy coats on a day like this!* his ego thought to himself.

Bemused, I then watched as his mind kicked into gear, halting his legs. I could tell what he was thinking. *Hold on, big boy. Maybe we ought to think about this for a minute.*

I could practically read his mind. I knew he had picked that jacket because it looked especially right with the rest of his clothes—and he had worn it the day before, and what was good the day before was good today. As his mental gears ground away, his furrowed brow told me that the heavy coat just wouldn't look right. Then, eureka! A broad, gleaming smile spread over his face when he announced, "I'll just throw that hooded jacket in the garage under this one. The wrestlers always did that with their letterman jackets, and they always looked so tough."

Wrestlers are the epitome of manhood in Fred's world. He paused for a moment, wearing the satisfied look of a man who'd just sold his house for fifty thousand dollars more than it was worth. He spun toward the garage door, disappearing with a wink. "Who knows?" he called out hopefully. "Maybe they'll mistake me for a wrestler out there."

I just smiled and shook my head as I stuffed another school lunch into a brown paper bag. That was so cute…something so simple, and yet his day had clearly taken a sweeping turn to the upside.

Maleness can be so special and fun to me. Why does a forty-seven-year-old guy still care if he looks like a wrestler? And when he imagines that he looks like one, where does that satisfied glow come from? In the end, I only know that this "being a guy" stuff hails from the deepest center of their beings.

But while this is mostly endearing to me these days, it wasn't always so. Fred was deeply wounded by his father while growing up, and once a man's been wounded in that guy place, most of what swirls up from there is not very funny at all—things like anger, distance, and rigidness. I think Fred's story can shed some light on how their wounds lead to sexual sin.

FROM FRED

Manhood is a confusing, foggy maze, even for men. Consider this: even though I was valedictorian and athlete of the year in high school, and even though I'd graduated with honors from Stanford University and beaten Dad head-to-head in career sales while working in separate territories for the same company, my father never accepted me as a real man. And for many of those years, I wasn't so sure he was wrong.

Manhood has little to do with accomplishments. Maybe you can get a glimpse of what it is as I share the only two situations in my life when I absolutely knew my dad accepted me as a man, at least momentarily.

The first happened when I was in second grade or so. I'd been playing with neighbor kids in my backyard when one of the boys got mad and punched me hard. I ran crying into the house and sat down wailing outside my dad's office, hoping for a hug and some sympathy. None was forthcoming.

Instead, my dad jumped out of his chair and bawled me out. "No son of mine is going to come running into the house every time he gets hurt!" he bellowed. "Now you get back out there like a man and punch him right in the nose."

Sniffling and in shock, I turned and marched back out to the yard as my dad watched from his ringside perch behind our big bay window. As I approached my adversary, he stood proudly with his hands on his hips and a sneering little grin playing across his lips. Then, as my dad would say in countless recounts of this story through the years, "Freddie really lowered the boom on the guy! Without a word, he just reared back and punched him in the nose, just like I said he should do! Now it was the *other* kid's turn to run home crying."

The second situation came at the end of the summer between my junior and senior years at Stanford. A friend and I had discovered this little thing called stock options. Stock options are financial instruments that allow you to buy a stock at a certain price at a set time in the future. The upside is that you can get rich really quick. The downside is, well, you can lose all your money.

Anyway, we'd both grabbed our life savings we'd earned in summer jobs during the years and plunked it all into options accounts at the local brokerage, about four thousand dollars each. The market was blazing, and within a few weeks we'd each grown our stakes to ten thousand dollars. We believed we were Wall Street's next whiz kids! It was Thursday with the Dow around 880, and our broker told us the Dow would be at 940 by Wednesday, so we loaded up. One more week, and our dreams of doubling our money again would come true!

The next day, the prime rate hit double digits for the first time in history. The market crashed, and it would be years before the Dow saw 940 on any day, let alone that Wednesday. Our investments vanished.

As whiz kids we were just certain this was a minor setback, and all we needed was another grubstake to prove it. So we each took our tuition money for the upcoming fall quarter and invested in more options, figuring we'd quickly double our money and then cash in to pay for that expensive Stanford tuition. Yes, we lost that money, too.

I flew home after the summer semester to see my family and figured I wouldn't see Stanford again anytime soon. I hated the thought of dropping out of school and pounding nails on a roofing crew to earn back the tuition money, but I was absolutely terrified by the thought of telling my dad what I'd done. Yet the fateful day arrived, and I told him the story straight up. I was stupefied by his response. He didn't yell. He didn't berate me. He simply told me I wouldn't have to drop out, but that I could borrow the money from him as long as I paid it back after I got a job following graduation.

And you know what? I'm sure I saw pride in his eyes, the kind of pride that says, "You know, my son has some real hair on his chest! That took guts to lay his tuition money on the line to prove he had what it takes! Maybe he's becoming a guy to be reckoned with after all."

You may be thinking, *You've got to be kidding! Punching a nose and losing your tuition money is manhood? That's crazy.* I guess so, but that's where guys live.

Worthiness is what manhood is all about, and that's why we say that men become men in the company of men. On the human level, only another man can declare us worthy, and when a father shows that kind of respect, that's worth a hundred times more. A father doesn't have to be a national wrestling champion to do this. He simply has to be a man. Fathers have size. They've got power. They've got wallets with real money in them. They've got beards like sandpaper. But most of all, they captured our hearts long ago, and because of that they have the words we're dying to hear: "You fit, boy. You belong here with the men. You're worthy— a man to be reckoned with."

But when we don't hear those words or sense that acceptance, that's when the father wounds crash in. The pain goes straight to the bone. My dad never abused me sexually or physically, but he emotionally abused me by withholding his full stamp of approval. He withheld this approval in part by spending very little time with me when I was a boy. He traveled five days a week, spent all day Saturday in his office to catch up with paperwork, and then he devoted each Sunday to watching pro sports from the couch. That was his way to rest up for the coming week.

Dad showed more interest in me when I made the high-school football team as the starting quarterback. Not only did he come to my football games on Friday nights, but he also regularly dropped in on my football practices to boot. But instead of cheering me on or even watching passively from the sidelines, he yelled constantly, ripping me for the slightest mistake. If I threw an interception in practice and hung my head a little, he'd bark, "Get your head up!" If I fumbled a snap, he'd shout, "Get your head out of your rear!"

I don't mean to dishonor him; I'm simply telling you what he did. It got so bad that my coach had to bar him from practices. But he couldn't bar him from games, and after those Friday night battles, Dad would deliver horrible verbal blitzes and name every mistake I had made. After one tirade I got so nauseous that I vomited into the cap I was wearing.

Needless to say, in spite of the respect I got around school from the coaches and my teammates, I never really felt like one of the guys. I never felt like I measured up as a man, because my dad never said I did.

Wounds like this—that form holes in our hearts—can launch us toward sexual sin. Think about it. Because of our brains' hardwiring, we're already handicapped regarding relationships in the first place, partly because our brains' hemispheres don't talk to each other very well. Then, since our verbal skills are rooted in the left hemisphere and our emotions are rooted in the right hemisphere, we can't easily access our emotions verbally. That explains why it's hard to articulate what we're feeling. We just know we don't fit in anywhere, and we aren't connecting with anyone intimately.

Here's where our hardwiring sets us up to fall. My dad wounded me deeply and left me lonely and aching. Do you remember the primary way guys give and receive intimacy? That's right, through the acts just prior to and during intercourse. What can give guys that feeling of intimacy, that feeling of love and acceptance? Right again—the always smiling, always available and unclothed girls of cyberspace who never reject you and who always offer you everything they've got while asking for nothing in return.

Without that connection with our fathers and that acceptance as men, we are practically guaranteed to fall into sexual sin during our teen years. Orgasmic relief is the medication for our pain. And once this becomes our crutch in our crippled interpersonal lives, we'll drag that crutch right into marriage. Wives often think their husbands used porn before marriage merely to release a little sexual pressure from time to time, so they expect the habit to vanish once the honeymoon begins. But I'm not talking sexual pressure; I am describing emotional wounds that run deep. If your husband still doubts his masculinity, then his porn habit won't disappear overnight no matter what you do for him sexually.

Here's the application. Wives often ask me, "As my husband fights this battle for purity, should I expect him to fall sometimes along the way?" The answer is yes, of course, and these underlying wounds are your clue why. These issues must be dealt with as he pulls away from porn, and that takes time. Brandon can attest to that confusing aspect:

> I am thirty-three and have used porn and masturbation as a means of coping with rejection, loneliness, and stress for about twenty years. I am a Christian, but I am just now trying to develop a genuine relationship with God.
>
> I quit porn and masturbation about a month ago and have no desire to go back to it. I'm not even tempted, but I am now dealing with some serious emotions. At times, I am feeling emptiness, anxiety, and depression, and then at other times, I'm normal. I can't tell if it's getting better or worse. I am trying to build new relationships with others, but sometimes I just feel so bad it is hard. I just want to know if this is normal.

Of course it's normal! It was never about sex in the first place. It was about the rejection, and once you stop the medication, the painful wound beneath it all is still there and still needs healing.

The sad thing is that when I talk to campus ministers around this country, they tell me that the most consistent thing they hear from their guys is that they had little relationship with their dads growing up. When you mix that broad lack of male affirmation with the natural weak links in our sexual hardwiring, you have a recipe for disaster of epidemic proportions. And of course, that's exactly what we have.

Quoting from our book *Preparing Your Son,* one expert said:

> "I deal with a lot of men, and it never fails that the men with the deeper sexual issues also have uninvolved or missing fathers. Their sexual issues are directly and severely impacted by their dad's failures as a father."
>
> That's to be expected because there's a point in the development of a boy into a man—say from eleven to thirteen—when the boy needs to move into an even deeper relationship with his dad. "I know this sounds a bit

weird," he continued, "but I've never found a better way to say it: Dad has to be close enough to his son to be able to call the 'heart of the man' out of the boy. If this does not happen, the next window of opportunity for a young man to try and feel like a man is through his emerging sexuality. So, if Dad isn't there early in adolescence to help answer questions, the boy will use his sexuality as an arena to answer his questions about being a man."

That was definitely true for me, with both porn and girls.

Still, the deepest wound my dad ever inflicted on me was his divorce. As I've said, masturbation is a way young men can salve deep insecurity or psychological pain, and nothing delivers a load of pain quite like divorce. Derrick said, "I've been a Christian all my life, and I had no problem with sexual sin until my parents divorced two years ago when I was seventeen. I was so upset. For some reason, I started up with some mild porn and masturbation. It felt good, but now it's gotten steadily worse. I don't know what to do."

I've heard many stories like Derrick's, and part of the reason is surely this: thirty percent of fathers who get divorced never see their kids again. These broken relationships cause great internal anguish and insecurity in the sons, leaving them to seek intimacy wherever they can find it.

Sexual sin flourishes in the wake of bad or broken family relationships. The splintering effects of divorce or parental death shatter our worlds. Teens, rather than feeling accepted and cherished by their parents, feel as though they've been cast aside. They spend their lives searching for love and meaning, when it should have been provided in the home by a loving mother and a loving father.

But even when a father sticks around, the wounds inflicted can lead to deep bondage, as Rich writes:

I was very insecure as a child. Dad was distant because he worked a lot (though he wasn't totally cold to me). So I bonded very closely with a domineering, legalistic mother. Consequently, I never really felt like one of the guys. At school, I wasn't much of an athlete, so I played in the band. On top of that, my classmates tormented me, so I found masturbation to cope.

My porn and masturbation was never really about sex. It was about medicating pain and seeking emotional intimacy. Sometimes I think women view porn habits the same way they view the guys whooping it up at the strip club. They think it is all about lust and nothing more.

But it never was that way for me. Masturbation was just my medication of choice. I could have easily gone the route of drugs or alcohol, because the wounds at the root of the problem would have been the same no matter what the substance.

But you know what eventually seemed to help the most? It turned out to be my best friend, Eric, who really turned the tide for me. He was the first guy who truly accepted me as a man and as a friend. He affirmed my masculinity through our hiking adventures and our talks. Sometimes I think that a strong, masculine friend was all I needed.

And now after a couple years, I can honestly say that I truly hate porn. I now dislike porn so much that I can sit down and write this e-mail at a home computer that no longer has any filter software.

Men need to be accepted as men, and this man found freedom through the heart of a friend. This is the very reason accountability groups can be so vital in this battle. The true intimacy of friendship and acceptance actually heals the wounds so that the false intimacy of masturbation and porn is no longer needed as a pain-killing medication.

Affirmation from a Different Source

Even more important, men need to be accepted and affirmed by God. In the end, that's where I found healing of my wounds and a washing away of the anger simmering in *my* soul.

I've shared much of my story in other books in this series, but I repeat this particular one again because it's important to this topic about the hole in men's hearts when they haven't been affirmed by their fathers.

When I reached age thirty-five, the lack of my father's acceptance rocked me deeply. This pain affected my relationship with my wife and kids. I was harsh in my tone, harsh in my words. You could say that I went around the house being harsh, harsh, harsh. Brenda tried to explain away my behavior, but after a year she became frustrated. One day she told me, "All right, then! Fine. Just tell all of us how long you plan to stay like this, so we can prepare for it!" Then she stormed out of the room.

I sat there speechless for quite some time. How long was I going to stay like this? Ten years? Why ten? Why not five? If I could decide to change at the end of five years, why not after one? And if after one, why not now?

Her question penetrated my heart like a stiletto. I knew it was time to change. Within days I found a counselor. Within weeks I attended a Promise Keepers conference in Boulder, Colorado, where Greg Laurie opened the seminar Friday evening with a salvation message. I'd been praying that God would give me some answers during my trip out west, but I never figured that some hip preacher from Southern California doing an altar call before a packed house in Boulder would break the logjam.

While referencing Revelation 3:20, Greg made a simple statement that just blew me away. "God just wants to put His arm around you and have a steak with you," he said. In that moment, God's revelation hit me like a comet.

God wants to put His arm around me and cut into a juicy steak with me? You're probably scratching your head and saying, *What's the big deal with that?* All I can tell you is that when that sentence was mixed with God's power into my spirit, years of pain, agony, and frustration over my dad crumbled and melted away instantly. My heavenly Father saw me as His son, and He didn't care a whit about what I achieved or what I did or if I was successful. All He really wanted was a relationship with me, a chance to just sit down with me, put an arm around me, and have a barbecue steak with me. Because of Jesus, I was already worthy to be called His son, a man to be reckoned with, with nothing to prove.

And you know what? Sitting that evening in the bleachers at the University of Colorado's Folsom Field, I felt the pain from my dad dispersing. From that moment, it seemed like every other one of my significant relationships changed too.

Sure, the vestiges of that little boy still live inside me. I like to wear hooded jackets under coats and look like a guy to be reckoned with when I walk outside.

But now that my wounds have healed, by the grace of God, I can go and sin no more in the sexual arena.

Unfortunately, those men who don't find that healing often experience deeper wounds, and these are self-inflicted. We'll talk about those types of wounds in our next chapter.

self-inflicted wounds

FROM FRED

Father wounds aren't the only ones that may drive men—young and old—into the soft arms of cyberspace. Cal's story is like countless others I've heard:

> Almost all my life I've been extremely shy and quiet. Making friends has been difficult since everyone always talks about sports, and I'm clueless about them. I always felt uncomfortable around people, especially girls. There were times in middle school when I'd talk to a girl just for a little bit, and I would really hear about it from the other guys—usually the jocks who didn't even know me. "Oooohhh, Cal's picking up girls now!" they'd taunt. Needless to say, all this loneliness has made me feel depressed.
>
> When my depression was mixed with the many sexually oriented things I saw on TV—and the guys and girls making out in the hallways at school—I just burned with envy and felt very sorry for myself. So I turned to masturbation. It simply offered something I'd never get in real life.

If you ask wives to explain porn's potent draw, they'll cite the sex appeal of limitless free and frisky women to the male eyes and mind. But there are more complex factors at work here. Porn provides instant soothing to emotional stress, and the easy access to Internet porn makes it difficult to wean men away from their emotional dependence on it.

Tanner said, "Sure, I've learned that sex does not fill the emptiness like I thought it would. But online porn offers the 'gentle stroking' that we males need. I can tell you this: it's better than nothing."

The trouble with this tack is that masturbation is an implosion of sexual pleasure that focuses a guy further and further into himself. Since the genuine need for interpersonal intimacy cannot be met by self-seeking sexual activity, the hunger for genuine intimacy is never fulfilled. But a "better than nothing" attitude sends him right back to the computer for that gentle stroking, which drives him further within himself, which leaves him feeling emptier still...and so it goes.

It's like being really thirsty and being handed a glass of salt water. The glass of water looks like it should slake your thirst, but taking a sip of salt water would be awful, and drinking a whole glass would be disastrous. Similarly, masturbation can't slake that loneliness, and the insecurity and isolation simply tighten their grip around a young man's heart.

It's Not a Real Encounter

Have you ever noticed that you feel more lonely and isolated after watching television alone? That's because there was no human contact. Masturbation is similar. There was no real sexual encounter. Sure, the act feels sexual and the resulting climax feels like intimacy, but it actually leaves a guy feeling more alone and more ashamed than when he woke up that morning.

What an awful, sucking whirlpool of pain. But it gets worse. When Tanner says that masturbation and porn are better than nothing, he doesn't realize that he is rewiring his male hardware in a way that will corrupt his future sexual relationship if and when he marries. These self-inflicted wounds have now been added to the other wounds in the mix.

It's like a computer virus, only worse. A computer virus can instantly destroy the efficiencies of the machine's software, but the hardware is left largely intact. Sadly, human hardwiring is not so rugged, and heavy wounding can warp the brain's hardware itself.

For instance, recent landmark studies suggest that child abuse and neglect create serious brain abnormalities that can last through adulthood. The medical journal *Cerebrum* reported on Martin Teicher's detailed study that demonstrated how childhood experiences affect brain development. Teicher looked closely at high-tech brain images of several hundred children and adults. His findings confirmed earlier studies showing that trauma resculpts the brain, resulting in the brain's becoming rewired both in function *and* structure.

Among the differences between normal brains and the brains of those abused as children are a poor development of the usually dominant left verbal hemisphere and electrical impulse disturbances in part of the brain. Sexually abused girls and neglected boys were most affected, resulting in potentially serious mood and personality disorders that can lead to aggression and self-destructive behavior.

How does this information fit in with porn and masturbation? As I said earlier, there are those who contend that masturbation can't hurt you physically. While I've not yet seen a study claiming that porn and masturbation actually resculpts the brain in the same manner as sexual abuse and neglect, there is plenty of evidence that porn and masturbation wreak significant havoc upon male sexual hardwiring in a number of miserable ways.

Decoupling Sex from Intimacy

For instance, God built my hardwiring on the basis that my sexuality is not really mine at all. My sexuality was not created for me or for my pleasure but for Brenda and for her pleasure. God never spoke of sexuality in the context of one in the Bible. He always spoke of it in the context of two.

In addition, my sexuality is a primary communication line for transmitting and receiving intimacy. When that line goes down, my emotional life shrivels, and the effects upon my marriage are disastrous.

Tragically, porn's first major blow does exactly this, decoupling sex entirely from the communication of intimacy. Over time, sexual *intensity* replaces *intimacy* as the man's primary focus. This is where significant damage to our hardwiring begins.

How in the world does this happen? Like a germ using a cell's own DNA to reproduce, porn and masturbation uses the man's own hardwiring to destroy itself. It all starts innocently enough, with the eyes feasting naturally on the sexual images, just as they were created to do. The orgasmic chemical responses hit the pleasure centers like a dream, again, just as they were created to do. Then the addictive component develops, which will keep him coming back for more porn. Once that happens, he's hooked, and looking at porn becomes part of his life.

It is here where porn initiates a cataclysmic feedback loop in our hardwiring. Pornography's effect on the brain is Pavlovian, and an orgasm is a huge reinforcer.

Now, if my hardwiring is normal, as God created it, my focus is not on me but on Brenda and her pleasure, and all my orgasms happen with her. Because of that, I associate my orgasms with my wife: her kiss, her scent, her body. Because of that reinforcement, that is what will turn me on over time and will keep me fascinated with the wife of my youth.

If I open my boundaries to endless transgressions in the harems of cyberspace, however, my sexual proclivities and tastes go in other directions. That is not good for me...or for Brenda.

Worse, my hardwiring morphs and brings in an unnatural obsession with looking at women rather than interacting with them. It brings an attitude that objectifies women and rates them by size, shape, and harmony of body parts. And the morphing? The visual side of my sexual hardwiring gets supersized, creating an obsession with visual stimulation (for instance, the bigger the breasts the better), while the "transmission of intimacy" side ("I so love your soul, honey") shrivels away.

Wives notice it when their husbands aren't totally there in bed. Rachel said:

I can tell that my husband seeks sex for the thrill in and of itself. He may think he's connecting intimately with me, but he really isn't. That's the reason why wives reject sex with their husbands—because it ends up being empty sex. I can feel the lack of relationship, so in my mind, what's the point of making love? I'm ready to skip this part of our marriage and move on to raising the kids.

The thing that my husband doesn't realize is that if he would seek intimacy, then we would have a very satisfactory sex life.

Why doesn't he realize it? Oftentimes, porn distorts a guy's perceptions. This warped hardwiring causes a sensual overload of intensity over intimacy, and the sheer heat of porn's intensity requires an escalation to more graphic depictions in order to reach the same high. Eventually, what once would have disgusted him now grants him the excitement he craves.

Matt said he was twelve years old when his brother got him started on porn, and now this addiction is killing him. "It started innocently with a *Sport Illustrated's* swimsuit issue back in grade school, but by now I'm looking for anything and everything sexual, including homosexual sex and even worse."

Whoa. Matt originally craved intimacy, but no genuine intimacy was passed. Faster and faster he gulped his sexual salt water, but his thirst went unquenched. All he got was the high and the thrill, and before long, that's all he knew to seek. Intimacy's transmitters were fried long ago, and the porn-related thrills are all he knows. He honestly doesn't know that marital sexual *intimacy* offers so much more than *intensity*.

Gordon's story is very enlightening:

My masturbation became practically ritualized. I would plan my time at home to take long, long showers just to build up the intensity and masturbate. After I married, I waited until my wife was in bed so I could surf the Net or watch the late-night sexy cable channels until two or three o'clock in the morning.

Each week I'd get excited about my plans for the upcoming Friday and Saturday nights because I knew that I would be doing it again, just like I was planning a date. My conscience was seared, as I didn't have any guilt at all after a while. I just did it, and then I began operating my life around my porn stars. I had to have it, and I had to have it more and more just to reach the same level of excitement. Sometimes that meant longer and longer hours, but other times that meant more bizarre photographs.

Once intensity takes the place of intimacy, and intimacy is then decoupled from sex, the sexual high is the end in itself. As we said, the transmitters get fried, which means the marriage bed is cooked. The souls and the spirits aren't meeting on the mattress…only the bodies are connecting.

And more often than not, the gentle affection and climactic touch that his wife needs will hold little of his interest or attention. His attitude: *All aboard my one-*

way express to Sex City! Grab what you can, honey, but I'm the one who counts! Pour the coal to my engine and don't you dare tap the brakes.

Where once his natural hardware prompted him to normal intimate connections, now it just prods him for another intense hit, sometimes with you, sometimes with the computer. The computer sex may be intense, but it's always soulless and cold, just like his sex with you. Afterward, you're still lonely, and he got nothing but high.

Destroying the Taste for the Real Thing

In a second self-inflicted blow to the hardwiring, porn eventually destroys the taste for the real thing, as this e-mail from Randy relates:

> I've hit bottom, and so has my poor, beaten-down wife who believes I'm not attracted to her anymore. Maybe she's right. My sex life with my wife has been virtually nonexistent since lust has been controlling my thought life, and yet here we are trying to have our first child!
>
> She's depressed. The clock is ticking because she's thirty-four and has this thing in her head that she doesn't want to get pregnant past the age of thirty-five. I've got about nine months until her birthday to deliver the goods, but the devil's stolen my sexual desire for the most beautiful woman I know.

Gabriella's experience is no different. When I asked her how the porn affected sexual intimacy with her husband, the floodgates of her heart broke wide open:

> When I asked my husband not to fantasize about other women during our lovemaking, it immediately became more difficult for him to get and maintain an erection, and our sex life has become so infrequent that it hardly exists now.

You know, it's strange. Hugh Hefner hoped to use *Playboy* to convince a generation of men that they *needn't* stay with their wives and take their sexual joy only in them. But the end result is that they *can't* stay with her, even within marriage. They have to fantasize. They have to think about Miss May and the other gorgeous girls with their come-hither poses. When that happens to a guy, his sexuality has been seriously wounded, and tragically, the wound was self-inflicted.

In this postmodern world, access to "adult" material is so cheap and widely available through various media that it's changed the landscape of how men and women interact sexually. What's actually happened is this onslaught of porn is responsible for *deadening* a male's appetite for real women and leading men to see fewer and fewer women as "porn worthy."

Afraid of Relationships

Has free access to porn really left men and women more liberated to connect sexually with each other or has it pushed them farther apart?

I think I know what many young women would say. In the secular world, young single women and college coeds aren't so worried about fending off porn-crazed swine as they are worried that they can scarcely get a guy's attention. They can't compete with the digitally retouched nudes, and they know it. How can a real woman—with pimples, unretouched breasts, and her own sexual needs—possibly compete with the perfection of cyber women?

Naomi Wolf wrote in *New York Metro* magazine, "The young women who talk to me on campuses about the effect of pornography on their intimate lives speak of feeling that they can never measure up, that they can never ask for what *they* want; and that if they do not offer what porn offers, they cannot expect to hold a guy. The young men talk about what it is like to grow up learning about sex from porn, and how it is not helpful to them in trying to figure out how to be with a real woman. Mostly, when I ask about loneliness, a deep, sad silence descends on audiences of young men and young women alike. They know they are lonely together, even when conjoined, and that this porn imagery is a big part of that loneliness. What they don't know is how to get out, how to find each other again erotically, face-to-face."

Is it any different in Christian marriages? Not if he's morphed his hardwiring. She can't compete, and in a way, she just looks like bad porn in his eyes.

If she's courageous enough to try something he's seen onscreen, all too often she can't quite get him where his own hands could take him. In the end, he can't even get aroused by the woman who should know his triggers best. They may be in bed together, but they might as well be on separate continents.

Self-Inflicted Sexual Wounds

Sadly, as a husband's hardwiring morphs out of control, a wife's hunger for sex can be easily extinguished.

It's very common for women in their twenties to like sex with their husbands. Cassie said:

> Younger generations of women are pretty inclined to sex—at least, that's
> the way I feel as a young wife and that was my anecdotal findings among
> women at my church last fall. We were studying the *Power of a Praying Wife,*
> and when it came to the section of wives praying about their sex lives, the
> author said, "It's hard to be in the mood all the time, but I find if I pray
> about it, God gives me the drive to enjoy sex with my husband."
>
> The younger women in the class were appalled. One said, "What, you
> older women don't enjoy sex? You don't frequently want it?" I found myself
> wondering if maybe their husbands just didn't have "the moves" or if I was a
> freak for actually liking and enjoying sex to a point that I was the one who
> normally initiated it at our house! When I asked around, it seemed like
> most of the women under thirty were more "in the mood" more often.

What destroys the hunger for marital sex? One obvious answer is porn. You aren't really meeting in bed, so there is no real relationship involved in the sexual encounter. Since a woman's sexual triggers are based on relationship, it becomes harder for her to find the desire. Without the relational connection, her husband simply doesn't arouse her anymore.

Self-Inflicted Spiritual Wounds

But the self-inflicted *spiritual* wounds run deep as well. Once a husband has given Satan a toehold into his life and marriage through porn, that's the only opening the Evil One needs to up the intensity of temptation for the wife.

Brenda tells me that my sexual purity defends her against the wiles of Satan. How can she be disloyal to look at another guy when I'm working hard to be true to her? But when a wife has had her spirit crushed by her husband's pornography addiction, who will inspire and protect her from going out and seeking solace in another man's arms? In instances like this, she can be an easy target for Satan's darts, as Brett describes:

> I'm thirty-seven, and I've known my wife since we were both fourteen. For twenty years it was like a lovely story until I dabbled with some mildly sensual magazines. As time passed, my choice of reading material got more explicit and more evil. My wife noticed a change in me and could not understand it. She asked me about what was happening, but how could I tell her about the sin in my heart?
>
> Well, to make a long story short, three years ago she left me for my best friend because of the distance between us. I was devastated. I have never loved anyone more in my life, but I couldn't blame her. It must have been so horrible for her, and even as I write this my heart breaks and tears flow.

Even if our wives manage to stay true to us, we open them up to the Enemy's direct attack as we bring sinful, corrupt sexual paraphernalia into our homes. It is foolish to think that our sexual impurity has no impact on our marriages or in the spirit realm.

Does an obsession with pornography release an element of spiritual oppression into your family's life? You be the judge after reading Sarah's letter:

> There was a period where our normally quiet home was disrupted for no apparent reason during the night. It started when the kids were six, eleven, and twelve and began having horrid dreams. Other times they awoke for no apparent reason and wandered around the house in the middle of the night. They reported odd occurrences, like seeing faces in windows or feeling something brushing against them in bed and awakening them. They even heard strange sounds and voices.

I couldn't figure out what was causing the disruptions. Was it their diet? the weather? school? I couldn't find a common denominator.

Then one night I was awakened out of a deep sleep by the feeling of a weight lifting off my body. It felt identical to that feeling when my husband gets up and rolls over onto his side of the bed after we've made love. It felt so real that I was certain he had made love to me while I was asleep, so I turned to look at him and saw him sleeping and heard him snoring. It was obvious that he had not been involved in the feeling I'd just experienced.

When I reported this to a Christian friend, she suggested that we might be experiencing demonic activity if my husband was bringing porn and sexual paraphernalia into the home. When I confronted my husband, he admitted that he had. I immediately burned his magazines, videos, and toys. Then my friend and I went through the house and prayed, room by room. The nighttime activity ceased immediately and has never returned. I told my husband that if he ever brought that junk into the house again, I would kick him out.

From Brenda

The stories we have related in this chapter, as hard as they are to believe sometimes, are real. As a woman, it seems so odd that a man can mete out such severe self-inflicted wounds apparently without noticing. After all, when intimacy gets decoupled from *any* part of my relationship with Fred, I notice it instantly. Perhaps I can make the generalization about men that because of their hardwired weaknesses, without strong teaching, they simply don't notice the damage as its occurring.

It takes a wise and spiritually discerning woman to notice when things have gone awry in the home. If you feel that something is not right with your husband or that he's changed for the worse, pray that God will reveal what is happening in his life. Your marriage may depend on it.

what now?

FROM FRED

I spent a couple of days speaking at a college campus recently when an attractive young woman drew me aside for a brief, private conversation.

"I have a problem," she said, hesitating a little. Something was churning painfully inside her.

"I'd love to help any way that I can," I encouraged.

"Well…it's my dad. He doesn't know about this, and it's even hard for me to admit it to you, because I've shared this with almost no one," she said, eyes darting about quickly to make sure no one could overhear. Then, she locked her eyes on mine. "I was five years old when I stumbled across my father's *Playboy* magazines in his study. I burst out crying because I knew something was just terribly wrong about those pictures. After discovering the stash of magazines, I quickly slammed the cabinet shut. My older sister tried to console me, but she couldn't. I never told her what I'd found."

Then her face drew tight, and tears welled up in her eyes. She stammered, "I have never felt beautiful a single day in my life since that moment. Anytime my dad tells me I'm pretty, I remember those pictures, and I know what he thinks is beautiful about women. I feel so dirty."

Her tears turned into sobs. "He's robbed so much from me! Tell me I can keep this from happening to my own children someday. Please help me!"

I helped that young woman as best I could. Gratefully, she had a godly fiancé, and I reminded her that while it's good to acknowledge God's Word regarding generational sin, she mustn't forget His Word regarding generational blessings. If she and her fiancé committed to holiness, I said, blessings of purity rather than sin would flow naturally to the next generation.

The next morning, as I reflected upon the incident on the flight home, I thought about the moments we spent together. A daughter's unrelenting, excruciating memory. Traumatized relationships that never heal. My tears were as real as hers in that quiet corner of the student union.

I will *never* forget the bottom line about our sexual sin as men. Our sin crushes women, and we need to take responsibility for that and stop it. Sure, I just spent eight chapters on our sexuality, explaining how, in significant ways, the deck is stacked against us guys, but don't think for a moment that I'm trying to absolve or excuse our sin.

God graced men with a high call as husbands and fathers, and our Lord is counting on us to stand with Him. We have such power to impart and heal, and we have a strong position to impact lives for a generation.

But as a group in this present day and age, we are disappointing. One woman acknowledged, "I love men for what they bring to the workplace, but I'm not sure how much I could ever trust another man after what I've been through with my husband." Too many women share this degrading view, and we deserve it.

Far too often we arrogantly lord over our wives while keeping a secret cyber-harem on the side, spitting on Scripture and summarily dismissing any inspection of our lives on the grounds that we have imperial immunity.

As a group, we are not living up to our high calling as men. As a wife, you have every reason to feel rotten about your husband's sexual sin, and it is critical you understand that. But regarding your marriage and your future, there's an even more critical issue at play: do you still have any reason to feel that his sin is a reflection on you? *Absolutely not!*

That's good, because you *have* to know it's not about your attractiveness or sexiness. It's that simple, and that's why I have spent so much time describing male sexuality. The tendrils of sexual sin that choke our lives aren't just sexual and aren't just physical—they reach throughout our being—body, soul, and spirit.

They're about addictions and old habits. They're about wounds and emotional dependence and ignorance and warped wiring. They're about sin—his sin. Your husband is at the root of it, not you.

The cry of your heart has been, *Tell me this is not about me!* One more time I'll say it: it's not about you. But we both knew from the beginning that this would not be enough. The sixty-four-thousand-dollar question is this: do you believe me? Until you do, you can't heal.

From Brenda

It's time for a midterm exam to see if you are ready for the second half of the semester.

Nobody likes exams, so I'll keep this to three simple questions, but you must have a perfect score if you expect to graduate to the next level:

1. Are you certain now that you are not alone in this battle and that your emotional pain is normal?
2. Can you see now that your husband's sexual sin is not about you or your attractiveness?
3. If you've stretched beyond your female perspective and peered at his sin through the prism of male sexuality, compassion and mercy should have replaced some of your rage. Have they?

Here's the answer key: every answer should be yes.

Regarding question 3, you may asking, *How much mercy do I need in order to pass this test?* Not much. If God works with faith the size of mustard seeds, no doubt He can work with a seed's worth of mercy.

By this point in the book, you should have at least that much mercy. As women, we must concede that in some parts of the sexual makeup of men, they have a tougher battle than we do, because they're saddled with challenges related to their sexuality that we simply don't have. If you can't muster a mustard seed's worth of mercy and compassion in light of what we've discussed about your husband's masculinity, it's likely that you are still too bitter and angry to open yourself to the Spirit's prompting in your heart. While that's difficult to face when you're hurting so, you must face it in order to heal.

If you remain bitter, you'll cause as much stress on your marriage as your husband's sexual sin. And you'll have to answer to God for your stagnant, damaged marriage as much as your husband will.

I say that softly and in the fear of the Lord. I had to face that same stark realization in my own marriage on other issues more than once, and it was no fun. Still, the truth is the truth, and just as I once faced *my* truth, you must face yours now. There's nothing to fear in that. God is certainly not harsh about these things. He's merciful. He knows your frame is but dust, and He's certainly not expecting perfection from you by next Tuesday. You are, however, His little girl, His precious one, the very apple of His eye. While He would never wink at sin, He can't look at you without a little skip in His heart, either. He loved you so much that He sent a Comforter so that you would never stand alone in such times as these.

And He knows that you'll struggle some days, oscillating between compassion and anger. He knows your feelings will ebb and flow with the tide of your husband's battle, because He can't forget what it was like to walk in this same dusty flesh and to suffer utter rejection Himself. His tears are as hot as yours in this battle.

Having said all that, the truth remains: God expects you to do well on this exam and to move on to grace and victory. That's why if you can't answer the three quiz questions affirmatively, you *must* go back into prayer and review the first three parts of this book.

If you do go back, what should you pray for? Pray that God will keep this promise in you:

I will give you a new heart and put a new spirit in you; I will remove from you your heart of stone and give you a heart of flesh. (Ezekiel 36:26)

Pray, too, for humility. Humility makes forgiveness possible and opens the door to oneness.

God is perfectly capable of dealing with your husband in His time once you've laid down your arms and allowed Him to take the center of your marriage. Your humility releases an opportunity for victory in your life.

But this opportunity alone does not guarantee victory. Laying down your arms is only the first step, because your decisions aren't the only ones responsible for winning the day. The root of the problem is your husband's behavior, and for total victory, he needs to repent. He has to accept his sin and engage the battle.

The reason that's true should be no secret to anyone. While it's true that your marriage has been a mirage in many ways, don't forget that your husband destroyed something that was very real—your trust in him. He demolished it, and there will be no victory until trust returns, because trust is the basis of all relationships. There can be no oneness and no intimacy without trust, sexual or otherwise.

Trouble is, when it comes to trust, there's a catch. No matter how desperately you want it, you can't manufacture trust on your own. Trust requires two ingredients: your husband must become trustworthy, and you must trust again. Each of you is responsible for bringing one of the ingredients to the table.

Neither will be easy to provide. Becoming trustworthy will require an immense character change on his part, and that's no small task. On your end, trusting your husband again will require obedience and submission to God in spite of your scars. That won't be easy, either. But we never said any of this would be a Sunday-afternoon drive, so we might as well get started. Let's take a look at your end of the bargain first.

Remember Valerie's sad story from chapter 2? We were talking about trust recently when she told me:

> I know you told me that trust has to do with obedience and submission. I have pondered what this means, and for the life of me I can't see it.
>
> In my experience, I can forgive my husband and wipe out the consequences of his sin, releasing him completely in my heart. But that does not mean that I will trust him again. I may submit to him, and I might obey him and do exactly what I am supposed to do, but to trust him—to feel confidence in his ability to be faithful—is something completely different to me.
>
> It's sort of like Lucy pulling away the football when Charlie Brown agrees to kick it one more time. He knows she is going to be unfaithful, no matter what she says. Sure, he can unilaterally choose to play along like he always does, even though he doubts her ability to keep her word. But he knows that he can't really trust her.

Valerie was right in her views about trust, but she was confused about what I meant when I told her that trust requires obedience and submission. She thought I was referring to blind obedience and limp submission to a wayward husband, playing along the lines of Lucy's farce with her football. Hardly.

No, I was referring to obedience and submission to *God* in spite of your scars and only *after* your husband has grown trustworthy. You can't do your part (trust him again) until he has done his part (become trustworthy).

Valerie was right on target when she continued, "It seems to me that forgiveness and commitment are different from trust. I can forgive my husband and keep my marital commitment by staying in relationship with him, but that doesn't mean that I can believe what he says or have confidence that he is being faithful or truthful."

I nodded, and then I listened as Valerie asked me another question. "A wife may be able to forgive her husband," she said, "and she may commit to work on the relationship, but trust goes far beyond forgiveness and commitment. I never figured out how to get that far, but you seem to know how, Brenda. You trust Fred implicitly. What's your trick?"

Valerie's right on one count—trust *does* go far beyond love, forgiveness, and commitment, but there is really no trick to trusting again. The fact of the matter is that Fred changed completely, so I trust him now. I reminded Valerie that her ex-husband never changed, so trust wasn't possible under any circumstance.

The fact is that love, forgiveness, and commitment are choices that I can make alone in a vacuum, regardless of Fred's actions toward me. I can choose to love Fred simply by choosing to do so, no matter how he treats me. I can forgive Fred over and over even if he never asks me to. I can commit my heart faithfully to him no matter how adulterous his heart may grow in return.

But trust can't exist in a vacuum like this. Trust can only exist in relationship. Oh, I can hope against hope that Fred'll keep his word, and I can certainly play mind games with myself like Charlie Brown does with Lucy, but real trust can only come when I have full confidence in Fred's faithfulness. Only one thing can bring that confidence—his consistent, faithful actions. My love, forgiveness, and commitment may require nothing of Fred, but my trust requires plenty. Without right actions, he can't have my trust, and if he wants my trust, it's all on him.

Husbands often hate this responsibility, but you needn't apologize for it. And you needn't feel guilty if your husband sneers, "If you loved me, you would trust me." Baloney. Trust and love are two different things. Even if your husband has been saying he's a Christian, he's been acting like a pagan:

> It is God's will that you should...learn to control [your] own body in a way
> that is holy and honorable, not in passionate lust like the heathen, who do
> not know God. (1 Thessalonians 4:3-5)

Your love could be as strong as the ages, but his sin will still crush your trust and will keep crushing it until he stops.

Don't allow your husband to reframe your lack of trust in him as a referendum about your love for him. He's simply untrustworthy, and if it's a referendum about anyone's love, it would be about *his* love—for you and for God.

FROM FRED

When Brenda and I were first married, our marriage quickly began a long, slow death spiral beneath the verbal barrages surrounding our in-law problems. In my often theatrical rage, I'd shred white dress shirts that Brenda inadvertently had colored in the wash, fling pots of soup, punch holes in the dry wall, and do anything to intimidate her and hammer home my point.

My favorite ploy was to stand over Brenda and holler until she backed away. I never hit her, but I wanted her to think I might. After I turned things around, though, she'd still flinch whenever I'd even slightly raise my voice. That went on for five or six years. When it did, I'd angrily snap, "If you loved me, you would stop that! You know I've changed!"

But on the inside, I wasn't really angry. I was crushed to my toes. I knew that it wasn't *her* fault that she couldn't trust me yet. It was mine, all on my shoulders, and it had nothing to do with her love for me.

It was years before Brenda stopped flinching, but there was no trick to getting there at all. I'd simply become trustworthy, and in time, she trusted me. That was all there was to it.

WHAT NOW? ⌐ 131

How will you know your husband's trustworthy? First, you'll see that he gets it, understanding what he's done to you through his pornographic infidelity. You'll *hear* a change of heart and *see* a response on his part. It might sound like this, from John:

What does my wife deserve from me? Lots of stuff, but what she most deserves is to know who I am. Part of me still wants her to have this idyllic image of me; godly, honest, hard-working, and a hunka-hunka-burnin'-love. I am all of these things some of the time…maybe even most of the time.

But I am also the guy who lusts after teenage girls, who downloads porn for hours a day, who masturbates until he's physically injured, who slinks out of his office after hours with ejaculation stains on his pants in such abject shame that he cannot look the lowly janitor in the eye. I'm the one who shouts at the kids to stay away from me when I'm on the computer and they peek into my home office, showing them by my actions how "real men" behave.

I used to be the only one who knew this side of me, but since I've come clean and submitted to counseling, my wife knows this side of me now too. Does she love me less? I'm not even sure what that question means. All I can say for sure is that she loves me differently, because it's authentic now. It isn't about some image of a perfect man anymore. And I don't ask her to believe she's insane anymore.

You see, my wife first suggested I was addicted to porn more than three years ago, catching enough snippets of my dark behavior to form her hypothesis. I reacted angrily, mostly because I knew she was right, but also because I didn't think it was really any of her business. It was, after all, "just pictures."

I insisted that she was insane to throw her off the trail, but my wife knew, just like so many other wives seem to know. Even though she had no real evidence, she *knew*. A wife may not know the specifics, and she may not know it's "just" porn or whether it's on the computer or in some seedy quarter booth at the porn hall, but she knows. She'll know because here is this man whom she loves with all of her heart and whom she has made into this fantasy figure of strength, godliness, and fidelity, and yet something is terribly wrong.

I spent years and years lying to her and telling her that her concerns were just a fantasy, and that everything was fine. I told her that her intuition was bogus, that her perception of my distance from her was ridiculous, and that the countless hours I wiled away on the computer each morning before she awoke were all spent on perfectly innocent pursuits. When I got home late from work, I'd say, "Everything is hunky-dory! I'm just feeling a little tired, so please don't bother me," when the truth was that I was just coming off another porn marathon and was in so much self-loathing and shame that I couldn't bear to be around anyone.

All the facades are now gone, and now she gets to choose whether to stay with the *real* me, not some cracked idol that I tried to convince her I was through lies and deception. Sure, her love feels different, but at least it's honest, and now I regret running from honesty all these years. I like things better now.

When I look into my wife's eyes, I see her loving me in spite of my faults, and she knows exactly what they are now. She knows exactly who she is married to.

And she loves me still, despite my wrongdoing. Now that I'm honest with her, she's being honest about herself in ways never possible before, admitting things she would have never told me in a million years before. That's breathtaking.

Christ is in my marriage in a way that He never was before, and I believe she's forgiven me and that she's going to stay. Now I'm not suggesting that this happy outcome was preordained. She could have just as well walked out the door or kicked me out, and she may yet. But at least I am in the light with her, and she gets to actually choose whether to be married to me. She couldn't choose before, because she didn't know who she was married to.

Even if the worst happens and she ditches me, it will still all happen in the light. And in my journey, I am learning to prefer the light over every other thing.

John's eyes are open and he seems repentant, doesn't he? But is he trustworthy? Only time will tell, and his choices will reveal the truth. The same will be true in your marriage.

But while trust will have to wait for tomorrow, hope is here today. While this man's marriage is still in ruins, hope bubbles up from every word. The mirage has evaporated, which places his marriage in one of the most hopeful positions possible. Honesty and truth can now reign. Light can prevail, if only he'll choose wisely. We're about to find out what his Christianity is really made of.

And what about you? Have you ever wondered what your Christianity is really made of behind all the Bible studies and potlucks and Easter pageant costumes you've sewn? Your moment of truth is upon you. The lethargy and blindness have been lifted from your marriage, and this is your chance to bring glory to God, your chance to live it all out in spite of the pain.

As we said earlier, this is your opportunity to live like a real Christian, to truly sacrifice, to truly rebuild on the foundation of Christian principles, and to truly align your thinking with Christ regarding your marriage.

A man has far more potential for blessing his wife than most women ever dream. As an author, I'm out to lift men to walk in the image of God, to stand regally and proudly in His light, trustworthy and fully Christian.

As a wife, you can help your husband go there. You must look to your husband to rise up and stand as a trustworthy man. What's the best way to help him stand? What's the best way to draw alongside him and help him along? We will spend the rest of the book exploring how you can do that.

a rebuilder's reflection

FROM FRED

We trust that by now you understand that your husband's sin is not about you and that your lack of trust is normal. So where do you go from here? What is your role? What does it look like in practice?

Interestingly enough, you have the same role here that God gave you to play in every other area of marriage…the role of helpmate. And just as interesting, the principles involved in rebuilding a marriage broken by sexual sin are the same principles required to fix *any* broken marriage, regardless of the type of sin. After all, if you've been trampled by sin, you've been trampled, and it doesn't matter what kind of sin crushed your heart and marriage. A wife's response must always be the same, and she will follow the same principles of healing and restoration no matter how her husband crushed her—because the challenge is always the same…that somehow, the trust must be reestablished, real accountability must be formulated, and romantic love must be revived.

That's important to understand, because while I was clearly hooked on sexual sin, *most* of our marital damage was caused by my sinful temper. You'll notice that the destruction I inflicted upon our marriage parallels yours in many obvious ways, and you'll find that there is much to learn from Brenda's responses through God's grace. We choose to use this next story to illustrate how these universal biblical principles work in practice so that you can apply them to your own rebuilding efforts.

under-the-radar mission

FROM FRED

So where should you start in helping your husband stand firm as a trustworthy man of God? Do you hover over his shoulder with a furrowed brow, arms crossed, jaws locked, tapping one foot impatiently, and intermittently glancing at your watch while rolling your eyes and sighing deeply, "You blew it again, pal. You aren't trustworthy yet!"

While that may be your first instinct, it wouldn't be your best one. The *actual* starting place is a quiet little spot waiting for you in front of your mirror.

Hey, wait a minute! This thing doesn't start with me!

I can empathize, so let me hasten to express clearly what I *didn't* say: I am *not* saying that every wife bears some of the blame for her husband's sexual sin.

Of course, you might, but I never start with that assumption. Brenda had absolutely nothing to do with my sexual sin. I schlepped my sinful baggage right up the gangway and on board the good ship USS *Matrimony* on my wedding day, and I carried those trunks freely about the decks with no help from her. She had no warped thinking. On the contrary, it was her healthy, holy thinking that challenged me to move closer to Christ and to eventually toss my baggage overboard.

But that doesn't mean she needn't check herself in the mirror once in a while, and I guess this is the tricky part. People are 100 percent responsible for their lives 100 percent of the time. Yet what spouses do or don't do has a direct influence on the situation. A wife can certainly make matters worse, but she can also make matters better if she plays her position well.

And *that's* why I'm asking you to step in front of the mirror—I want you to play your position well. I know that's a sports term, but its applicable here. As you step up to take a look, ask yourself a little question: *How much do I look like Christ these days in my marriage?*

FROM BRENDA

Why must we look like Jesus? The snap answer is that we're Christians, and we love Him. He is beautiful beyond description, our bright morning star. But for His purposes here on Earth, don't the reasons go deeper than that? He's not just our morning star. He's our North Star, our reference point in this chaotic, sinful world. What does the capital *N* at the top of our moral compass stand for? That's right— it stands for *normal.*

And that's a good thing, because in this murky gloom of sexual sin, you will need your compass in the worst way. The emotional fog is thick, and the hurt and loneliness can be so disorienting that you can walk in circles for months, even years. Maybe you've already been saying to yourself, *I don't know where to go from here or what to do. I don't even know what is right or wrong anymore. Nothing feels normal to me these days.*

Jesus is your mark in the distance, your reference point. When God speaks of normal life and character, He speaks along these lines: *Jesus is My beloved Son, in whom I am well pleased. He is the most normal person ever to walk the planet Earth. You are a believer, My child. Are you walking normally like My Son, Jesus?*

You've been called to a normal married life, and Jesus is the magnetic pole of all things normal. The arrow in your compass must point directly at *N.*

Becoming normal is what Christianity is all about. Your husband needs to become normal like Jesus and stop hurting you. At the same time, this is your chance to normalize your relationship and stop inflicting your husband with more wounds from your cold shoulder and biting tongue. The wounding on both sides has got to stop or you'll never be normal.

Which brings us back to the mirror. If you want to stand shoulder to shoulder with your husband one day in a restored marriage, a great first step is to see that you're standing shoulder to shoulder with Christ and taking on His normal, broader view of marriage as well as His normal view of your husband's sin. Without Christ at your side, you'll lack the foresight and the compassion to play your position well.

From Fred

It's all too easy to pick up a narrow perspective on marriage. Brenda grew up in perfect peace, a precious lamb of God with sparkling eyes and a soft heart. Except for her dad's premature death, her Christian life, for the most part, had been full of joy and fun and wonder before she met me. After we exchanged our wedding vows, she expected marriage to deliver that same package of personal joy to her front door.

But then she awoke one bright September morning next to the husband who'd taken the wraps off a short, hot temper the night before, frightening her to her toes. Within two short years, her feelings for that man—me—had been buried in the matrimonial graveyard. All was rubble.

Where was the joy and fun and wonder? She thought, *I have obviously missed God's plan for my marriage!* Or had she? It all depends on the perspective.

From Brenda

Our perspectives are usually uneven from the start. In the premarriage classes we taught, Fred and I used to ask the young couples, "What do you hope to get out of marriage that you could not get if you stayed single?"

We heard just about every answer under the sun, but many could be distilled down to the promise they would make at the altar: the promise to honor and cherish till death do they part. Most engaged couples said they were seeking a soul mate who would bring lifetime personal fulfillment—sexually, emotionally, and spiritually.

When we later posed the same question to newlywed couples in our young-marrieds class, however, the answers weren't soaked in the same starry-eyed optimism. In fact, our question prompted answers that sounded more like marital gripes:

- "We're just so incompatible."
- "He just doesn't respect me."

- "How can I respect her lousy attitude?"
- "I'll start forgiving him when he starts forgiving me!"
- "I'll start treating her better when she starts being happier again!"

My goodness, what happened after a few short months or a few short years? Answer: there had been a collision between their lower ways of thinking and God's higher, broader thinking on marriage. Remember what God says about our ways and thoughts:

> As the heavens are higher than the earth
> so are my ways higher than your ways
> and my thoughts than your thoughts. (Isaiah 55:9)

The blinders were certainly off now! Just a few months earlier, many of these couples were convinced that God had personally put two of His wonderful children together in holy matrimony, to have and to hold, for better or worse, for richer or poorer, in sickness and in health, to love and to cherish until death do they part. It was like He would turn down the marriage bed every night and place a chocolate on each pillow. God would be their quiet, benevolent, behind-the-scenes partner in their marriage of three.

But things didn't always work out that way. Why? Because God has higher purposes for marriage, and those purposes may not necessarily be all about you. Let me illustrate this with a story about our four children.

FROM FRED

When the kids were young, each child was assigned chores to do at night, varying according to their ages and abilities. When Michael, our youngest, was a toddler, we staggered their chores so that they all weren't doing them at the same time. This ensured there would always be at least one brother or sister free to play with Michael and keep him from gumming up the works.

But Saturday's long, fun days precluded a staggered chore schedule on Saturday night, which meant we'd all be working our jobs at the same time. Thus it came as no surprise when Michael usually slowed things down or made more messes during his awkward attempts to help out. Whenever that happened, we asked Rebecca, the second youngest, to watch Michael, and we *also* asked Jasen and Laura to pick up the slack by splitting Rebecca's chores between them.

Jasen thought he was getting gypped. "Can't we take turns watching Michael each week?" he asked. "It isn't fair that we have to do Rebecca's chores all the time!"

"I hear you, Son," I replied, "and I know it may not seem fair to you, but as a father, I have a lot more to consider than your fairness." Pausing, I grinned and said, "My ways are higher than your ways, big boy!"

What I meant was that I was concerned with fairness for Jasen, but I had *other* concerns as well, like:

- *What was fair to Rebecca?* Had I made Jasen the baby-sitter, his chores would have been too much for Rebecca to handle at her age. That wouldn't have been fair to Rebecca.
- *What was fair to Michael?* Rebecca was his favorite playmate because she was closest to his age, so she was better suited to the task.
- *Who was committed?* When Rebecca baby-sat Michael, she actually stayed and played with him to the end. When Jasen or Laura baby-sat, they often got bored and wandered off, leaving Michael free to roam and rattle.
- *Who needed to learn to submit to authority, even when it wasn't fair?* Hmmm, I wonder?

Jasen's fairness *was* on my mind, but his fairness could only come through my higher ways of thinking. I wanted fairness for Jasen, but I *also* wanted what was best for the rest of the family.

In response to my little higher-ways joke, Jasen grunted, "I don't care about all that, Dad. It still isn't fair." (He wasn't being a smart aleck, by the way. He was just being honest.)

In short, Jasen was saying, "Dad, you aren't listening to me! It is so clear that my way is the right way. Why can't you see that as clearly as I?"

His young mind lacked the maturity to grasp the big picture, and it's similar to how we sometimes do not see the big picture regarding the way God designed marriage. We choose to marry based on similarities and compatibility, but when the honeymoon's over, we sometimes believe we've made a mistake, not thinking for one moment that God *also* brings us together for our differences and even our wounds, since living happily ever after is not the only thing He has in mind for us. We're blinded and trapped by our less-mature, lower-ways view like Jasen was.

But God has much more on His mind, and it may not be until all is said and done that we can understand why God brought the two of us together. So we whine, "God, I didn't ask for this! You promised a soul mate, but I got this sexual pervert instead. It isn't fair! Why did this have to happen to me?"

But like Jasen, we aren't grasping the big picture. Providing a lifetime soul mate *is* on God's list, but how soon we'll *seem* like soul mates on a day-to-day basis depends upon the softness of our hearts to His sanctification work, both inside and outside the bedroom. That's part of God's higher ways.

He wants happiness for you, but He *also* wants what is best for you *and* what is best for your husband. He knows that this sexual disaster in your marriage will force you to learn how to love the unlovely, the very bedrock trait of Christian character, and He knows that what's happened will shatter your husband's defenses so that the Lord can move in closer and begin healing his long-festering wounds.

Jasen told us he didn't care for our little character-training episode. "You are treating Beck better than me, and you don't even care," he stated.

We say the same thing to God, and it sounds something like this: "I don't care, Lord! His sexual junk is just filthy and sick. I don't even want to touch him anymore. And how can I trust You now, God? You didn't care enough to keep me away from this pervert. Well, I quit, and I'm getting out of this marriage!"

But God *is* caring. Isn't it caring and right for God to improve your character? We *are* His, after all. Besides, marriage never was all about you. What if God needs to change your husband by making him struggle through these problems with you? Is it not fair for God to ask you to serve Him this way after everything He's done for you? We aren't truly a marriage of three until we accept His higher ways of thinking on marriage. Consider this verse:

> If your first concern is to look after yourself, you'll never find yourself. But if you forget about yourself and look to me, you'll find both yourself and me. (Matthew 10:39, MSG)

And if we don't accept His higher ways of thinking, guess what continues to happen? While you're thinking everything is wrong, everything may actually be going perfectly, from God's perspective, and you'll remain totally confused and frustrated even while your husband is healing.

FROM BRENDA

If you're to avoid confusion and frustration, you must accept this pair of possibilities:

1. God may have created your marriage in part for the messy work of helping Him heal your husband's wounds, of assisting your husband in his journey to Christian maturity.

2. God may have picked you to be the central figure in this work of restoration from the very beginning. How do you know this marriage isn't among God's highest dreams for your life?

I know what you're thinking: *If it is, then I've been duped. I didn't sign up for this.* Maybe so. But all too often we ignore God's higher-ways point of view and miss His vision for our marriages, which He's intended as our very own under-the-radar, no-headline, home mission field. Perhaps you've spent years asking God to reveal His will for your life, when all along He's been asking in return, *How are you doing with that little part of My will that I've already revealed to you regarding your marriage?*

Emily wrote, "I feel like God has fed me to the wolves in this marriage. I feel like I was conned into what you call a mission field."

We're easily thrown off by our husbands' filth, aren't we? We resent having married into this dark, sexual underside of humanity.

I've been right there with you, especially after reading through e-mail after painful e-mail from women confronting a husband's sexual sin. But recently God challenged me through another counselor's view of sexual sinners, and I had to admit I wasn't looking enough like Christ.

I no longer view these guys as the dark underside of humanity. A big change happened in me when God moved me beyond *There but for the grace of God go I* and on to *There go I.* Not that I did any of the severe things that many of my men have done, but I am a sinner and just as capable of this type of fallen, compulsive, sinful behavior.

What changed me most was the revelation that I am not my brother's keeper. I am my brother's brother, and these brothers need help. And when one of these brothers really gets it, really turns things around, it's like watching Lazarus walk out of the tomb, fully alive. And then when that new life spills over into whole families, it's simply breathtaking.

What about you? There's no question that you are your husband's wife. But when you look in that mirror of your heart, what do you see? Are you also your husband's sister? If you're to handle his wounds well on Christ's behalf, you'll have to act like a loving sister, too.

Christ's example is clear. Jesus was wounded plenty, just like you—it happens to all of us. But while it's okay to *be* wounded, it's not okay to *stay* wounded.

Christ refused to stay wounded, and He didn't dwell on how He was being mistreated (as we're so prone to do). Instead, Jesus chose to be His brother's brother and to help the wounded around Him, the very ones who had wounded Him and who would eventually nail Him to the Cross. If He focused at all upon His own wounds, it was to turn them around in order to bring glory to His Father's grace and to change the entire world. In the end, He could pray, "I have brought you glory on earth by completing the work you gave me to do" (John 17:4).

You, too, can bring God glory on earth by completing the work He gave you to do. And what is your work? To be your husband's sister in Christ, and not just his wife. You, too, can refuse to stay wounded, fixing your gaze upon the Cross, the Word, and the regenerative power of the Holy Spirit and turning your focus toward your hurting brother. It isn't easy at all and you certainly won't change the whole world like Jesus did, but you'll surely change that smaller world around you and the relationships that God has placed in your hands.

FROM FRED

Brenda did exactly that in setting a standard of normal into my life. Before that time, I couldn't look God in the eye because of my sin. I couldn't pray, I had no peace, and I felt no strength before the Enemy. Today, I have a wonderful intimacy with God. When I walk outside in the morning, I'm absolutely certain that I'm walking with Lord, and the Enemy jumps to the alert. Obviously, Christ authored this work from the beginning, but Brenda's ministry to me has had a vast impact upon my life. Somewhere from beneath the barrage of my awful temper, Brenda somehow caught God's higher vision of marriage.

Now that doesn't mean she was perfect. She may not have been punching holes in walls, but she had a bag of tricks of her own. For instance, while she hated my temper and demanded I control it under threat of separation, she later confessed to me that she deliberately used my own temper against me on occasion, out of pure frustration. When my "superior" logic threatened to win arguments, she purposely played dense and pushed the right buttons to drive my temper over the edge. That way she won no matter how much I was right!

In spite of all that, at the end of the day Brenda shone magnificently for Christ in my life. She found the grace and mercy to see the big picture with the help of Christ's eyes. Our marriage was no longer all about her. For Brenda, our marriage had become a ministry.

She saw a hurting young man who had never been taught the truth, a son whose father had rejected him early in life, and a young man who'd never had a completely faithful friend or family member. As my Christian sister, she once declared her faithfulness with these indelible words: *You have never had a completely faithful and trustworthy person in your life. I'm going to be that person, no matter what. I won't hurt you, and I won't leave you for as long as I live.*

With that note of unconditional love ringing in my ears, she began a long, torturous journey, working with God to heal my wounds and rebuild my mind. Forgetting her own wounds, she chose to focus instead upon God's call on her life as my sister in Christ, and today she can honestly pray, "I have done all that You asked me to do. I have brought glory to You, Father."

I am so grateful. Without her, there would be no Every Man series, and I would be no author. Of course, this was never where Brenda thought the marriage gig would take her. She's a homebody, a busy and happy mother who would have preferred that our private troubles never became public. But she knew she had a part to play in encouraging and lifting me, just like God does for us:

> He raises the poor from the dust
>> and lifts the needy from the ash heap;
> he seats them with princes,
>> with the princes of their people. (Psalm 113:7-8)

Brenda put her shoulder to the task, helping me *look* like a prince in practice, not only in title. And for that, a family tree has been shaken and its destiny altered. A picture of God's love has been painted, and a few books have been written. But most of all, a young man who couldn't believe in hope now writes hopefully of God's unfathomable grace and power to heal.

God could very well be asking you to stand in the gap for your Christian brother. He's counting on you, His daughter, as the last line of defense.

The church has let your husband down through its collective silence. His father and friends have let him down along the way. Will you call back the straying one and live righteously before him? Will you show him mercy?

God's eyes are going to and fro throughout the whole earth looking for someone on whose behalf He can show His power. You've been called to let that someone be you, as you'll see even more clearly in the next chapter.

helpmate

I will make him an help meet.

GENESIS 2:18, KJV

FROM BRENDA

As you stepped before the mirror in the last chapter, we encouraged you to ask yourself, *How much do I look like Christ these days in my marriage?* Before you step away, I would like you to take one more good look into your heart's mirror and ask yourself this question: *How am I doing in my role as helpmate?* It is in this role as helper where most wives make their biggest mistakes in marriage. Let's return once more to Genesis and review why we were created as women:

> The LORD God took the man and put him in the Garden of Eden to work it and take care of it....
>
> The LORD God said, "It is not good for the man to be alone. I will make a helper suitable for him."...
>
> For this reason a man will leave his father and mother and be united to his wife, and they will become one flesh. (Genesis 2:15,18,24)

Why was it not good for man to be alone? I can assure you it was not because Adam needed some help hanging vines or running a backhoe in the garden. And it was more than Adam's needing someone to talk to or have sex with.

God knew what sin was about to do to Adam and to all who came after him. He knew the wounds that would be meted out on innocent bystanders through the sin of friends, families, and even churches. He'd even seen ahead to the days when Internet porn would enslave millions of men. He *had* to have known all this was going to happen, because that's what being omniscient means. Given that He knew what the future would bring, He knew it wouldn't be good for Adam (and his future male offspring) to be alone.

As we've said, the word *helper* in Genesis comes from a Hebrew word that means "a help as his counterpart." So what does a helper do? Fred explains it this way: as a helper, a wife's role is to help lift up her husband—boost him, assist him, encourage him—to Christian greatness, whatever that may entail. This isn't an easy role to fill, even when your husband is *asking* for your help.

Recently, Fred was asked to appear on a video project called *Porn Nation,* produced by Campus Crusade/Braveheart. Braveheart's production team was insistent, though, that I be interviewed on camera with Fred. Well, it's one thing to disclose our story in a book; it's quite another to do it with the cameras whirling under the hot lights. When Fred told me about this opportunity, he added that we would have to fly to Braveheart's production studio in Atlanta for filming on December 21, just four days before Christmas.

That news didn't please me at all. The timing was horrible. All the kids would be home on holiday break, and I would have a houseful of company arriving two days later. *Auugh!*

There was only one person I could direct my wrath at, and that was Fred, because this *Every Man's Battle* stuff was *his* thing. So I unloaded these beauties for his consideration:

- "You're probably just caught up in something that sounds really cool, but it'll turn out to be some dumb little thing that neither one of us should have taken the time to be involved in."
- "You're only thinking of yourself! I can't think of anything that I dread more than speaking in public, let alone having my inadequacies taped for everyone to see for years to come."
- "You couldn't care less about leaving your kids alone! Well, I care, and I don't want to leave my kids home alone for any reason." (In Fred's defense, our oldest is in college, and two are in high school.)

- "You know that I hate flying, and here you are making me fly when I don't really have to. Plus, it's insane to fly during the Christmas holidays."
- "I heard no call from God on this, pal. This is your thing, not mine. Do it yourself!"

I also felt offended when Fred told me he had been sitting on this news for a day or two. He claimed that he had been waiting for an opportunity to approach me with it when I would be relaxed. So there I was, resting on the couch one Saturday morning and looking forward to a nice weekend when he suddenly sprang this film project on me like some big hairy spider.

I felt betrayed that he waited until I was relaxed before he dropped his big bomb. I suppose there isn't any good time for that kind of news, but I felt so angry over the whole thing that I figured our weekend would be ruined. From that moment, I knew that it would be very hard for me to get over my feelings.

For his part, Fred was appalled at my initial refusal to go, asking incredulously, "This film will be shown on more than two hundred campuses every year and draw thousands to Christ. How can you turn your back on God after all He's done for us?"

Great. Play the God card, Fred.

"Why can't you see *my* point?" I responded. "I don't feel called to this, and I don't feel I have anything important to say. Besides, I don't believe anyone cares to hear what I have to say."

It's not that I have a low image of myself. I just know that people listen to those famous folks, and I'm not one of them.

Fred has a definite calling to write and speak, and sometimes it worries me that I don't *feel* called like he does. On the other hand, I do feel called to *support* his call. Huldah Buntain, wife of the great missionary Mark Buntain of Calcutta, openly admitted that for as long as her husband lived, she never had the same call for the people of India that he did, but she had an unmistakable call to support him in his work.

Public speaking was the worst thing that Fred could have asked me to do. Several times that day I felt tears behind my eyes, and my heart was broken that he'd asked me to do something for him that was this hard for me. *How could he be so cruel?*

All this churned away inside me until I prayed to God for direction later that day while taking a shower. While I rinsed my hair, I just *knew* I had to be a help-mate to Fred and go to Atlanta with him. After toweling off, throwing on some clothes, and blowing my hair dry, I wrote this note to Fred:

Even as I write this, in my own flesh I have tears and a deep dread in my heart right now. But I've made the decision to not fight it anymore. For once in my life, I choose to walk as boldly and confidently as I can with the Lord's help. I'm counting on seeing His strength and faithfulness before the camera when I have no strength of my own, and I trust that He can use me somehow. I figure that if I'm being obedient to him, He can do nothing less than honor that obedience.

Fred was in shock. Later, he asked me what had happened to change my mind. "Two things, I guess," I responded. "The first was that I gave in for *your* sake this time, even more than I did it for the Lord. I love you and how you do so much for me, and I knew how important this must be to you.

"Second, I guess I just saw this as an obedience issue for me. Sure, I may not *feel* your call, but I know that He's called me to *support* you. I believe God wants me to go with you, and because I love Him so much, I don't like the thought of disappointing Him."

Well, the taping in Atlanta went smoothly, for which I'm very grateful, but my story illustrates how hard it is to play our helper role when our husbands are *asking* for help. But what are you supposed to do in that role when your husbands are *not* asking? What happens then?

It can be confusing, and most of that confusion revolves around the choice between these two courses of action:

1. When your husband needs your help, but he obviously can't see it, should you simply be quiet and pray for his insight to improve, submitting in silence for the sake of peace?
2. Or should you bravely speak up directly and forcefully in the face of his blindness to challenge him to Christian greatness? What is your role?

Maybe it would be useful to step back and take a look at the roles your husband should be playing alongside your own. It can be enlightening to see how interrelated our roles as husband and wife really are.

Each of us has two major roles in marriage. Fred plays the headship role and is the overall leader in the home. He's also been called by God to be the high priest of our home, the spiritual leader responsible for building a normal Christian home.

As his wife, I play the parallel submissive role to Fred's leadership at home, and the parallel helper role to prod, lift, and strengthen him to carry out his roles as head and high priest.

Note how God expects the husband and wife to play essentially the same spiritual role for the other spouse. As a high priest, Fred is to *lead* me into Christian greatness. As a helpmate, I'm to work alongside the Holy Spirit to *lift* Fred to Christian greatness. Sadly, we've noticed that both of these roles are routinely ignored in Christian homes these days, although for different reasons.

FROM FRED

Why do men ignore their role as high priest? Mostly out of laziness and natural rebelliousness. We'd rather kick back and flow with the lazy tides as long as we can do what we want.

But if we're ignoring that high priest's role out of rebelliousness, why are women ignoring their helpmate role? The answer is simple: they've been wounded by the church's silence in much the same way as young men have been wounded by the church's silence on sexual issues. While their helper role is rarely supported from the pulpit, countless sermons and books pound at our wives to submit, submit, submit, no matter how their husbands act and no matter how blind we have become.

And so their helper role, which might have helped strengthen us husbands to become great leaders in our homes, has been stripped away from our wives, while the better Christian male leadership we might have provided is compromised.

Which brings us right back to the questions posed earlier: when your husband needs your help but can't see that he *needs* help, which role are you to play? Should you simply be quiet and pray for his insight to improve, submitting in silence for the sake of peace? Or does the Lord expect you to step out boldly to actively defend your home and to encourage your husband toward God?

For answers, we can look to the story of Abigail and David from 1 Samuel in the Old Testament. Abigail was an intelligent and beautiful woman, while her husband, Nabal, was surly and mean in his dealings throughout their region.

David and his men settled nearby and asked Nabal if he might be able to spare some food in exchange for the protection that David's army had been affording Nabal's household. Nabal—not the sharpest tool in the shed—harshly dismissed his request, and David was furious. David told four hundred of his men to strap on their swords, as he fully intended to make Nabal pay for his insolence. But suddenly, Nabal's helper—that's right, his wife, Abigail—intervened. After hearing from a servant that disaster was hanging over her house and without telling Nabal, she loaded up the donkeys with food and cut David off at the pass.

She bowed low before him and said (my paraphrase), "My lord, pay no attention to my husband. He can be so foolish. Let my gift of food be given to your men, and please forgive our offense. When God makes you king over this nation, as He has promised, and you are enjoying broad success, I don't want you to have to look back and regret this day of bloodshed. I want you to remember us well."

David was overwhelmed by her boldness, and he graciously accepted her gift. Abigail could have been divorced for opposing her husband's wishes, but she stood bravely to protect Nabal and her house from his foolishness. She also could have been sliced to ribbons by David's men, but she trusted God that as she spoke the Lord's words into David's heart, he would respond and rise up to be the merciful, spiritual leader that was his calling. Her reward? Peace for her house.

As women, sometimes you'll be called upon to stand up to your husband's foolishness to protect your house, and you'll have to trust the Holy Spirit that as you speak His words into your husband's heart, your husband will listen and the fruit of the Spirit will blossom broadly in his life. Your reward will be peace for your house. Quiet submission is not the only path to peace and health in marriage.

We would have never had lasting peace in our home had Brenda not also played her hard-nosed, audible helper's role for God and for me. It isn't normal for a Christian man to be surly, mean, or foolishly blind like I was, and had Brenda not intervened strongly as my helper when she did, my leadership would have been devastated and I would have crushed our home. None of us would have had a chance to become all that Christ intends us to be.

I'll never forget the day when I blasted Brenda with a bellowing frenzy and crushed a hole in the dry wall with my bare fist as an exclamation point. Pleased with the drama of my little display, I arrogantly turned back toward her, glaring fiercely.

She'd been letting a number of these instances slide in the past, but things were escalating dangerously, and by now she'd finally had it. After I punched this hole, rage now covered *her* face. Brenda menacingly leaned in and jabbed her finger up under my nose. With a pair of narrowed eyes that would make Clint Eastwood proud, she snapped, "I thought I married a Christian, and I did it for a reason! I didn't want to live with something like this. I don't care what you grew up like, this isn't normal. You are going to fix this temper, or we'll be separated so fast it'll make your head spin. I'm not going to live like this for the rest of my life, and you better not doubt me!"

Spinning away, she made her own stormy exit, stage right. I was stunned.

Where does she get the right after two months of marriage to talk to me like that? I huffed. The answer: from God.

Brenda had said, "I thought I married a Christian, and I did it for a reason. I didn't want to live with something like this." God had painted a picture of what a Christian man looks like in the Bible, and Brenda's dad and uncles had lived out that picture for her first twenty years. She knew what normal looked like.

The truth is, when I became a follower of Christ, I gave up my right to look like anything but normal as a Christian. As spiritual leaders, men are to *lead* their families to Christian greatness, which is another way of saying normal Christian behavior. As helpers, women are to *lift* their husbands to Christian greatness by revealing the blind spots keeping them from normal, Christian behavior. (Please note that "lift them" is not a synonym for "control them" or "take them over.")

Without a doubt, this is where Brenda has excelled as my helper. She could have just as easily backed off under my withering outbursts. She had heard well-meaning girlfriends tell her to "be still and let Fred lead." It gives me nightmares to think where we'd be today if she had listened to them. I know *so* many men who have the same temperament flaws twenty years after their weddings because they wouldn't let their wives play that helper role.

It is so vital that we both play our roles well in marriage because sin is rampant everywhere, and the percentage of folks in our pews with little Christian heritage is growing rapidly. Most of us just don't know what normal looks like anymore.

Brenda knew what normal was, and she loved me enough to fight on until I could see it for myself. As you can see in these verses, it was good that I listened to her:

> So I tell you this, and insist on it in the Lord, that you must no longer
> live as the Gentiles do, in the futility of their thinking. They are darkened
> in their understanding and separated from the life of God because of
> the ignorance that is in them due to the hardening of their hearts.
> Having lost all sensitivity, they have given themselves over to sensuality
> so as to indulge in every kind of impurity, with a continual lust for more.
>
> You, however, did not come to know Christ that way.... You were
> taught, with regard to your former way of life, to put off your old self,
> which is being corrupted by its deceitful desires; to be made new in the atti-
> tude of your minds; and to put on the new self, created to be like God in
> true righteousness and holiness.
>
> Therefore each of you must put off falsehood and *speak truthfully to his*
> *neighbor,* for we are all members of one body. (Ephesians 4:17-20, 22-25)

As my Christian sister, Brenda had a right and a duty to speak out truthfully (and even sharply) to me when I was still living in the futility of my thinking, darkened in my understanding and separated from full life in God because of my ignorance of normal Christianity.

And when it comes to your husband's sexual sin, you have every right to stand up and help him win. To be a helpmate means that you will never allow your husband to drift to his lowest level. Instead, you'll help him be great.

Now, it's not always easy to help a man. Our egos can be maddening, and since you'll rarely seem like a submissive wife while showing your husband his blind spots, he'll likely object to your attitude on some trumped-up biblical grounds. I've done it myself. But you are not being godless—you are simply playing your other God-given role in his life.

It's normal. Being iron sharpening iron is part of Christian friendship and fellowship, as the previous scripture (Ephesians 4:25) suggests. Like it or not, sometimes you're required to encourage (and perhaps even force) your husband to consider a higher train of thought and behavior in your marriage, and when you do this, its okay. You are just doing your job.

Women often write, "My husband and I have this serious problem. Is there some way to bring it up to him so that I don't irritate him? He doesn't like it when I question him, and I don't want to push him away."

Can you sense how continual, quiet submission can destroy communication between spouses and allow us to drift to our lowest natural bents? If you only play "submitter" and never play your helper role, the laws of reaping and sowing will be suspended in your husband's life and he'll pay no price for his abnormal behavior.

What will God think? Don't worry. God knows that husbands need to pay a stiff price sometimes, and so do husbands. Sometimes I *need* to be irritated, or I won't listen. Sometimes I *need* to be pushed away, or I won't see. I need my helper's voice!

When Brenda stands up for her right to speak into my life, she's actually standing up for *me,* though it rarely feels like it at the time. When she refuses to be still regarding my crushing behavior, is it an abdication of her call to submit to my authority? Heavens no! It is the proper discharge of her call to help me see and to lift me towards Christian greatness. It is a sign of her unconditional love for me.

From Brenda

Of course, a husband must respond. It can't be forgotten that if Fred was to answer God's call to holiness and seek Christian greatness by walking closely to Christ, he had the responsibility to commit to kindness and sexual purity on his own. But my job as his counterpart was to help him seek purity and normal living in any way that I could, especially by pointing out blind spots and insisting he address them.

You, too, will have to step into the role of being a helper to your husband in the wake of all this pain, and we'll spend some time in the next chapter showing you how this looks in practice. If you do it right, it'll make it easier for him to respond to your help and to God's call to walk Christianly.

dressings and iron

FROM FRED

Thanks to my volcanic temper and clumsy leadership surrounding our in-law problems, it took just two years for Brenda to switch from panting, "Oh boy," when she'd see my face across a crowded room to breathing a tense, "Oh no," when I came home from work. I single-handedly destroyed nearly every trace of romantic love in just twenty-four months. Then it took me *five years* to restore what I had decimated in only two.

My struggle with sexual sin was no different. While it took me just six weeks to get my eyes trained and under control, it took quite a bit longer to train my mind to capture my wandering thoughts. I was developing a complicated new skill, and I wasn't used to it. Once the major fighting had ceased, though, my newly installed Christian government had to gain control of my borders. I think two or three years passed before I'd mastered all the emotional triggers that had tripped me up sexually in the past, which was right in line with the two- to five-year time line predicted by most counselors.

The good news is that total victory is possible for your husband. I've lived that victory, and for fifteen years I haven't experienced any sort of trip or stumble. But victory requires patience by all involved, and I know patience is not easy when your heart has taken deep wounds from a husband's betrayal. Extending patience will require great focus in you, and it will take balance.

After all, problems don't crop up in a day, and neither do they vanish overnight. Overcoming sexual sin is a process and a journey. Accountability, counseling, communication, support, and continual prayer are mandatory. Surrendering and forgiving are daily requirements, and discouragement can abound.

Any isolated slip or fall by a husband can send emotions cascading like hail over a wife's delicate young crop of trust. You may want to cry out, "Have we lost everything again?"

I know that hailstones were falling when Kristie wrote us this note:

I just feel like we're not getting anywhere. Kyle has read the first two chapters of *Every Man's Marriage,* but now he hasn't picked up the book for two weeks. I really think he has no clue about changing his approach toward me. He said he is trying, but he feels he's not getting any credit from me, and he feels like I'm demanding a lot from him.

Kristie has every right to take Kyle to task because her husband broke his promise about reading the book. When a hurting wife just wants the torment to stop, however, she may demand too much too soon. How much patience must she offer in the midst of her pain?

Balancing the forceful action of your helper role and the tender patience of your submissive role is critical. Brenda kept a remarkable balance between holding my feet to the fire and holding out mercy. Sometimes, she'd bark at me after one of my anger outbursts, while at other times she'd patiently say nothing.

FROM BRENDA

If we're to honor both of our roles as wives, balanced accountability must always arise from these two cornerstones:

1. My marriage is not all about me.
2. When I hold him accountable, my focus must be on my choices as well as his.

Christ's broader view of marriage prevented pain from dominating my heart and kept Fred's pain on my mind, enabling me to consider mercy and patience, regardless of the sin involved.

You need that broader view too. Sure, his sin is betraying and crushing you, but it is also revealing his deeper wounds and addictions below the surface. He's not just a straying husband but a brother lost in the futility of his thinking and now corrupted by his deceitful desires. It's not just about you.

The way I came to view things, I was not just Fred's wife, called to respectfully submit to his leadership and to always be ravished in his arms. I was *also* his good Samaritan, compelled by my love to dress his wounds, and *also* his friend, taking on the "iron sharpens iron" role described in Proverbs 27:17.

That dual picture of applying the dressing and grinding the iron portrays our helper role pretty well. When we make sure to include that mental picture of applying dressings to our husbands' wounds, our primary focus remains on our own choices in the situation, rather than on our husbands', which is the second cornerstone for balanced accountability.

When we limit ourselves to the "iron sharpens iron" role, we women exhibit a tendency to overdo the sharpening, as if we are in some sort of motherly-correcting role. After all, *he's not behaving right and needs to get his little rear in gear!*

But you are not your husband's mother, and he is not your misbehaving child who just needs to get his little rear in gear. He is a man, and if he's anything like Fred, he's been wounded by years of emotional trauma, and those wounds aren't just going to skip away under your scolding. Yes, sparks can fly when iron sharpens iron, but the results sought should always be mutual and healing and constructive. Fred's wounds, which became bound up with his temper and his sexuality for years, had also infiltrated his mental tapes and discolored his view of the world. This was his mind-sent in those dark days:

- I'm no good.
- I'm not worthy.
- The louder I am, the righter I am.
- No one loves me enough to be faithful to me.

Changing tapes takes time under the best of circumstances, but if you stop and consider the phrases recorded here, you can't miss how your harsh pounding with angry, bitter ultimatums may easily torpedo your efforts. You need to be erasing his tapes, not confirming what's recorded there.

Again, that's why a "dressing his wounds" mind-set is crucial to a wife's approach to any of her husband's sins, whether it's anger or porn. Of course, there will always be times when you must reach for the iron bar to sharpen his ways. I'll talk about that side of your role first before having Fred delve into the dressings mode.

I always made sure Fred understood that the iron was within my reach even when out of sight, like the lump from a handgun in the pocket of a trench coat. By that I mean that there could be no doubt in Fred's mind that I had the right to use my iron to sharpen his and would do it when necessary.

Verbally, I absolutely refused to be muzzled in our relationship, in spite of his frightening, intimidating tantrums. That would have stripped me of my helper role, and it would have perpetually doomed us as a family. Sorry. I couldn't do that to God, Fred, or my kids.

I was never afraid to use the iron, and I could be extremely confrontational about his temper, depending on how badly he'd just lost it. If he threw a pot of soup or grabbed me physically by the arm, he could count on a ferocious, toe-to-toe response.

But I was always careful to hold myself as accountable for my choices in responding to him as I was in holding him accountable for his temper. I understood where the outbursts were ultimately coming from—his tapes—so I was careful to affirm him as best I could. When he really blew it, though, I let him have it. But if he had a mild outburst, or if I had already banged him over the head about his anger several times in a row, I'd leave him alone, knowing that he couldn't miss what he had just done and that he didn't need to be chastised every time he flew off the handle.

He was a man, which meant that nagging him would have been very discouraging. Besides, he had committed to win this battle, and he had given me his word on it as a man. From time to time, I had to let him know that his word was good enough for me. That is always encouraging to a guy.

He also knew that I cared a lot more about his *attitude* toward change than about his careless trips and stumbles along the way. If I ever sensed he'd begun dogging it in his efforts to overcome his temper problem, my iron would vigorously move into play. I needed a normal, holy Christian husband as quickly as possible, since the future of our home was at stake. My patience was there to give him hope, not to give him space to goof off.

Some would say I had no right to change my husband. Baloney! Of course I had that right and, because of my role as helpmate, I also had the *responsibility* before God to insist upon change. When Fred claims Christ but continues to harbor sin, he pollutes our stream. We are *one flesh,* and because our lives are so intertwined spiritually, I have as much right to expect him to change as I have the right and responsibility to inspect myself and change. In marriage, my spiritual health depends not only upon my choices but also upon his. I have every right to insist that he handle that responsibility well, in one form or another. We're one.

Granted, we must manage our expectations between short-term goals and long-term change. In the short term, for instance, you can expect *nothing* from your spouse. You might demand, "Get that temper under control," but he can't possibly reply, "Okay, sugarplum, I'll have that changed by Tuesday." Change is hard, and old habits die slowly on the battlefield.

But in the long term, you can expect *everything* from your spouse, because we can do all things though Christ who strengthens us. In the long term, there is no wiggle room. The mate with the temper can only say, "I married my wife, for better or worse, and she traded away all her rights and freedoms to marry me. I have a responsibility to her before God to walk a godly path and to be conformed to Christ. I will not rest until my temper is under control."

One of the reasons why I was diligently honest with Fred was because I wanted him to understand the full extent of the damage he was causing our relationship. If anything would keep him from dogging it, my honesty would. I once told him that my respect for him was in a free fall in nearly every area of our relationship, and that I was having an especially hard time respecting him spiritually and as a father when he was rough with the kids. These damage assessments were brutal for him to hear, and they were also brutal for me to pronounce.

Believe it or not, I have a peaceful, phlegmatic temperament, which prompts me to avoid conflict at every turn. I found it difficult to stand up to him because I knew that when I did, my words would only provoke another wave of anger that would flood over my spirit as well. I was determined, though, that it was "Normality or Bust" for my marriage, and I would never just let these things go without doing everything I could do. I knew it was all on me, because I wanted a calm, healthy home, just like the one I grew up in. And Fred wouldn't know how to lead us there without my help.

You cannot afford to ignore the roles God asks you to play in marriage, whether you hate confrontation or not. You must do it for God, and you must do it for yourself. If you are asking your husband to fight this withering battle for sexual purity, shouldn't you be willing to carry the iron as his helpmate, no matter how hard it is for you?

FROM FRED

How did my heart soften toward change? Brenda's approach with the dressings had a lot to do with it. Though she could be quite a spitfire, Brenda never seemed like a scolding mother or a wild-eyed shrew.

Retaliation was not in her arsenal. Brenda has a razor wit, and I'm certain she could have verbally sliced my emotions to ribbons on countless occasions, but she never did, no matter how badly I'd hurt her. Her incredible restraint kept her focus from failing. No matter how much the confrontations hurt me, the absence of after-the-fact retaliation forever reminded me that she was only interested in my good.

Manipulation was not in her arsenal, either, and its absence did more than any single thing to soften my heart to her help. If I'd reach out after a fight to touch her, she wouldn't pull away. If I'd stomp downstairs in manipulative fury, she'd calmly wait up until I snuck back upstairs. She wouldn't play my games, and she wouldn't start her own.

That doesn't mean her stinging rebukes never hurt, of course. In fact, they always did. Like any guy, I hated to be called out on my character flaws, and she was always dead-on right, much to my private consternation. I often struck back like a wounded rattler.

But unlike my sorry tactics, she never belittled or demeaned me, and she never attacked me personally. Her words were meant to switch on a light in my mind, not shoot a flaming arrow through my head. Though she often stung me, she never wounded me further.

I asked her about her approach one time, and she said, "My reactions to you are always a choice, and when I can't love you for your sake because you are being so harsh, I can always find a way to love you for Jesus's sake because of what He's done for me."

So she hugged me because she loved Jesus, and when she couldn't summon any love and grace for me, she'd forgive me because of what Christ meant to both of us. She was so disciplined in that! She was not out to hurt me or to have her own way. She was out to help me and to have things God's way, normal and true.

But in the end, her greatest gift was teaching me how Christians think, and she had this wonderful, nonthreatening approach to that. For instance, let's say we were headed home after a dinner party. Given my past and my discomfort in those situations, I would naturally assume that most of the guests had thought I'd been a dork all night. If I'd express something along those lines to Brenda, she'd simply turn toward me with raised eyebrows and ask softly, "Is that really how you think? Normal Christians don't think that way, sweetheart."

Startled, I'd reply, "Really? That's how I've always thought. Are you sure?"

"Of course," she'd giggle. "Normal Christians have a good self-image, and they don't assume the worst like that."

I'd be mesmerized and silently ponder her words for miles while she'd fume in the background about the years of torture I must have endured to come out thinking this way. These revelations were like priceless dressings with miraculous powers applied to my life, and I'm forever grateful. Sure, she was an expert with the iron, but what a grand master she was with the dressings!

Balanced accountability is the loam in which the seeds of trust will sprout again. In the end, each couple's story will look different from every other, as temperaments will vary and response times will differ.

But one thing must always remain consistent: each Christian couple is called to be sanctified, to become normal in Christ. You are both wounded now, and you'll both have to work together to heal and to be accountable to living a normal life together.

What is normal living in the wake of sexual sin? Well, it's up to your husband. Has he fully repented? Is his repentance lagging or even nonexistent? We'll take a look at what you must do in response to each case in the next part.

what's normal?

Everything you've read up to this point is critical to you, regardless of your husband's response regarding God's call to purity. No matter what your situation, your feelings are valid and quite normal. No matter how it's coming down in your home, you must understand that it's not all about you. Yet you have a crucial healing role to play as you encourage your husband to seek Christian greatness and to make your home normal.

We concede that the way your husband responds is a wild card here. For instance, if he becomes a zealot for purity and grows quickly in his intimacy with God, it could leave some confusing responses in you, which we'll discuss in chapter 18. If he dawdles between right and wrong for months or even years, you'll need to pay close attention to chapters 19–23. And if he never turns away from sexual sin, then chapter 24 addresses that situation.

No matter where your husband is emotionally and spiritually, we suggest you read on through to the end of the book. We have included several key stories that offer much insight and advice for many circumstances. These stories from women just like you will help you understand how the principles of restoration look when applied in practice.

your lagging heart

FROM FRED

You were shattered when your husband confessed his sin to you, but you have to admit he has been nothing short of magnificent since then. He's read *Every Man's Battle,* he's teamed up with a couple of guys for accountability, and he's told you that he's never felt closer to God in his life. So why aren't you happy? Okay, maybe you are ecstatic about his turnaround, but many wives echo what's inside Jenny's heart:

> I just found out a month ago—after three kids and twelve years of marriage—that my husband has been into pornographic movies and magazines. I now understand why Lee could say that he loved me all these years, yet he couldn't give me the sexual intimacy I desired.
>
> I am amazed how just getting the secret out has made us so much closer. Believe it or not, Lee is the one bringing it up and talking a lot these days. We are really together now. Everything is awesome, and I am doing all that I know to help him stay strong in this.
>
> Still, is there anything to convince me that this wasn't really about me? I need to understand that there was nothing I could have done—like look prettier or have breast implants.
>
> Lee tells me this had nothing to do with me or the way I look, but I just can't help taking it personal. Can you help me with something to read?

Jenny keeps bouncing from hope to dismay. Her husband's now living the life she always hoped for from the beginning, so she should be happy. Then why are her feelings lagging far behind the new condition of her husband's heart?

The answer: nothing's wrong. She's responding quite normally, and if you're feeling anything like Jenny, you're normal too. After all, there practically *has* to be a lag in how you respond here. While you and your husband may be chasing the same *goal* (a strong marriage), you're not at all starting from the same *place*. Take a look at the following comparisons:

HIS REALITIES	HER REALITIES
I'm becoming a man of integrity.	I've been betrayed.
I've never loved her more.	I've never felt less loved, less valuable, or less safe.
I'm beginning to see how much I value our marriage.	I've never realized until now how little our marriage meant to him.
Finally, I'm an honest man.	How could he live a lie like this?
I understand the healing process sometimes takes three to five years, but I think I can speed up the timetable because I want so badly to be whole.	Three years seems like a lifetime to deal with this pain—and it could go longer.
I finally have accountability.	How many people know that I am married to a pervert?

See what I mean? Your husband wants to give you a high-five for something that's still making your stomach turn. If only the confusion stopped there!

But it doesn't, because your eyes are playing tricks on you these days. When you look at this muddled marriage through the eyes of your emotions, you see it's not your fault that you're lagging behind. You're mired in the sloppy muck of broken trust, and it was his masturbation and lies that put you in this hole.

But when you look at your lousy state through the eyes of logic, it can almost appear to be *your* fault now. After all, *you* are the one who's lagging behind while *he's* turned the corner and is making tracks. These push-pull emotions were captured well by Kelly, who told me her story:

For Christmas I asked my fiancé to purchase *Every Man's Battle* for me, while I bought *Every Man's Marriage* for him. The truth is, I already felt like I had a pretty good understanding of the problems guys have with porn and masturbation, but while reading *Every Man's Battle*, I remembered a comment that Ben had made several months before. "I need to stop masturbating," he said one day out of the blue. I'm not sure why he brought it up, so I let it drop. Like most girls I know, masturbation seems quite unnecessary; we prefer intimacy and love.

One weekend recently, I asked Ben how the battle was going for him. He replied that the masturbation was still a problem, and so I shared with him the justification I'd been making for him in an attempt to get a discussion going.

"Since it isn't possible to think about algebra or sports while you're masturbating, I'm glad you're thinking about me!" I said.

He agreed, but something in his manner froze my heart. Call it women's intuition, but in that moment I somehow knew that he was digging up other images and memories to make those times with himself satisfying.

"You're thinking about other girls, aren't you?" I demanded, looking him dead in the eye.

He just put his head down. He couldn't say anything, nor could he look at me. A flood of emotions surged over me, while sickening confirmations hammered me broadside over the next few days.

Since then we've talked about this over and over again. On the outside I've told him that I've forgiven him, but on the inside my heart hurts so badly that I've built a wall between us. I don't want him to kiss me or hug me or to even tell me that he loves me, even though that's exactly what I wanted before.

So here's my dilemma. When he finished reading *Every Man's Marriage*, Ben said that he has learned more about love than we could have ever dreamed. He said that he finally "gets it," that he's become this new man, but I can't even respond to this new man.

I am now the one who's cold and busy and moody while he's the one constantly chatting or hugging or loving me. In one sense he's become the man I've always wanted, but now it's like I'm on another planet.

How do I not take all this personally? He feels horrible about it all and apologizes to me a hundred times a day—but I just want to punch him. I don't want to throw our love or our engagement away—but I feel so cheated. What do I do?

The answer to Kelly's question may seem deceptively simple: she needs to fight the right battle. If her fiancé—or your husband—has fully repented, and your emotions are still lagging behind the changes in his life, you're no longer dealing with sexual sin. The battlefield has changed. You're now dealing with broken trust.

As we discussed in chapter 14, trust cannot exist in a vacuum, and you can't manufacture trust on your own. Trust requires two ingredients: your husband must become trustworthy, and you must trust again. Each of you is responsible for bringing one ingredient to the table.

Practically speaking, it no longer matters that it was your husband (or fiancé) who demolished your trust in him. You're on to a new battlefield now, and all that matters is that both of you have roles in rebuilding that trust. In light of that, let's take a look at both roles, starting with yours.

Trusting Again

In Kelly's situation, she didn't recognize she was on a new battlefield, but think back to what we learned in chapter 14:

As women, we must concede that in some parts of the sexual makeup of men, they have a tougher battle than we do, because they're saddled with challenges related to their sexuality that we simply don't have. If you can't muster a mustard seed's worth of mercy and compassion in light of what we've discussed about your husband's masculinity, it's likely that you are still too bitter and angry to open yourself to the Spirit's prompting in your heart.

While that's difficult to face when you're hurting so, you must face it in order to heal.

If you remain bitter, you'll cause as much stress on your marriage as your husband's sexual sin. And you'll have to answer to God for your stagnant, damaged marriage as much as your husband will.

Remember the midterm exam? You must stretch beyond your female perspective and peer at his sin through the prism of male sexuality if you're to understand that his sexual sin is not about you. If you don't, compassion and mercy can't replace your rage, and you can't lay down your arms in humility before God.

Kelly hadn't yet laid down her arms because she hasn't seen how this sin does not reflect on her. If you're still ready to punch your husband, that's a red flag saying you haven't either.

By now you should know that he can compartmentalize porn and masturbation and that his sexual sin doesn't mean that you don't have what it takes. You also know that dysfunctional families and our sensual culture can push a man into an addictive quicksand, and it takes discipline and training in God's truth to break free. His sexual sin really wasn't as sexual as it first appeared.

But most of all, you should know that marriage is not about you but about God and the picture He wants to paint with your life together. And since you know these things, you can lay down your arms and decide what your future will look like.

You can choose to love the unlovely and to do everything in your power to encourage your husband in his brave stand for righteousness. No, he doesn't deserve grace like this, and it certainly would be unmerited favor from you. Still, this looks a lot like what Jesus did for us.

Your second option is to remain on Kelly's path, and I wouldn't blame you if you did. However, that choice will lock in some real losses for the both of you. In Kelly's case, this choice would weaken a Christian brother who, like a newborn babe, had just had his eyes opened and was ready to grow quickly in Christ. It would also lose her quite a catch—a rare guy who passionately embraced the message of servant leadership in *Every Man's Marriage*.

Christianity is always about choices. Whose ideals do you love the most—yours or Christ's? Your anger or His grace?

Brenda has been amazed how often she hears about the husband who creates the mess by lusting after porn while the wife keeps things messy by breaking his spirit and judging him into oblivion. Which is worse?

When it came to my temper, Brenda always said that no matter what I threw or what wall I punched, her reaction was a choice. If she couldn't love me for my sake, then she always found a way to love me and do the right thing for Jesus' sake because of what He did for her.

Was this easy for her? I can't say it was, but I *can* say that Brenda's choices gave me the freedom and grace to live again in our relationship and to grow into all I was supposed to be, in spite of my sin. That's what helpmates do.

That's exactly what I told Kelly. "Here is your chance to practice doing just that, the very thing that you will be spending the next seventy years of your life doing if you marry him," I said. "Seek God's face on this, and then, if you can find it in your heart, be his helpmate. Love the unlovely, and watch what God will do in your Ben's life."

Kelly nodded her head.

"Kelly, the best part is that you will reap as many blessings as Ben will," I continued, "and oneness *will* arise for having gone through this all together. If you're looking for someone better, you'll have to go a long way to find another young man who embraces servanthood like Ben does and besides, most men have this same challenge to stay sexually pure. You can look further, but why not stay and help him grow, since he has so many other things working right in his heart already?"

Kelly chose to trust again, and because she chose grace, she and Ben are *very* happily married now. "I can't believe how close I was to throwing away everything I'd dreamed of," she exclaimed recently. "Fred, I owe you one!"

FROM BRENDA

But let's not forget your husband's role in rebuilding trust. You can't do your part (trust him again) until he has done his part (become trustworthy).

I'll say it again here for emphasis: there is really no trick to trusting again. Only one thing can bring confidence—his consistent, faithful actions. Without right actions, he can't have your trust, and if he wants your trust, it's all on him.

Husbands often hate this responsibility, but you needn't apologize for it. You can expect it and even fight for it, applying the iron for the sake of your relationship. How so? Well, your husband wounded you. Use your iron to insist that he apply the dressings to your wounds as you need them applied.

To get your emotions back up to speed, you'll need the following from your husband:

- complete openness and honesty
- his patience as you heal
- trustworthy acts

First, how much detail and honesty can you expect? As much as you need. John explained it pretty well from his experience:

It's tough to answer the question, *How much detail do I give my wife?* Different women want different levels of detail, but my wife was one who wanted to know everything, down to the smallest nit. That was one of the reasons it was so agonizing for her to have to go through the drip torture with me for a couple years as she plumbed the depths of my past.

A far easier question to answer would be, *How much detail should I* be willing *to give her?* The answer: everything. If she wants to know if you used Kleenex or a handkerchief to clean up the semen after you masturbated, you have to be willing to tell her. If she asks you to describe in minute detail how you touched yourself, or what you thought about when you did, you have to be willing to tell her. If she wants to know if the real reason you were late on such and such a date is because you were out doing your porn thing, you need to tell her. Ditto on the questions: *What kind of porn? How old were the girls? Did you do anything with the other guys in the quarter booth area?* Any question, any time.

I'm not saying you can't have any boundaries, because I know that you can only talk so much about the details before you go bonkers with shame. But the willingness to answer has got to be there, and at worst, you should say, "I can't talk about it any more right now, but I will later, sweetheart."

Second, how much patience can you expect from your husband? Again, as much as you need. This kind of damage demands gentle care, and he owes that much to you simply out of restitution, if nothing else. He put you there.

His patience is a sign of deep repentance. If that sign isn't there, it's a troubling red flag. When your husband demands immediate forgiveness and doesn't show patience, then that's an indication that he's not where he needs to be. A husband may even complain, "What kind of Christian woman are you that you won't relax and forgive me?" That is outright spiritual abuse and comes from the same weak character that sent him into sexual sin in the first place.

Third, if he's truly repented, trustworthy acts will become second nature to him. As his helpmate, you have every right to play a role in defining what trustworthiness means to you, and you can expect him to come through for you.

For instance, if he doesn't like to read, but you need him to read *Every Man's Marriage* as a follow-up to *Every Man's Battle,* he'll show his trustworthiness by reading it anyway or listening to the audio version of that book.

In addition, *he* will be the one buying the porn filters for the Internet, rather than you. *He* will be the one placing his computer in an open area like the family room or breakfast nook. And *he* will be the one limiting his time on the Web. He will also be telling you about the action steps he is taking and will ask you for more ways that he can build your trust.

One of the primary things he did was to write me a contract, and the best part was that this was his idea. He committed to join an accountability group, began investing in marriage builder books and tapes, and learned some steps he could take to stay pure while traveling out of town. Really, the list goes on. I'm pretty proud of him. He has kept his promises—other than a few delays in finishing some of the books he's promised to read. I think it came to a point where he realized this trap could cost him everything he loves, and it just wasn't worth it.

Melissa told us this about her better-late-than-never husband, Jerry:

He hadn't been able to keep his promises until he lost his job over the porn.
It was the biggest life changer for the both of us. After he attended an *Every
Man's Battle* conference, he went straight to our pastor—something he
would never have done before—and he connected with a men's group and
began taking steps on his own, without my suggesting to him what to do.
That felt like a wonderful dream to me.

It has been nine months since he was fired. We used all our savings to
get by, and now we live on a meager weekly wage. We have literally gone
from middle class to poverty level with no backup whatsoever.

I had quit my job last year to stay home with our new baby, but now
I've had to go back to work because he lost his job. Scratching by daily is a
constant reminder of his sin, but I keep looking forward and wouldn't dare
mention it to him, because I now see him as a new person. We seem to be
on the same path in a healing sense. We both have a better understanding,
and we're resolved to take each day one at a time.

Thankfully, there's a bright silver lining. Because I see a change in him,
I am freer to love him. When he finally took responsibility for this sin, I was
drawn closer to him.

Taking things one day at a time is good advice because complete openness and
honesty, patience as you heal, and trustworthy acts don't happen overnight, but they
will happen quickly once your husband turns his whole heart to God. Once
they do, your emotions will finally catch up to his new life, and you'll experience
the loving freedom of your dreams.

SUGGESTED READING

These books will help challenge your husband to Christian greatness.
> *Every Man's Challenge* by Stephen Arterburn and Fred Stoeker: *teaches men to
> deepen their walk on the other side of sexual purity*

Every Man's Marriage (formerly titled *Every Woman's Desire*) by Stephen Arterburn and Fred Stoeker: *teaches men how to rebuild intimacy with their wives*

Always Daddy's Girl by H. Norman Wright: *fathers escaping sexual sin need
to learn how to touch, hug, and interact with their daughters in normal,
healthy ways*

Through Gates of Splendor by Elisabeth Elliot: *biography to encourage men
to think boldly as Christians*

God's Smuggler by Brother Andrew: *biography to encourage men to trust God in
all battles*

a Merle Hay Road moment

FROM FRED

You want your husband to stand as a pure Christian man. Until he does, you'll feel crushed and your family will be open to assault from the Enemy. But what do you do when his repentance is lagging? We've said that you have a right to stand up and sharpen some iron, and you do. Increasing the pressure to change can help him see the light, and we'll talk more about that in the next chapter.

Nothing will change, though, until he makes a hard, firm decision to fight for purity. Once he truly makes up his mind that things are going to change in his life, you should see some sort of progress, some sort of mental shift, but such a decision can be a long time coming.

Maybe you're wondering, *Why is that decision so hard?* It's a bit difficult to explain. It's not that guys don't want out—even unbelievers often want out. I was haunted by my pornography and masturbation even before I turned to Christ— after all, it had begun as a medication and a soothing friend, but before long I sensed it was making me less secure with women and more withdrawn from my friends.

Turning to Christ should have eased that decision, especially since He gave me an obvious leg up from the outset. Just a few weeks after I'd asked Him into my heart, He led me to leave the San Francisco Bay Area, where I had sown some corn-high oats, and move back to Iowa for a fresh start on life. I packed everything I could into the back of my Bonneville and found the eastbound lanes of Interstate 80.

On my way back home, I stopped in Steamboat Springs, Colorado, to visit a couple of Stanford buddies. The father of one owned a ranch just outside of town, so I was looking forward to grabbing a few days of relaxation as I passed through. Call it my Rocky Mountain high.

When I arrived at this rural ranch, I badly needed a pit stop, so I headed straight for the bathroom. When I opened the door, I found the walls papered with *Playboy* centerfolds. Now check this out: I was instantly repulsed by those glossy, full-frontal photos of Miss May, Miss October, and her friends. My reaction shocked me because just a month earlier, I wouldn't have reacted this way.

Obviously, the Holy Spirit had wasted no time in transforming my heart and conscience. But was I totally turned around? No, not by a long shot. Nor did getting married eighteen months later spur a rock-hard decision for purity. While I did stop buying porn magazines, I've told you how I continued snapping up eye candy.

In spite of His work in me, it took me four years before I finally reached a moment of decision for purity. It happened when God showed me Job 31:1, which said that it is possible for a man to make a covenant with his eyes not to look lustfully at another woman. As I meditated on this passage, this revelation rocked my soul: *If Job could do it, so can I!*

I'll never forget the moment—or the exact spot on Merle Hay Road in Des Moines—when everything broke loose. Minutes before, I had failed God with my eyes for the thirty millionth time. A female jogger, her glistening body capturing my eyes as I drove past her, made me all excited. Yet as soon as I passed her, my heart churned in guilt, pain, and sorrow for having given her the "look." Driving down Merle Hay Road, I gripped the wheel and through clenched teeth, I yelled out: "That's it! I'm through with this! I'm making a covenant with my eyes. I don't care what it takes, and I don't care if I die trying. It stops here. It stops here!"

I made a clear decision and decided once and for all to make a change. I can't describe how much that decision meant to me. Floods of frustration from years of failure poured from my heart. I wasn't sure what would happen next, and I wasn't convinced I could trust myself even then, but I did know I'd finally engaged all my mental and spiritual resources on a single target—my impurity.

Your husband must also have a Merle Hay Road moment of decision and make that decision with all of his heart. Now, I know what you're thinking—*God's call to purity is so obvious!* You're wondering what's taking your husband so long? When will he have a Merle Hay Road moment like I did?

It's so hard to answer that question because every man is in a different place in life. What is the same for all of us is that our hardwiring gums up the works, and that goes a long way in explaining our sluggish moves toward repentance. First, from as far back as your husband can remember, his eyes have naturally run to the sensual, appreciating the beauty of the women around him. It's hard for his mind to grasp that something this natural should be eliminated. That's confusing to him as well as agonizing.

Second, his fragile ego can't stand the fears that bubble up from his core as he ponders, *Do real men submit to this kind of discipline with their eyes? What if sex becomes boring? What if purity hinders my ability to perform in the bedroom?*

Third, the damage to his softwiring just piles it on as his wounds keep crying for those medicating highs that keep him bound. In short, it's not that men are being purposely obtuse regarding this decision. In fact, your husband's torture can be as agonizing as yours over his sin. He may want to pull the trigger on a new life in the worst way, but he just can't find that trigger in the midst of the confusing din in his soul. Joey cried:

> This sin is destroying my marriage. My adultery and self-defilement has separated me from my wife and separated me from God. I feel so lonely and lost, asking myself, *Why do I do the things I do? Why won't this monster leave me alone?*
>
> I want to know God and walk with my Lord daily, and know that His blood washes whiter than snow; but I feel dirty, eternally stained. I do not want to hurt my wife anymore than I already have. Besides, I'm beginning to think I don't even belong in God's kingdom. What good am I to God? There are times when I pray, "Oh God, do you still love me when I bleed?"

You see? Joey wants to break free, but he can't quite let go. Why doesn't Joey just make the decision? Why did it take me so long? Sometimes we need a good, stout revelation of truth to pop us free.

FROM BRENDA

How do we deal with such a frustrating wait? We begin in front of the mirror, by recognizing that we're no different. Has your obedience ever lagged? I know I've been slow to see the truth like this. During the fifteenth year of our marriage, God touched Fred in some ways that I'd never experienced spiritually. As a result, for eight months I fought his spiritual leadership in our relationship, even to the point of killing our prayer life together. The funny thing is, I knew that my attitude was wrong, and I desperately wanted to change the whole time, but I just couldn't seem to figure out how to do it—perhaps not unlike our husbands feel in regards to their sin.

While we had many a stormy row over this, the last one broke Fred into tears. He finally gave up, moaning, "Why can't you see your pride in this? If something was never experienced within the branches of your perfect family tree, it can't possibly be of God, can it?"

In that moment, the Holy Spirit finally broke through my walls. Instantly, everything was clear—I'd been horribly wrong. For eight months I'd been torn wildly about our spiritual relationship, assuming I could see yet blindly kicking about helter-skelter in my pride. The moment of decision had finally arrived. I chose to fall into line, and we were at peace.

I am so grateful that Fred patiently waited for that moment of decision—that revelation—to arrive. He believed in me, but more important, he believed that God would find a way to reach my heart and save the day for all of us. Faith was easier because he had gotten much closer to God, which gave him the strength, patience, and discernment to endure this trial and to keep loving and ministering to me in spite of my blindness and his pain. Couldn't you use stronger patience as you wait on your husband's repentance and deal with your simmering pain? Move in closer.

And don't miss this: Fred recognized that this was as much a timing issue as a sin issue with me. Since I was a Christian, he believed that I would eventually see the light. He merely had to endure the storms until that day. This mind-set balanced his emotions until the day I could see.

Your situation is the same. If your husband is a Christian but has not yet fully repented, he is to be pitied—he is either blind with a veiled heart or he is trapped and can't quite see how to get out, just as I couldn't quite see how to get the right attitude in my situation with Fred. But since he's a Christian, you must believe that God is trying to lift that blindness, though the scales are still there now. Yours is a timing issue too. God has authored something in your husband and simply needs time to finish it. He's counting on you to persevere as Christ endured the Cross:

> Let us fix our eyes on Jesus, the author and perfecter of our faith, who *for the joy* set before him *endured* the cross, scorning its shame, and sat down at the right hand of the throne of God. Consider him who endured such opposition from sinful men, so that you will not grow weary and lose heart. (Hebrews 12:2-3)

If you can endure the wait, there is marital joy set before you on the other side. God has such plans for your marriage!

What should you do then—just watch and pray? Not exactly. Praying for revelation is crucial, but your ministry as a helpmate stretches well past your knees. You are to enhance your husband's Christian growth, whatever that may entail. That means keeping the truth before him at all times by speaking the truth and living the truth before him.

Endurance and prayer play a part in any ministry. But remember you are not just your husband's helper, but God's. If you expect to minister in His strength and with His heart in your helper role, getting closer to the Lord yourself is critical. According to Paul, it'll help anyone keep her head emotionally to serve the Lord well in ministry:

> But you, keep your head in all situations, endure hardship…discharge all the duties of your ministry. (2 Timothy 4:5)

And make no mistake, marriage is ministry. This is a time to get tight with God as never before. Dorie found a catalyst there:

I was getting further and further away from God during the years leading up to my husband's disclosure of his sexual sin. I was so caught up in looking at my husband and trying to figure out what was wrong with him—trying to pull him back to where we once were. My focus was entirely upon my husband and my family, but that's because our marriage was in trouble. After finding out about the sin, I realized that this was bigger than me. I needed God's help.

As you get closer to the One who created you, you'll pick up God's higher-ways view of your marriage, and that's vital. God doesn't see marriage as an end in itself but as a restorative process for both of you, and He puts us in relationships like these to allow us to work out our sin so that we can be of more use to Him.

FROM FRED

Remember Jasen's lower-ways view of our Saturday-night chores? He could only see fairness from his perspective, but as his father, I had higher ways. I was also concerned with what was best for him and for the family.

As you get closer to your Father, you will see things from His perspective, and you'll find that God is asking you a favor, which is to pick up the iron and to apply the dressings to your husband's life. God wants restoration because that's what's best and fair for your family.

Jesus came to Earth to heal the broken, to have mercy on the ones who couldn't stand on their own, the ones who would never deserve it:

> [The Pharisees] asked his disciples, "Why does your teacher eat with tax collectors and 'sinners'?"
>
> On hearing this, Jesus said, "It is not the healthy who need a doctor, but the sick. But go and learn what this means: 'I desire mercy, not sacrifice.' For I have not come to call the righteous, but sinners." (Matthew 9:11-13)

Christ always chose mercy when it came to sin, and He's asking you to move closer to Him so that you might choose mercy too. Your husband has probably been deeply wounded and warped by sin, like many husbands are. Jake wrote us this:

I've been a slave to sexual sin since the age of eleven when my father first introduced me to pornography. He had me lie in bed with him and his magazines while he taught me to masturbate, and this began five years of sexual abuse. His actions paved the road for a lifelong struggle with compulsive masturbation, casual sex, and drug addiction.

Needless to say, my marriage has always had it difficulties, and we have both withdrawn from each other and the intimacy we dreamed of. My wife and I are now separated, but we are committed to reconciliation, though the only thing we've agreed on so far is that we don't want to return to the marriage we had.

Every Man's Battle has helped me understand the events in my life and my marriage in a new way. Because of my sexual abuse as a child, I grew up to be a very self-reliant man with a very guarded heart and a selfish, self-protective spirit. I have never trusted God completely and have withheld some of my heart from Him. My lack of true relationship with my wife has been a reflection of my lack of true relationship with Christ.

At the first sign of trouble or rejection, I immediately withdraw to a place within myself that is only safe in its familiarity. In that place, I justify masturbation and porn and fantasy as a release from the perceived rebuffs from my wife and as a defiant act of rebellion against God. During our separation, I binged sexually to the point of crying out to God for help, and He answered through your book.

Do you sense your ministry opportunities? Aligning ourselves with Jesus means being about our Father's business as Jesus was. And what is that business? Simple: healing the broken—especially those who don't deserve it.

FROM BRENDA

Your husband has veered off the track and crashed hard, so you're obviously in business. You're the last line of defense, and God's counting on you to defend His name and His boundaries before your husband. The Lord wants him walking again in His image.

After months of struggling with her emotions, Kim caught God's perspective and began to see her struggling marriage as a ministry. "I had to realize that my husband, Carl, made his own choices when it came to being sinful or not, and I didn't have full control of that," she said. "My job was to trust God, be the person God wanted me to be, and help my husband."

As Kim trusted God, she became less critical about her husband's choices, and this one step has produced more fruit in their marriage than anything else she could have done. "As I've gotten my angry eyes off my husband's issues, I've come to realize that I cannot judge his sin of lust as somehow worse than my own sins."

God expects you to give this situation to Him, and He deserves that from you as your Father. And if you are asking your husband to move closer to God, shouldn't he be able to expect that you'll move closer to God as well? I think so.

FROM FRED

This discussion brings to mind something Brenda once told me about submission. "Submission never came naturally to me," she said. "It was even harder to submit when my respect for Fred's spirituality was at its all-time low. During our days of severe fighting and in-law problems, I would ask myself, *Why should I submit to someone who is worse off spiritually than I am?* But I knew I should submit for the sake of the Lord. I knew His ways were for the best."

Your complete trust in God can be the very thing that jars your husband to his senses, as Debbie found out recently:

> After my husband's affair, God really ministered to me. He had me study
> the life of David and encouraged me to believe that although my husband
> struggled with sexual sins, he could still be a man after God's heart.

Maybe that is why the second incident a few years later rocked me as much as it did. I felt like I had *already* paid the ultimate price to save our marriage, and yet here we go again. I cannot say that mercy rose up in me this time! Although it may have sounded like a harsh threat when I told my husband I was leaving, my fearless confidence in God and in His ability to take care of me shook my husband to his toes.

For the first time, I think Jay realized that marriage was something fragile, and he could lose everything he loved by participating in sexual trysts and downloading a bunch of stupid pictures. This time he found someone who could counsel him on this struggle—a godly accountability partner.

There was something different and lasting now. I guess you could say he was ready to grow up, take the hard steps, and make the hard choices to open his life up to others and to humble himself before God. Oddly enough, our sex life quickly became better than ever. For the first time in a long time, I felt like he really knew I was there in bed with him. Maybe there was more of a reason to invest in my pleasure since the other wells had run dry, but who really cares? All I knew is that I liked his efforts.

Debbie's happy ending is encouraging, isn't it? Once you've moved in close and have a kind, humble spirit before God, He can deliver the spiritual tools you'll need to discharge the duties of your ministry well. After all, if you plan to be iron sharpening iron in defending God's truth in your husband's life and character, your husband will need you to have God's tender heart as you grind and sharpen—as well as discernment.

Read what happened to Naomi when she felt her intuition telling her to do some checking up on her husband. She learned to her dismay that he hadn't quit leering at Internet porn like he had promised:

I calmly told him that I knew about his porn usage and that he'd never quit at all. His first reaction was anger that I'd checked up on him, and he railed to the heavens that I didn't trust him.

I firmly pointed out that for the past ten months I had tried to trust him, but in doing so, I'd been played for a fool. I informed him that I wouldn't take this in our marriage anymore, especially if we kept ending up in this situation. His reply was that I'd have to answer to God if I broke our marriage vows and filed for divorce.

Hearing him say that hurt me more than you can imagine—here he was trying to make me out as the bad guy when it was *his* sin breaking those vows. But I had the discernment to know that behind that finger-pointing was a hurting guy screaming, "No, I love you! Please don't leave me!"

You'll need God's discernment to see through your husband's bluster as he tries to wriggle out of the light. That bluster can cause many wives to believe their husbands' excuses, which is a form of denial.

As you may know, there can be an overwhelming urge to sweep everything under your heart's rug and to bury the emotion of it all. Like the heart-wrenching scene from *Gone with the Wind*, you naively trust that everything will work out somehow, passionately muttering like Scarlett O'Hara, "I can't think about this today… I'll go crazy if I do. I'll think about it tomorrow."

God already has one naive, blind, broken child on the scene in the form of your husband, and He can't afford to have two. He's asking you to move closer to Him so He might make your sight completely whole. He needs one trustworthy child on hand to work with Him in this, and He wants to make you strong.

As your husband's helpmate, it's best for you and him if you inform him in a low-key manner that you'll be actively seeking out God and asking the Lord for discernment in holding him accountable.

While this statement may give him pause, tell him that he should be encouraged because you will have his back and will follow through on whatever the Lord says you need to do to help him. This was Molly's approach in her relationship:

My husband, Randy, who is a pastor, recently revealed his unfaithfulness to me. He said that he had been having affairs throughout our seven-year marriage. I praise God that I had just completed a great Bible study on breaking free from strong generational bonds, because I was walking closer to Him than I had ever experienced before, and let me tell you, I needed to walk close to my Lord.

When my husband confessed, I felt I had been slit open with someone's fingernail. I was so distraught that I gathered up the kids and left the house immediately, saying it was only temporary but knowing that my true motive was to never return. I quickly found that I had the wrong motive. Because I'd been seeking God with all my heart and our communication lines were clear, I knew beyond a shadow of a doubt that God was asking me to stay with my husband—with no conditions, if you can believe that.

I stayed, but only out of pure obedience. I can honestly say that I didn't stay for our children, for financial support, or for fear of being alone. There were many times over the next three years when I was tempted to bolt, but obedience stopped me each time.

I was feeling pretty proud of myself, but I shouldn't have been. As I stayed close to God over the next few months, He kindly revealed that while I hadn't left my husband *physically,* I had divorced myself emotionally, mentally, physically, and spiritually from Randy. I had been begging God constantly to release me from this marriage, rather than completely giving my heart to restoration.

After Molly repented, she told the Lord that she would obey Him by moving in closer to Randy. This is what happened when she did:

Seeking godly counsel and praying like never before, I finally committed my heart 100 percent to restoration, preferring to go through the pain of marital healing rather than the pain of walking away. Believe me, this was not the popular decision with my extended family.

But God had asked me to choose mercy and to stay one more time. You might ask, *Where does mercy start and stop in this situation?* Well, how can I deny showing mercy to Randy when I have received so much from Christ? Mercy will *never* cease flowing from me. Now, if he chooses to continue in this enslavement of sin, separation or divorce may yet come, but I will follow God faithfully and help Randy until then.

I think we'll make it, though. A breakthrough came when Randy read *Every Man's Battle,* and he called me and told me specifically what he had learned. Needless to say, some of those things were not easy to hear. But that information, coupled with visible changes in his lifestyle, speech, habits, spiritual hunger, and humility, have encouraged me to stay married.

At some point I suspect that God's next lesson for Molly will be to teach her to trust Randy again, which won't be easy and won't happen overnight. But in the meantime, she will have to continue to discharge her duties well as helper, and we'll take a look at what these duties look like in our next chapter.

SUGGESTED READING

The Power of a Praying Wife by Stormie Omartian: *to help you to get closer to God through prayer*

The Wounded Heart: Hope for Adult Victims of Childhood Sexual Abuse by Dan B. Allender: *to help you and your husband heal childhood wounds*

Every Woman's Battle by Shannon Ethridge: *to make sure your own sexual purity is up to God's standards*

moving even closer

FROM FRED

Take a moment to read Jennifer's e-mail:

> When I met my husband-to-be, I found magazines and videos lying around
> his apartment on occasion, but once we got married, I told him that I did
> not want those kind of things in our house. Little changed until about
> eighteen months ago when I found a video that he made of himself mas-
> turbating.
>
> I confronted him in tears, and while he said he would take care of the
> situation, I bought *Every Man's Battle* as a precaution. Your book was a real
> eyeopener for me, and I have been taking care of my husband sexually
> much more than I did before. Still, he has refused to read the book himself,
> claiming he needs no help.
>
> So here we are today. We just bought our first computer, so we have a
> new battlefront. When I confronted him about cyberporn, he got mad and
> sneered that I obviously have personal problems to deal with. I pray every
> day that God will open his eyes, and I love him so much that I am willing
> to do anything for him, but I do not know what to do anymore. He denies
> that he has done anything wrong and believes that he does not have a prob-
> lem. What can I do that won't push him away?

We know that you love your husband, but love sometimes requires pushing
him a little toward normal. If his repentance is lagging, you must speak the truth,
even though the truth can be disruptive.

Your husband made promises to you the day you were married, and you have every right to speak up when he doesn't keep them. Sure, he may not recognize your rights and may try to wriggle out by sniffing, "You're not so perfect yourself! Who are you to judge me?"

Well, you are his sister in Christ. By God's reckoning, that gives you the right to judge his actions, and you needn't be perfect to do so:

> It isn't my responsibility to judge outsiders, but it certainly is your job to
> judge those inside the church who are sinning in these ways. God will judge
> those on the outside; but as the Scriptures say, "You must remove the evil
> person from among you." (1 Corinthians 5:12-13, NLT)

If your husband is a Christian, he had better be open to inspection, because you are called to speak the truth as his Christian sister.

FROM BRENDA

So what do you say to him? Fred and I have said all along that it's vital for wives to understand porn from the male perspective, but it's also vital for men to understand porn from the female perspective: while porn may rest in its own mental silo and have little effect on a husband's love for his wife, that same porn is devastating to his wife's emotions because of her differing hardwiring—she has no silo to hide it in.

This means that if you're willing to rebuild your marriage after your husband has destroyed the most precious, intimate area of your being, then he owes you big time—and he likely has no idea what a precious gift you've offered. While the Christian life is about forgiveness and turning the other cheek, it is also about commitment and keeping promises. Calling oneself a Christian while dancing openly with sexual immorality is reprehensible and degrading, and it also gives a false testimony of Christ to the world.

Furthermore, there are inescapable laws of life, like reaping what you sow. Perhaps your husband needs to be reminded of this principle. When Fred heard me say that I'd leave him in a heartbeat if his violent behavior didn't change, that clarified for him what normal means to me and to God, and it encouraged him to rise up to God's standard quickly.

Women often ask, *But after all this, I'm not even sure I know what normal looks like anymore!* Let me try to paint a picture of normal as best I can.

I feel incredible security knowing that I'm married to a man who keeps his eyes to himself. Even after four babies and twenty-four years of aging together, I live unthreatened by any women around me. Fred loves me for me and is very satisfied with who I am and what I've become.

When my husband prays, I'm confident that nothing is hindering his connection with God. If I knew of dark, hidden areas, I'd have no faith that his prayers would even rise to the ceiling, but I've seen how a pure man's prayer packs a spiritual punch.

My confidence in Fred's spiritual protection is unbounded. I never wonder if there are open cracks in our spiritual defenses where the Enemy can slip into our lives. Christianity is not a game to Fred, and image means nothing. He'd rather *be* a Christian than seem like one.

Fred has every right to make the decisions for our family because it's God's plan, but even if it weren't, he's earned that right through his actions. He's proven in battle that his commitment to the Lord and his love for his family are the highest priorities in his life, and we simply rest in his strength.

This normal, godly pattern leaves everyone flourishing, and this wouldn't be possible if blatant sin were clogging things up. I know who Fred is, and in the secret places of life, I know where he will not go.

Let's freeze that frame for a moment. What I'm describing should be normal family life, and every wife deserves a shot at normalcy. I sure didn't start at normal in my marriage, and heaven knows that most of us don't. But with our help and Christ's grace, our marriages can get there. It won't happen over a long weekend, but this is what you deserve, this is what God has promised you, and in the long run, this is what God calls your husband to deliver.

What is the foundation of this road back to normalcy? Take another look at the normal picture of marriage. Implicit trust permeates every corner. Fred's consistent, faithful actions stir confidence within me that he conducts himself in a godly manner when it comes to sexual purity. And it's right there, faintly visible among the weaving threads of this tapestry, where this whole picture turns. Peer closely once more, and you'll catch a glimpse of the foundation: if your husband's ever going to be trustworthy to you, he must first be trustworthy to God.

Your husband hasn't been conducting himself in the same manner. Like Adam, he is hiding behind the bushes after leaving a bite impression on porn's fruit. Since God is long-suffering and didn't hit him immediately with a lightning bolt, all your husband has ever had to do is convince everyone around him that he hasn't been crouching in the bushes at all but standing upright in the image of God along with everyone else. But God knows the truth, and now so do you.

As his helper, you can hasten the arrival of your husband's turnaround by burning these bushes to the ground. Expose that false image for what it is. It isn't enough to seem Christian in marriage—you have to be Christian, to live His Word. Only then can God trust him, and only then can you trust him again.

In short, it can backfire to focus primarily upon your husband's trustworthiness to you, per se. It is not uncommon for a wife to focus on her husband's behavior, looking earnestly for anything from him that demonstrates that she should trust him again. She watches every move intently, and more often than not, the husband fails under that pressure.

It's far wiser to work on your husband's trustworthiness *to God* by defending God's boundaries in your marriage and exposing your husband's well-crafted image to the light. Not only does that take the pressure off of everyone, but it is also the proper target. Your job is to help him see and open his heart and ears to God.

Men are slower at understanding relationships, and we can't forget that our husbands have blind spots that result from their hardwiring. Your goal is to speed up his learning curve by grinding with the iron and pointing out clearly what God means by being trustworthy.

Confront him. Be excruciatingly honest about your pain. Remove the wiggle room with the precision of a surgeon, talking straight about how he is failing you and how you are losing respect for him.

At the same time, don't retaliate, don't manipulate, and don't play games.

You're not here to hurt him but to help him. You're not fighting for your way but to have things God's way.

Never withdraw from him verbally—the silent treatment must never happen in your home, because that's just another form of anger out of control. Your silence can inflict more cruel damage on a relationship than an open storm.

When Fred spoke of my style with the dressings and the iron in chapter 17, perhaps you wondered, *Given how I'm feeling, how can I do all this like Brenda did without retaliation and manipulation? Sometimes I just want to punch him!*

You do it by defending God's boundaries and not your own. Be transparent, persistent, and resolute. Say something like this: "Honey, this is how we're called to act, and we really have no choice. God won't let us live any other way, and I can't live any other way." Don't try to control him, because you can't. Just stand normally and in Christ.

You aren't there to attack the man—you are there to boost the man. It's not your ministry to bring him back to you sexually. It's your ministry to bring him back to God spiritually. It may be hard to keep this as your focus, but it's the right focus.

This is ultimately between your husband and the King. You needn't jump him every time he blows it. Trust God. When you aren't speaking, you can be certain that God is.

FROM FRED

Let's take a look at a few of God's boundaries you might defend.

Insist that your husband stop drawing his own lines for sin. He needs to accept God's definitions of sin, not those of the guys he plays pickup basketball with during lunchtime on Tuesdays and Thursdays. Your husband must accept God's terms, or else He can't trust your husband, just like Justine wrote:

> One night during our engagement, Caleb showed me a calendar he'd gotten from a tool dealer. Since he was an auto mechanic, I'm sure he was excited about the cars, but all I could see were the blatantly sexual, scantily clad women in serpentine poses suggestively draped all over the cars.

I objected to the calendar and asked him to throw it out, but he huffed, "They're not pornographic… These women aren't even nude!"

We argued some more, but a little piece of me died when he icily chided, "You are so insecure and immature!" Patronizingly, he then added, "I chose *you*, not some model. Can't you even see that?"

Clearly, I'd lost the argument. But a small voice inside me inquired persistently, *Isn't he really choosing those models over you by not honoring your request?* I've heard that voice grow louder throughout the years.

Those pictures are pornographic, and this voice should get louder, because it's telling the truth. You mustn't muzzle the Spirit's voice in your helper role, because if your husband is stuck in sexual sin, his eardrums have been cauterized to the whispers of the Holy Spirit, and his conscience has been seared. You must speak for God and call sin "sin" so your husband can hear and learn what it is.

Insist on the truth. Perhaps your husband can't deliver on sexual purity by the weekend, but he *can* be man enough to start telling the truth today. Normal Christian men tell the truth, and if he expects God to trust him, his lying has got to go. Call him out every time you know he's lying to you.

Obviously, lies undermine relationships, as this e-mail from Mary Beth reminds us:

I cannot trust my husband, but I *am* trying to trust God with my husband. He has been able to hide everything so well that I have no idea when he is lying or telling the truth, and this has definitely put a distance between us.

I found out about his affair a year ago in June, and we slopped through that muck for almost a year. This past June, I asked him some pointed questions, and I told him that I wanted to put it all behind us. I forgave him, but I told him I would never go through this again. He seemed very happy I'd forgiven him and quite humble.

Yet only six weeks later, I found out that he was still involved with that woman—and had been all along. He had looked me in the eyes and lied to my face every time I had questioned him. That whole past year I had seen him run the gamut of emotions…the anger at himself for having the affair, the hurt, and the sorrow. He snookered me good. He had played the loving, accountable-husband act to a T, but he had been lying through his teeth the entire time.

Your husband must stop lying immediately. You need open communication regarding his sin, and he must truthfully answer any question you might pop his way.

Insist he stop posing as a strong Christian man. Remember, your husband has been hiding behind a good Christian image, but that must change. Since image is everything these days, "Showtime Christianity" is pandemic. Brody's part of the show went like this, according to his wife:

> After arguing about his porn again, I left the room and went to God in prayer, sobbing. I really didn't see how Brody's pride, shame, or defensiveness would budge, but I asked God to jar them anyway. I proposed to Brody that we go see the youth pastor at our church, since he is also a licensed marriage and family therapist.
>
> If Brody refused to go, I'd know he'd rather save his pride and be comfortable than work things out with me. Brody finally agreed to go, but protesting loudly, "That pastor's never going to look at me the same way again."

Who cares if the youth pastor won't look at you the same way, buddy? Get real! Your wife already can't look at you the same way, and God's eyebrows are arched askew too. Being Christian should have total priority over looking Christian any day of the week, and if God is to ever trust your husband, you must encourage your husband in that direction.

Insist that he quit posing at church. If he's a deacon or elder, he ought to step down until he's free of sexual sin. If he's a lay worship leader, he ought to step down. If he's on a mission board, he ought to step down. His image may mean something in the visible realm, but only substance counts in the spiritual realm.

If he won't do it, consult the pastor. Your husband needs to face the truth that he isn't who he says he is. Those bushes must burn, and this charade must end.

FROM BRENDA

Full repentance can take time, and I ought to know, since I spoke to Fred about his temper for more than two years before he finally had a revelation experience. Once he did, things healed quickly, but until then, I had to move closer to God, endure, grind away, and pray, as much for my sake as for Fred's.

But what if there is *still* no sign of his turning after you do all those things? When your marital ship has stopped dead in the water and your voyage seems over for good, it's tough to get moving in the right direction again without a friendly supporting wind in your sails. But you must be careful that this support doesn't blow in from the wrong direction, which can easily happen when you're living in vulnerable times.

Tina recently reminisced about the stormiest days of her marriage: "Once I had realized that it might take years for Rick to have a turnaround, I resigned myself to finding my friendship needs met outside of marriage. Fortunately, I was working at a very close-knit company, and there was a fairly large group of us who went jogging most afternoons after work. I loved this group, and in many ways we were like family. When you practically live with your coworkers for eight years it can get that way, but that became my trap."

Tina had good relationships with all of the joggers, both gals and guys. The single guys felt safe with her because she was married, and they'd often ask her advice about certain young women they were interested in. Tina, emotionally needy, was flattered and only too happy to have an audience hear what she thought. They chattered endlessly as they ran and afterward when they cooled down with Cokes.

"I began to find more fulfillment in those conversations than I did in any other aspect of my life—more than I found in Jesus, in prayer, and especially in my marriage," Tina confessed. "The friendships seemed quite unguarded and innocent at the time, but they turned out to be very, very dangerous. I realized way too late that I felt an attraction to one of my jogging partners, a male, and shortly there-after, I found out several of the guys were struggling with their feelings for me. By the grace of God, there was no physical unfaithfulness among any of us, but the emotional entanglements were very painful to sever on all sides."

Tina learned what so many have learned through the years: women must hold themselves emotionally separate from any man other than their husbands, and women should be careful discussing their dreams and desires with men (unless they are in a professional counseling situation).

"Oddly enough," Tina told me, "I even had to place romance novels into the same danger zone. They provided an emotional high that took away from my focus on Rick. Those novels made it easy for me to compare my warts-and-all husband against those too-good-to-be-true fictional characters. Reading those romance novels impacted my ability to be content in my marriage, marginal as it was at the time. Just like fairy tales, the all-too-perfect characters in the romance novels set the expectations for the relationship way too high."

Having offered these warnings, we definitely urge you to be purposeful about surrounding yourself with godly sisters who are navigating the same waters, because confiding in them can make all the difference in the world. You don't want to blab your husband's problems all over town, but being able to vent and pray with someone who cares for you can do wonders for your sanity.

Consider what Megan had to go through after the police dropped by her house and announced, "Ma'am, we don't know how to say this, but we must insist that your husband stop exposing himself to the girls in the drive-thru lines at McDonald's and Wendy's."

Then Megan discovered that her husband, Ryan, had been having an affair with a woman at church—but that's not all. Ryan lost his job when he was caught viewing porn at work, which really sent their marriage into a tailspin. Megan was flat-out crazy with fury and dead set on divorcing her husband.

"I had decided that I would leave Ryan, although I didn't want to rush any decisions. I just wanted to wait for God's timing," she said.

While she waited, Megan made a very smart move. She described everything to her best friend, Holly, who was a great listener and said Megan could call any time, day or night, and use her as a sounding board.

"I cannot put enough value on having a friend like her in my situation," Megan said. "The grace she gave me when I would lose my temper, her persistent attention to my moods, her ability to leave me alone when I didn't want anyone around, and that look she would give me at church that let me know she was watching out for me when others were talking behind my back.

"During those days, I stayed busy by helping Holly with her flower business after the kids went to school each day. We'd deliver flowers, run around the lake, and even play some tennis. During these days God ministered to me through our talks together."

Megan says that Holly helped her see that Ryan was repenting for what he had done. You see, Ryan had finally reached rock bottom and realized that he needed to make massive changes in his life or lose Megan. I thought back on how Fred never quite got the message about himself until I told him that my feelings for him were dead and that I was about to leave. How tragic it would have been for Megan to have endured Ryan's lagging heart all those years, only to be too enraged to see or care when he finally reached that point of repentance. Holly kept that from happening.

"You know, I was *very* angry, and I had little tolerance for any opinion that was different from mine. I often just walked around in my jacket and sunglasses with my headphones on, full blast. I wanted to be invisible, and I tried to retreat into myself," Megan said.

"But Holly wouldn't let me stay there. She was my friend, my staunchest ally, and more often than not, the voice on the phone that forced me out of bed to try to make it through one more day.

"Then Holly started telling me, 'Megan, he's different. He's really different.' Naturally, I was irritated and very much the skeptic. You see, during his addiction Ryan's personality was that of a weak man—a boy, really. I respected him less and less with each passing day, and he just sickened me. I was *never* going to stay with *that* Ryan, and now that I had my chance to get out, I wasn't going to let it slip away. So I told him I wanted—and needed—a separation, knowing full well a divorce would follow closely on its heels.

"But Holly was persistent that we get back together. Sometimes I would argue vehemently, but she didn't waver on her opinion as time went by. I refused to admit it was possible that Ryan had repented, but inside I grudgingly decided to look for changes in Ryan from a distance."

About this time, Holly's perseverance broke Megan down further. "I wanted to be more like Holly, to be that woman that God wanted me to be. I knew that my anger had taken me over. For weeks, I had no desire to even speak to Ryan."

Relentlessly, Holly reasoned with her, "You're not being fair to God or your kids! If you don't talk to Ryan, you won't be able to see the changes God is making in him." Megan knew she was right and finally agreed to talk to him.

"And you know what? I *did* notice some things about Ryan. He seemed more confident, and he wasn't that 'boy' I had come to despise—he was even being quite open with people that the separation was all his fault."

He started writing love letters too. Amazing ones. To be honest, Megan was skeptical about his sincerity and read most of them to Holly to see if they were in line with what she was seeing in him. She confirmed that they were totally consistent with the new Ryan. "To make a long story short, when I read those letters, I learned that I actually did still love Ryan, which I thought had been completely gutted from me. Without Holly's encouragement, I would have ended up in divorce court."

FROM FRED

The secret weapon in helping your husband come around is something close to my heart—prayer. Brenda and I met Tammy, whose husband, Mick, was sexually abused repeatedly as a young boy by his brother and was raped at age twelve by his school's Christian choir director, laying deep roots for the sexual addiction to come. For years he'd had affair after affair, and Mick was even prosecuted and imprisoned for statutory rape in relation to a teenager in his neighborhood. We stayed in touch with Tammy off and on through the years, and we've always wondered how she managed to stay with Mick—her commitment to him was breathtaking. Her secret? Gut-wrenching, nuclear-tipped prayer with a scriptural guidance system.

"It would be easy to believe that I'll never have what God intended for marriage after all this time, but I somehow still believe that I'll have it," she told us. "I believe that we will have the most godly, romantic, and awesome marriage that one can possibly have someday. It may take countless hours of prayer to see it come to pass, and I realize that it won't come without faith, but God can change any wrong and make it right."

Tammy says that at the beginning her prayers consisted of thanking Jesus for the man of God that her husband would someday be, even during the midst of her worst suffering.

> Then I began to pray Scripture over him, sometimes for hours. I prayed that God would create a pure heart in him, and that he would choose to set no vile things before his eyes. I asked God to give him the mind of Christ so that he would not be conformed to the world but rather be transformed by the renewing of his mind. I prayed that God would bind our marriage with cords that could never be severed, and that what God has joined together, no man or woman could tear asunder. I asked that God would renew a right spirit in Mick, and that he would know the good and perfect will of the Father.
>
> I also prayed for myself. I asked God to help me respect the man I had zero respect for, and I asked the Lord to help me trust a man unworthy of trust. Amazingly, God began to do both. If Christ can forgive Mick and still love him, how could I refuse to do the same? This brings freedom to me, as well as to Mick.
>
> Many ask me why I've pressed in so hard in prayer, but it was simple to me. Even in my pain and suffering—even when I was crying, *Why me Lord? It isn't fair to treat me like this when I've obeyed You and trusted You all my life*—I knew that Mick loved God somewhere deep inside, somewhere beneath all those wounds. I knew that he wanted to live for Him and bring our children up in a strong Christian home. Tragically, he just kept slipping into sin, but I've seen his tears and I've seen his sorrow and I never stopped believing that he has a heart for God."

That sure sounded familiar. I thought back to when Brenda desperately wanted to accept the spiritual changes God had been making in me, but for eight months she struggled to find a way to do it. I remembered how grateful she was that I never stopped believing in her underlying commitment to God during those months. Tammy has faithfully believed in Mick's heart for *years*—imagine how grateful Mick must be as he wrestles with the demons of his sexually abused past!

Some have accused Tammy of being a foolish Pollyanna who simply couldn't face the truth about Mick. Others say her blind, unreasonable faith was just one more bank of sand she stuck her head into, and she had never faced her pain or fear. But she faced them all right.

I'm not saying there weren't times that I just felt I *had* to leave, like the time I saw the police handcuff Mick and take him to jail for sexual assault. I was pregnant at the time [and already had] three small children. What do I do? Where do I go? I cried so much that I was afraid I would lose the baby.

The hardest part was that even when he came home from jail, he only thought of *his* feelings and *his* pain. He would lie down in a fetal position and cry, wanting to take his life. Many times I wished that he would. I remember thinking that death would be a breeze compared to all this.

He eventually lost his job, and then we lost the company we began after that. He would stay up late just listening to worship music and crying out to God, and I believe that is what kept him alive. We often wondered, *Will we ever be happy again? Will we ever laugh again?*

At times, death seemed to be a comforting thought to me, too—a way of escape from the shame of what my husband had done to me and to others. When those thoughts came, I would quickly rebuke the Enemy's lies and God would sustain me each day. He was also there during sleepless nights when I thought I couldn't endure the pain, groaning, *God, what am I going to do? How can I go on?* I became certain that none of my tears fell unnoticed, so in my heart, I simply embraced the day when all this would be only a memory. Thank God, we're almost there.

Tammy managed to love in the midst of sexual sin, business ruin, and many broken dreams because she chose to believe that God would bless her home in spite of Mick's sin and disobedience. She knew she had a biblical right to divorce him, but her ultimate dream was that one day they would together testify to God's power to restore, renew, and rebuild broken marriages.

There is great freedom in casting your cares and your worries at the Lord's feet. He'll give you supernatural peace, joy, and strength. Brenda and I urge you to continue to endure and persevere because great is His faithfulness, mercy, and grace.

SUGGESTED READING

Boundaries by John Townsend and Henry Cloud: *to help you set and protect rightful boundaries in your relationships*

Every Heart Restored Workbook

Into Abba's Arms by Sandra Wilson: *to help you deal with your current, natural feelings of abandonment and to guide you into deeper intimacy with God*

With Christ in the School of Prayer by Andrew Murray: *to help you enter a deeper intimacy of prayer with God*

the long and winding road

Women are relationally driven, and they need to share their stories with each other for the emotional support they bring, but they also need the wise instruction from those who've traveled these seas before them.

Toward that end, we've included snippets from other women throughout this book in hopes of providing a support team for you. In that same spirit, we're including this important story from Cindy, a godly woman dealing with a husband who couldn't say no to Internet porn. Our sincere hope is that her words will be an encouragement to you as you wait for your husband's heart to turn fully to the Lord.

CINDY'S TALE

Five years ago I was a junior in college having to write heavy-duty papers, so my husband, Will, and I purchased a top-of-the-line computer with our tax refund and subscribed to the Internet for both research and entertainment purposes. I was gone frequently at night for study groups, and on other nights I'd go to bed early in hopes of acing some big test in the morning.

I suspected nothing until various porn sites began spamming our e-mail. When I checked our Web browser's history, I was devastated to find that Will had been surfing for flesh whenever I was away or asleep. I was shocked because I thought he was different from other guys. After all, he was a Christian.

He wants them instead of me! I thought. The extra sixty pounds from taking birth-control pills hung heavy on me as I surveyed the slim, perfect women with their perky breasts sprawled across the screen. I was crushed to the core.

I discovered I was pregnant soon thereafter, right before our second anniversary.

We were *so* excited about the baby, and Will was especially fond of my pregnant figure. I teased him about him being a caveman, and the action in our bedroom went through the roof. I was quite accommodating, as my pregnancy had suddenly turned me into quite a seductress. But alas, all good things must come to an end.

Near the end of that pregnancy, I experienced my most scarring incident with pornography. Will worked just a few blocks from our apartment, so he joined me for lunch at home nearly every day. Since we had a membership at a gym across the street, I was taking a late-morning aqua-aerobics class to burn up some calories.

One day my class ran late, and I scrambled home to see Will's car already in the lot. Excited to see him, I hurried up the stairs but found the door locked. Puzzled, I got out my keys and let myself in. Will was in the bathroom, and the computer was on in the living room. I immediately knew what the scoop was, but I didn't want to. As Will came out of the bathroom, I noticed his face was rather flushed. I asked innocently, "Honey, did you know the door was locked? I thought that was really strange since you knew I'd be home any minute."

"It was locked?" he responded just as innocently. "Maybe I moved my key around too far and relocked it by accident when I shut the door."

I knew he was lying because you don't have to use a key to lock the front door, but I didn't want to fight it. I have this thing about being called an overemotional woman who argues without solid facts to back me up. So instead, we ate our lunch quietly.

After he left, I checked the computer and noticed he'd gone to several discreetly named sites, probably so if I checked up on him I wouldn't know they were porn by their Web addresses. When I clicked on one of them, I saw naked and flat-tummied young women, mocking my seven-month pregnant frame. Will had told me that my pregnancy turned him on, but now I wondered if that, too, was a lie like the one he'd just told. Maybe he'd found a sneakier way to get his kicks, like having sex with me while all his airbrushed beauties danced through his mind. That thought alone just killed me.

I just sat there, crumbling into emotional and spiritual rubble. I'd just been wasted by my Christian husband, the man I looked to for spiritual protection and guidance, the love of my life who'd vowed to forsake all others for me. He lied.

How was I ever to believe anything he told me again when he could lie to me so boldly and easily?

I eventually called him at work, now a sobbing mess. Add the crazy-making hormones of pregnancy to this betrayal, and you can only imagine how pitiful I was at that moment. What a dreadful conversation!

"Mary, I knew that you knew at lunch," he confessed.

"So why did you stand there and lie to me then?" I blubbered.

"Because I didn't want to hurt you."

"You thought that my knowing that you stood right there and lied to me wouldn't hurt me?" I shrieked.

"I didn't know… I didn't think," he stammered weakly.

For an instant I hated him. I hated him for making me emotional Jell-O, and I was angry at him for taking my trust away. But somehow, bouncing between hate and anger and sorrow and desperation, I found I still had love for him. Love for the part of him that was my best friend, the part of him that made me feel more special than anyone on Earth, the cute little crinkle his eyes made when he smiled—the list went on and on.

I'd begun to calm down when the baby kicked, which launched me into hysterics again. *What if he doesn't love me anymore? What if he really wants them over me? How will the baby and I ever get by?*

Satan's demons of rejection, self-loathing, and insecurity—my old bullies—raced in and made themselves comfortable: *Will doesn't really love you—no one ever will, you know! You're too fat anyway… Did you really think that you were beautiful to him?*

God tried in vain to reach me: *Will does love you, My daughter! I love you even more, and I'll never fail you. You're made in My image, and there is nothing ugly about you. Satan sends lies, but remember, I sent you the Truth!*

I still felt defeated, dejected, and hopeless, and suicidal thoughts showed up at my mind's door: *Will wouldn't miss you, you know. He'd probably even be happier. Either way, this would be a great way to teach him a good lesson.*

Those hours until Will got home were the most hopeless, painful, and terrifying moments I'd endured in my life. I cried out to God, *Am I not worthy of love? Why do you let Satan torment me like this? It's not fair!*

But when Will got home, things didn't get much better. He was defensive and angry at my snooping around. "Those women aren't real!" he responded. "What's the big deal?"

I told him I couldn't do this anymore—that he had to choose between porn or me. He chose me, or so he said. I began to pray daily for Will to stand up to his temptations and find me enough for him. The one thing I could never pray for, however, was for my healing. Meanwhile, I could tell that Will was trying over the next few weeks, and it was clear that we were both doing what we could to get back on track.

Just six weeks later our daughter, Britney, was born. All the women's magazines promised that Will would be begging me for sex well before the doctor approved it, but once the doctor gave the all-clear sign, weeks passed with nothing between us, despite my efforts to stir the pot in the bedroom.

I'd also read that couples sometimes grow apart sexually after childbirth, and I was trying to be as proactive as possible. When he finally caved to my pressures, all he offered was obligatory sex, the kind with no foreplay, no tender words—nothing but him lying naked on his back while I got on top and did my business. He obliged me this way once a month, and needless to say, I became very insecure, hoping against hope that this was just some rough transition into parenthood and not another trip down our pornographic trail of tears.

Soon it was the day after Christmas, and all of the relatives had finally left. While I loved playing hostess, I was exhausted, so I went to bed early that night without Will. I had extremely disturbing dreams about him and his pornography that night, and the next morning I was still reeling from those nightmares.

As soon as I could, I went online to a message board and asked how I might check out the sites visited on the computer if the history didn't show anything. Some good Samaritan out there gave me the technical info I needed, and before long, there it was—a list of every site he or I had visited on the Internet since the day we bought the cursed computer. And sure enough, the previous night he'd indulged in some serious porn while my nightmares raged. Then I looked back to that week in September when Britney and I were visiting grandma for a week. Sure enough—straight, hard-core porn, for hours every night.

I felt assaulted, violated, betrayed, and kicked down. But I'd been growing closer to the Lord and praying my heart out, so I felt I wasn't totally alone. This time I waited to confront him until he got home.

We had a terrible row, with my side of the conversation going like this: "You've broken our covenant of marriage, but I am staying, at least this time. I can't say that I will go ahead and divorce you over this, but I can't say that I won't either. We've dealt with this many times, and every time you say you're sorry, but then you find trickier ways to cover your tracks.

"In the meantime, I have been driving myself crazy trying to prove my worth as a woman to you, and you aren't even interested. Can you imagine what an awful way that is to live every day? I've prayed daily for God to remove this temptation from you, and I am confident that He has provided you a way of escape every time, but you have not taken any of them. I'm asking you to take some responsibility here! If you can't or won't change, that will probably end the marriage, so it's really up to you."

After that storm, I left the room and went sobbing to the Lord in prayer. It felt like we were back at square one, except that I distrusted Will far more this time around. I went into controller mode, checking his Internet activity at every turn, but really I was just trying to protect myself from getting too wounded again. I didn't want to be vulnerable.

Meanwhile, in January, after seven months of rejection letters, I finally found a job. My coworkers were therapists and people that I really got along well with, and I grew more confident in myself. I think Will was also happier because we now shared the burden of providing for our family. I began checking the computer less often, and each time it was free of porn. He had no computer access at work, and we had no cable television with adult shows or channels. All things considered, he was doing well, and we started to grow as a couple.

The next fall our church began a women's study on the book called *The Power of a Praying Wife* by Stormie Omartian. As I grew spiritually, I put fewer pressures on Will. The results bordered on shocking. We grew closer emotionally, spiritually, and sexually than we'd ever been, and one night Will surprised me when he asked if we should try for another baby. I was thrilled that he wanted a second child, and I felt the timing was perfect to provide a sibling for Britney. So we began trying, and I was pregnant in a month—there must have been something in the water.

I began praying like never before, and I felt such oneness with God. We still weren't very spiritual as a couple, but there was always hope.

The pregnancy went off without a hitch, and baby Tyler came a month early. What a miracle he was, so tiny, so precious. I loved watching him and his daddy napping on the couch together. This time the transition went a lot smoother— until I wanted to resume sex again.

Oddly, Will was hesitant, and he made excuses about being either too hot or too tired or too stressed. We had conversations about this every two weeks for months. By September I'd gone back to work, but it was different this time because I was doing most of my work from home or in the evenings so that I could be with my children and avoid day-care expenses. As a result, my contact with my friends was minimal, and I couldn't keep the household up as well. As I tried to juggle it all, I became more stressed, and then to my horror I noticed Will emotionally withdrawing from me, which was so characteristic of a pornographic backslide. I couldn't talk to him about it because he'd tune me out for a football game, a video game, or an engrossing television show. To make matters worse, we'd finally gotten a satellite dish for our television so we could watch the channels like Discovery and the Learning Channel again.

The insecurity came flooding back. Trying to get Will's attention, I quickly lost all of Tyler's pregnancy weight and the extra ten pounds I still carried from Britney's. I then got a flattering haircut and began receiving three or four compliments a day from people I'd run into, but the only person I really cared to hear from was Will. Those kind words never came.

In late autumn our church put on a seminar called *Fighting the Battles,* and the speaker, over the course of five hours, addressed pornography and revealed how this insidious stuff was infiltrating Christian lives today. On the way home, Will said, "For the first time in years I finally feel somewhat normal." I began crying, because his shame had finally been moved enough to where we could talk. As I slowly and carefully prodded over the next couple of weeks, things began to make sense. We still had a long way to go, but for the first time I felt like we were empowered together to destroy this stranglehold.

In December I went to bed one night after a coy remark, and I thought Will would be right up to accept my sexual invitation. But as I lay there, something didn't feel right. So I slowly came down the stairs and quietly opened the door to the living room. Will quickly switched to ESPN's *SportsCenter.*

"Honey, what are you doing? I thought you were coming to bed!" Will said he was just checking the weather, but I didn't believe him. I asked him if he would push the recall button on the remote, and he did. It turned out that he'd been watching a soft-core feature on Cinemax. I had blocked all of the other adult channels, but since Cinemax showed family-friendly movies during the day, I didn't want to block that one. I guess I should have.

"But I didn't see anything—I had just turned it there," he protested.

"Maybe so," I replied evenly, "but you turned it there in hopes of seeing something, didn't you? And you did it right after I'd just offered myself to you! Don't you have any idea how that hurts me?"

I was fiercely angry at first, mostly because I'd dropped my guard once more, only to get popped again. The next few days I was sad and weepy but praying constantly. I called Will one day at work and asked him, "I just can't handle doing this on our own anymore. I would like to call an elder and his wife from church and talk to them about this."

He agreed, and I picked an elder who was considerably older than us, and he had so much love and so little condemnation about him that I just knew he would be the best choice as a confidant. Besides, his wife was also a paragon of discretion, and I knew her quite well, so I felt at ease when we met with them. They were so encouraging during our first meeting that I left their home feeling as if God had lifted a horrible, secret burden off our shoulders.

Happily, our church had just begun a couples class one week after the latest confrontation, and it was based on the Every Man series. Will had confided in me that he was so glad and relieved to have this being discussed in church. Because of his shame, he had been afraid to just come out on his own and admit his addiction.

It's been five years since our first encounter with intimacy problems, and we've both finally talked out the things that have been hang-ups for us. We are finally effectively praying about these things together too. I used to say, "Yeah, we're going to make it now," only to be crushed by another backslide.

Now I can honestly say, "Yeah, we're going to make it with God's help, despite the backslides." That may sound like a small attitude adjustment on the surface, but it goes as deep as the seabed. I know that it is possible for my husband to live without the backsliding, and I'm praying that he can. But Christ has strengthened me to a point that I didn't even know existed, and much of my outlook has changed.

For instance, many people have divorced in my situation, and I believe they were justified to do so. But still I wonder, *Wouldn't God want us to try to forgive and move on together, as long as both parties are willing?* Years ago, I was the person who'd think, *If Will ever wanted an easy way out, all he'd have to do is cheat on me and I'd be gone.* But now look at me. He *has* cheated on me countless times with porn, but I have forgiven him, and I *still* love him so much.

I still struggle with the pain from time to time, and the other day I even thought, *Does love always have to hurt, or is it just me?* But then the Lord spoke to my heart, *Remember, My child, you live in a fallen world, and humans are fallen people. Their love is not what I intended it to be. You can strive to follow My Son, but you will still have struggles. Let My love alone be sufficient for you, because it will never fail you.*

In the early struggles I wasn't very merciful, and I wasn't quick to forgive, wallowing in deep self-pity and depression. Things only got better after I gave all that up and relied upon God instead.

Some might say, "That is just an illusion! Will wasn't better. After all, he kept sinning even after you thought things were better!"

True, but I wasn't talking about *Will's* getting better—I was talking about *my* getting better. I was healing and growing in God so that with each backslide I took it better, and now with the seminar and classes at our church, Will is getting better too.

Shame is powerful. Why else would Satan use it so often? It wasn't until Will's shame was jarred loose that he could begin to heal and go to God himself, and I didn't realize that until about halfway through all of this.

The sins of pornography will lead you to question yourself, your femininity, and your sexuality. Please don't listen to those doubts. Would alcoholism or substance abuse in your spouse lead you to question those things? Not likely. Well, it's been shown that porn produces the same highs that substance abuse does, and it's been noted that those who fall prey usually have low self-esteem and internal pain that they are trying to medicate, just like an alcoholic or drug addict.

If these things are true, then none of the lies that Satan tells us—*you aren't pretty enough, you aren't woman enough*—can be true. And it's also true that we wives can be a contributing factor to our husbands' porn usage by being critical, unforgiving, and hateful, which increases his inner pain and the need to medicate.

The best thing you can do is set the proper boundaries and hold him accountable, asking the Lord to give you healing and discernment to deal with your husband's wandering eyes. If you stay close to Him, then all the changes can come.

FROM BRENDA

Cindy's story is so inspirational. She hung in there against tremendous odds and worked to get her marriage bed back to normal. We'll talk more about how to do that in our next chapter.

SUGGESTED READING

If you are to get closer to the Lord and endure long-suffering in your marriage, it is encouraging and insightful to read books by other women who have endured long-suffering as well.

> *Evidence Not Seen: A Woman's Miraculous Faith in the Jungles of World War II*
> by Darlene Deibler Rose
>
> *The Five Silent Years of Corrie ten Boom* by Pamela Rosewell Moore
>
> *The Hiding Place* by Corrie ten Boom
>
> *Papa's Place* by Margaret Jensen

lagging sexuality

FROM BRENDA

Before we move on to discuss the husband who won't repent, we need to pause a moment and talk about sex. If peace and oneness are lagging in the relationship because of his sexual sin, your sexual desire for your husband will be lagging along with it.

Clarissa wrote, "The biggest problem is letting go of the hurt to make myself available again to my husband. Who has experience at such a thing? Who seeks out *any* kind of intimacy in relationships with damaged trust? But this cannot be avoided.... We are married and we are one, and whether we like it or not, sex is part of that."

By this point in the book, you easily recognize that we're fighting on the battlefield of broken trust, more than anything else. But Clarissa's last line is also crucial. Sex *is* part of a normal marriage, and if you're going to turn your marriage around, you need to get the marriage bed back to normal.

So where do you start? Your sexuality is your most guarded possession, your secret garden. You trusted that he would be worthy of your precious gift, but he cavalierly viewed all kinds of sensual garbage, polluting and littering your garden. You deserve so much more.

We cannot offer too many specifics here because there are just too many variables defining each situation—your temperament, your maturity in Christ, his level of repentance, his level of addiction, and the time you've spent enduring his lies and relapses.

Still, there are constants for all of us. As long as you're married, you have an irrevocable call of God to be your husband's helpmate. As we said in chapter 15, as his helpmate you must accept this pair of possibilities:

1. God may have created your marriage in part for the messy work of helping Him heal your husband's wounds, of assisting your husband in his journey to Christian maturity.

2. God may have picked you to be the central figure in this work of restoration from the very beginning. How do you know this marriage isn't among God's highest dreams for your life as His servant?

Perhaps He's intended this as your very own under-the-radar, no-headline, home mission field, as we've said. Part of this vital ministry is helping your husband maintain sexual purity and turning your marriage bed toward normalcy, no matter how you're feeling. As Christians we can never allow our ministries to be left up to the vagaries of our emotions. If we did, I can assure you that this book wouldn't exist because my feeling from the outset was: *Run for the hills!*

Nowhere is that more true than in marriage. It has been my experience that spouses should never wait until the situation is perfect or until their feelings are just right before moving ahead and doing the right thing in relational issues, especially regarding sex. The right feelings will generally follow the right actions soon enough. Besides, if we plan to love our husbands as ourselves, we must make room for their needs and their intimacy. Attaining normal, sexual oneness calls for personal sacrifices—sacrifices that you may have to make.

And why shouldn't you expect to make sacrifices even in the marriage bed? Remember, you are not just your husband's wife. You are also his Christian sister. As we've said, the church often has let your husband down through its collective silence, and his father and friends may have also let him down along the way. Will you show him mercy?

God could very well be asking you to stand in the gap for your Christian brother. God could be counting on you, His daughter, to be the last line of defense in the battle for your husband's restoration and freedom. All political freedom comes from sacrifice on the battlefield. Sexual freedom is no different.

On the battlefield of broken sexual trust, your husband must become trustworthy and you must eventually choose to trust again, and that'll mean sexual sacrifice. It's self-defeating to worry about which should come first—you need to keep your eyes on your own knitting first. Because sex is such an important part of his natural language of intimacy, and he needs interpersonal intimacy with you so badly, you will likely have to respond sexually as if you *do* trust him long before you actually do. As the Bible suggests, you'll likely have to model Christ (and normal sexuality) by doing the right thing (loving him sexually even when he doesn't deserve it).

Remember your wedding-day vow "for better or for worse"? Well, this time it's worse, and it's time to keep your vow to God. It's time to answer your call as helpmate by applying the iron to your husband's hide and dressings to his wounds, bringing your sexual ship back around to that course heading of *N* on your moral compass—*normal.*

But what's normal? After all this mess, you may not even be sure what normal sex is anymore. In the next chapter we'll paint a picture of what that looks like and explore your role in applying iron and dressings as you choose to trust again sexually. But before we do, we'll spend this chapter exploring your husband's role in restoring trust and what you can expect of him.

The first thing you can expect from your husband is that he returns your prized possession—his body—to you and stops using it without your permission. It's no laughing matter when a scoundrel makes off with your valuables, and in a very real sense, your husband has done just that to you:

> The wife's body does not belong to her alone but also to her husband. In
> the same way, *the husband's body does not belong to him alone but also to his*
> *wife.* (1 Corinthians 7:4)

Your husband's body is your prized possession, your *only* legitimate vessel of sexual satisfaction on the face of the earth. His sexuality was created as much for you as it was for him. And yet your husband has lifted your property for his own use, covering his tracks at every turn to hide the truth.

FROM FRED

When the Scriptures proclaim that "the wife's body does not belong to her alone but also to her husband," God is speaking directly to His precious daughter, gently reminding her of His expectations of her in the marriage bed and hoping to foster a servant's willingness in her heart through His grace.

Yet many husbands pretend that these verses were spoken directly to *them*, as if God is some omnipotent buddy calling out, "Come and get it, men—as much and as often as you like! It's all on Me and My daughters any way you like it!"

Some men twist this verse into a perverse entitlement that sounds something like this: *my wife is my very own call girl on retainer, and if she isn't up to snuff, I can head off to the harems of cyberspace to make up for it. God will understand!*

Nope, that's not how it goes. *The Message* translation of this scripture clarifies the spirit behind this passage:

> The marriage bed must be a place of mutuality—the husband seeking to satisfy his wife, the wife seeking to satisfy her husband. *Marriage is not a place to "stand up for your rights."* Marriage is a decision to serve the other, whether in bed or out. (1 Corinthians 7:3-4)

These verses were never intended to be used as a claim for individual rights, but rather as a reminder to both spouses to seek mutuality as a couple in the marriage bed. God's message to your husband here is *not* that you are his call girl—not even close. His actual message is that your husband's sexuality must always and only be used to serve and to satisfy you, his wife. You are the co-owner of his body, and he has no right to use his body any way he wants.

As my wedding approached, I knew that soon my money would no longer be mine alone, even when it came out of my paycheck. Because of Brenda's ironclad commitment to being a good financial steward of the money God would entrust to us as a couple, I began to seriously contemplate the monetary costs of my pornographic magazines. I knew in a million years she wouldn't approve of spending a dime on such smut.

So, since our wedding bells rang, I've spent no more on pornographic magazines and pay-per-view Web sites than Brenda has—a big, fat zero. Too bad, however, that I didn't see my body as hers. If I had, I would have been thinking, *I have no right to use my body—especially my eyes—on things she disapproves of.*

Of course, in time I adopted the same mind-set with my body as I had with our finances, and it's a very good thing that I did. After all, it is one thing to use her prized possession without asking. It's quite another to return it to her broken. Let me share a story to illustrate.

When Brenda was in high school, her mom and dad saved to buy her a sewing machine. As you might expect, she cherished it far beyond your average household tool—it was a symbol of her parents' deep love for her.

Years later, we befriended Colin and Amber in our young-couples group at church. Like us, they had small children and little money. But unlike us, they had no sewing machine, and Amber needed to patch up some of her kid's clothes. With deep reservations, Brenda lent her "symbol of love" to Amber, awaiting its return with bated breath.

Months passed while Brenda fretted, but finally Amber dropped it back to us with a friendly smile and grateful thanks. With a deep sigh of relief, Brenda returned her priceless gift to its honored place while chiding herself for her Scroogish attitudes at the start.

But when Brenda pulled it out a few weeks later to fire it up, she found that Amber had returned the machine without mentioning she'd broken it—and without offering to repair it. Understandably, our relationship with Colin and Amber was never quite the same after that. Our sewing machine was kaput, and so was our trust in them.

Your relationship with your husband may be kaput as well, because he has taken his body into his own hands without asking you. Now you find that when you go to use it, his body no longer works the way it should for you. He's broken it, yet he coolly returns it to your bed every night without a word of admission.

While tools can be borrowed and returned unscathed, bodies can't. Porn and masturbation inevitably inflict wounds. Remember what happens? His eyes begin to dominate his sexuality. A boorish clamoring for his own sexual intensity replaces his normal desire for interpersonal intimacy. His body, originally created for your sexual pleasure, now pleasures you far less, and we needn't search far to understand why.

Researchers like professors Dolf Zillman of Indiana University and Jennings Bryant of the University of Houston have found that men register a major increase in the importance of sex *without intimate attachment* after regularly viewing porn. Sound familiar? Intimacy's transmitters get fried.

In addition, these men using porn became more callous to female sexuality, and their concern for their wives' pleasure fell off significantly. How much porn is necessary to elicit such a dreadful, measurable change? Answer from the researchers: only six one-hour weekly sessions. Based on that, how likely is it your husband can borrow his body for porn and masturbation and return it to you unbroken? Very unlikely.

With longer, repeated exposure, men became significantly less satisfied with their wives' sexual curiosity and even less concerned about her end of the bargain in bed. In short, they've broken their normal, God-given sexuality that was created to be used to serve and satisfy you. Now their sexuality demands more and better and different from you to satisfy themselves!

Remember how Brenda knew her sewing machine was broken? When she pulled it out to use it, it didn't work right. In a similar vein, does your husband's body work right when you want to enjoy it? Considering what you now know about male sexuality, you can predict where you'll find the damage. Caroline discerned the damage in her husband, Cliff, in this telling way:

About six months into our marriage, I noticed our sex life losing momentum. The frequency had dropped markedly, and while this could have easily been explained away had it been the only sign of trouble, it wasn't. We'd always been compatible—technique, frequency, timing—in every area.

But now it was different. When we *did* make love, it felt like, *Wham, bam, thank you, ma'am,* meaning Cliff got his satisfaction while I was left high and dry. I even have a journal entry that reads, *I feel like Peg Bundy when it comes to sex. I have to nag him to do me like a chore.* It's like he stopped caring about my pleasure at all, and in retrospect, that was my first clue that porn was breaking him down.

Another woman, Loralee—after five kids and seventeen years of marriage—has never had an orgasm. Her husband is so self-centered during sex and so quick to hit the heights that he's never considered taking her along for the ride.

Nikki feels used, lonely, and vaguely dirty afterward, as she explains:

Over the years, our basic bedroom pattern was me being manipulated into having sex out of guilt and then laying there and tolerating the act until it was over. It was never about mutual satisfaction at all. It was one-way satisfaction, yet oddly enough, Lance never even seemed truly satisfied either.

Perhaps if Nikki better understood male sexuality, it wouldn't seem odd. Lance's broken body now searches for intensity over intimacy, and she can't possibly dial up the desired intensity for him by merely tolerating the act.

And if Lance better understood his own sexuality, he'd know that his lack of satisfaction isn't her fault. But since he doesn't, he complains and wants her to follow her pastor's orders—shape up and deliver like the girls on his computer screen. But it's Lance who needs shaping up, as Nikki relates:

Although we never slept in separate rooms, we definitely lived as separately as we could. I always felt him looking at me whenever the pastor would say, *The wife's body is not her own.* I knew our pastor was preaching the Word of God, but I wanted to leap up and shout, *You don't know what it's like in my bedroom!*

Of course, I knew it wasn't my pastor's fault. It's just that few people talk about marital sexuality that is out of balance or a place of continual wounding.

Lance is dissatisfied with his wife in bed, but there's nothing wrong with Nikki. He's simply been perverted by the porn, and whenever that happens, dissatisfaction with a wife's sexual curiosity follows hard on its heels, as Nikki describes:

It cycles again and again. For a while he tries hard to be pure, but then, like always, I begin sensing another world going on in his head while we're having sex. Eventually, he always speaks that dreaded word—*variation.* I steel myself for it for weeks before it happens, because I know it is coming. The end result is always the same blowout—he says he can't survive without variation, and I just can't give it.

A husband's craving for variety reveals a consuming desire for sexual intensity over intimacy, and it also unmasks the fierce, concealed struggle with tolerance. Any frequent masturbator knows about tolerance, which is the unnatural demand for more and more stimulation to reach the same point of excitement. If a man is pursuing sexual intensity through pictures, tolerance demands an escalation to more stimulating material and fantasy. We caught a glimpse of this in chapter 13, when Gordon said, "I had to have…more just to reach the same level of excitement. Sometimes that meant longer and longer hours, but other times that meant more bizarre photographs."

But when a real wife is involved, *variance* is required to escalate beyond the tolerance. Without the escalation provided by variance, a man can never expect to reach the same point of excitement. Once intensity takes the place of intimacy, and intimacy is decoupled from sex, the sexual high is the end in itself, and nothing but the bodies are connecting. That explains why Nikki always feels used, lonely, and vaguely dirty afterward.

That's not to say that all variation is a bad sign in the marriage bed. Some variation will be the natural result of a couple's creativity as they're mutually expressing their sexual intimacy. But an insistent, unilateral cry for variation often reflects an abnormal shift in a husband's sexual focus toward intensity due to porn. Normal male sexuality needn't clamor for constant variation to scale the heights of intimacy.

Mark can paint that picture of normal for you because his sexuality hasn't been broken by porn:

> My wife and I don't embrace fringe sexual activities—in fact, some would say we are pretty boring, but not me. I find our sexual life thrilling, even after twenty-three years of marriage, and I think it's because I have never made love to the same woman twice.
>
> Susan is always growing, and for that matter, so am I. It is not some new activity that keeps sex exhilarating each time. Rather, it is our newness to each other that makes sex so powerful. Sex stays hot and fresh not because we are exploring different ways to have sex, but because we are constantly exploring each other to a new depth every day of our lives.

Get the picture? Brenda and I have also been married for twenty-three years, and our story matches theirs perfectly. Brenda told me, "It's great that as we both keep our eyes and minds pure in terms of television, movies, and books, we've never once slowed down sexually. It's always fresh and new, even after all this time."

Have you been experiencing this normal picture throughout your marriage? If not, you're likely recognizing some of these damage signs in your husband's sexuality. Perhaps you've even felt an urge to pull away from him.

If you're married, though, pulling away is not the best answer for either of you—the best answer is simply for your husband to fix what he's broken. Unlike Amber with the sewing machine, he must admit he's broken things and offer to repair the damage. To fix things, he must do the following:

1. Give up porn to break the domination of his eyes in his sexuality.
2. Give up masturbation and choose intimacy over intensity.
3. Get an accountability group to help him explore intimacy further.

If the above actions do not resolve matters, he must get professional help through counseling.

First, he must get his eyes back to normal. God says it's normal for a Christian guy to keep his way pure (see Psalm 119:9) and to set no vile thing before his eyes (see Psalm 101:3). It's normal for a Christian to avoid lusting after women in any setting (see Job 31:1).

But for too many of us our sexuality is still dominated by our eyes, even after we get them bouncing and under control. While we would never say it to our wives, our attitude is clearly saying, *Okay, I've gotten my eyes under control, and you are looking better than ever before! I've done my part. I've gotten rid of my porn stash and stopped looking at the hotties in the string bikinis. But you have to do your part, babe. Become one of them! Always thin. Always available. Always smiling with that come-on look, ready for action. Become what I've given up for you!*

We want a seductive tigress on the prowl whose wardrobe comes straight out of a Victoria's Secret catalog and whose come-hither look reminds us of a certain porn star. The problem with that? There's been no underlying transformation of our corrupted sexuality. Our sexuality is still not about our wives or an intimate inner connection—it's about us, our eyes, and our pleasure.

Look, outer beauty will always have its allure, but it shouldn't dominate our sexuality, and neither should our eyes. My eyes don't dominate my sexuality anymore. When I sweep Brenda into my arms, it's not just her body I'm after. I want to connect with all of her, both inside and out.

Second, masturbation must stop. Masturbation is the ultimate in self-centered sexuality and causes men to depend upon themselves for gratification rather than their wives. His sexuality was given for your pleasure, not his own, and when measured against this intent of the Designer, masturbation is clearly counterfeit.

Bonding and intimacy is the whole point of sex, and masturbation clearly misses the point. Masturbation does not produce intimacy, but instead is a flight from intimacy. Your husband can quite effectively stop masturbating by using the techniques outlined in *Every Man's Battle,* but that doesn't mean that the pull of the masturbation will diminish overnight. Remember, there are often wounded emotions behind it all.

He does need to make a strong decision to stop, which includes eliminating as many temptations as possible—cable, videos, Internet, catalogs, and magazines. But he also needs to make a strong decision to deal with any of the underlying issues whenever they become clear. That means going to a counselor, even if that makes him feel weak. That probably means seeking accountability through a transparent relationship with a godly, mature man or finding a men's accountability group where the honest expression of feelings and true intimacy can replace his dependency upon the false intimacy of masturbation. He also needs to develop an ongoing relationship with God that involves all the spiritual disciplines, especially prayer and worship. (Our book *Every Man's Challenge* will challenge your husband on these issues.)

And what comes with this journey for your husband? Sex as God intended—real intimacy—and a relationship with God that will blow him away.

What happens for you? The return to normal.

You'll know if he has actually quit masturbating when you sense a basic change in his character. Certain things that may have vanished in his search for intensity—like intimate, gentle kissing—will return. You can expect a focus on your pleasure too.

No more frustration.

No more fantasy.

No more feeling rushed.

No more feeling pressure to do something uncomfortable.

If his sexuality has been given to you primarily for your pleasure, what commitment should you naturally see in him? For openers, your climax should be as important to him as his own. His knowledge of what makes you feel good should be as deep as his knowledge of what makes himself feel good.

You should expect him to study you. Has he studied your sexual responses? Is he going slow enough for you? Faster when he should? If you can't respond sexually in the early morning hours, is he waiting until nightfall?

One thing to keep in mind, though, is that he is still a guy, and he won't always be as intuitive about these things as you might like. In other words, you can't expect him to do this alone without your help. Women are built so differently! He may not know how to please you unless you tell him, as Jerry discovered:

> It came out last week that she has been holding on to frustration and resentment for years because I touch her in ways that stimulate me, but I touch her very little in the ways that stimulate her.
>
> She claims that I have not been creative in giving her pleasure, and while there are certainly more issues than that, she is right to some degree. I need to honor her by putting more energy into listening to her and touching her in pleasurable ways.

As women, your physical triggers are hard enough for us to pick up on, but the rest is such an absolute mystery that we are hopeless without your help. Lisa told us that because of hormones or exhaustion, there are times when she wants to have sex but she doesn't really care if she has an orgasm. She just wants the closeness of it all. Brenda can easily relate to this statement, but it is counterintuitive to a guy's nature.

Even then, however, your husband can learn. Brenda so appreciates it when I listen well and take these things by faith in the bedroom. She's granted me permission to include this snippet from a letter she wrote me years ago:

When you allow me to let you know that it is just one of those times that I'm beyond responding, it leaves me free to just enjoy being with you without the pressure that I'm disappointing you and ruining your experience.

And as you've noticed, lifting the pressure on me to respond can actually free me to be able to respond after all. It would be a good thing if all men could understand that this simple kind of sacrificial love for her husband can be as satisfying to her as his orgasm is to him.

When you simply accept that I'm willing to give of myself without putting pressure on me to climax, both of us learn something. I learn that I am very happy to help meet your needs, and you learn how I'm different and how you might best allow me to meet your needs.

Do I really understand everything that Brenda has shared here? No, not really. Do I respond as if I do? Sure! That's mutuality, and that's love. Compatibility is not necessary for oneness—sacrifice is—and that's something every man—and wife—has to learn. We'll take a deeper look at sacrifices in the next chapter.

normal sexuality

FROM BRENDA

Fred becomes a bit scarce around the house whenever he's writing a book, and things have been no different this time, even though we're writing this one together. Writing has cut into our time with the kids and with each other, and has also affected many other pressing, out-of-the-norm things that demand our time.

For instance, our daughter Laura is graduating from high school this spring, so there have been college tours and admissions meetings and countless conversations with her—labeled URGENT—regarding her academic future. Our other daughter, Rebecca, has her sights set on a driver's license this year, and she needs many hours behind the wheel with Fred before we can turn her loose on the unsuspecting Iowa public. Our younger son, Michael, is in the midst of his first wrestling season, so whenever Fred has a spare moment, he's been dropping by practice and helping Michael bone up on attacks and counters so that he can quickly improve.

When you combine all that with the regular urgencies of work and family, most of Fred's writing time is grabbed in the early mornings and the late evenings. What this means, in effect, is that during this writing season, I see very little of him in the morning and often go to bed without him at night. So even though we are working together, this has been a lonely time. I've missed him in many ways.

One recent night Fred put his writing aside, and we came together for some intimate time. We were both looking forward to breaking the dry spell.

But then an odd thought flashed through my mind. *Why are we doing this?* For a moment, sexual intercourse seemed out of place in the context of our relationship, because we had gone for a spell without it due to our hectic writing schedule. It felt odd, in the way it might if we were two dear old school chums who had known each other for as long as we could remember, who suddenly and inexplicably found ourselves in bed together. *What in the world? How'd we end up in bed? We're just friends, aren't we? Weird!*

As we were drifting off to sleep afterward, the same thought flashed in my mind again, and I chuckled as I mentioned it to Fred. We burst out laughing because, for us, we knew this temporary whirl of commotion would soon end, bringing our marriage bed back to normal.

But for many married couples, sporadic sex *is* the norm. It shouldn't be that way and, biblically, it can never be shrugged off as no big deal. Fred and I agree that infrequent lovemaking serves as a red flag to mark that something's gone wrong. Regular sex between a husband and wife is normal.

Remember, for a Christian, *normal* means to be like Christ. While Christ was never married, we know that Jesus was the Word in flesh, so we also know that when we follow the Word of God, we will always be like Christ. And what does the Word say about normal sex?

> The husband should give to his wife her conjugal rights (goodwill, kindness, and what is due her as his wife), and likewise the wife to her husband. For the wife does not have [exclusive] authority and control over her own body, but the husband [has his rights]; likewise also the husband does not have [exclusive] authority and control over his body, but the wife [has her rights]. Do not refuse and deprive and defraud each other [of your due marital rights], except perhaps by mutual consent for a time, so that you may devote yourselves unhindered to prayer. But afterwards resume marital relations, lest Satan tempt you [to sin] through your lack of restraint of sexual desire. (1 Corinthians 7:3-5, AMP)

What was God's intent? That neither party would have total control of their yes or their no in the marriage bed. For instance, sex under the total control of the husband's yes isn't God's plan. If the husband is consistently forcing his wife to have sex against her will, then something is wrong with the relationship.

At the same time, the wife can't have full control of her no, always waiting until she's in the mood. If the husband is being consistently forced to *not* have sex against his will, then something is just as wrong with the relationship. Neither is normal, and God wanted us to know that.

I'd like to try to paint a normal picture of marital sex by using a portion of my open letter to wives at the end of *Every Man's Marriage.* Some of you may have read it already, but I need to draw this picture again as a lead-in to some further discussions about God's expectations of us in the bedroom.

What does normal look like? When it comes to men, nothing seems normal at first. As I've said,

Initially, in my early years of marriage, I was shocked by male sexuality, especially by its visual orientation and its regularity. Male sexuality seemed rather shallow and almost weird to me, but I started to wonder about that. I discovered that it really isn't shallow. It's just different. And given the obvious struggle men have with sexual purity when they're without sex, I began to understand why God would tell me, "Your body is not your own." I can see where at times sex is vital to Fred's purity and his emotional intimacy with me. And I can really help him out. In fact, God expects me to do it.

While we're quick to expect our husbands to toe God's line of sexual purity, we're often slow to toe His other line and admit that our bodies aren't our own. We have no right to expect our husbands to stay sexually pure if we constantly pull away. We're his sole vessel of sexual satisfaction, and guys need regular sexual fulfillment two or three times a week.

A friend of mine, Cindy, related her husband's observation that she had all the power in their sexual relationship, every speck of it. Every single time, he was the one who had to lock the door and ask for it. She, on the other hand, was always either freezing or tired.

"I know you have no real interest," he said to her. "But it's tough knowing that 90 percent of the time when we have sex you can't even pretend to find me desirable. All you understand is that I need something you don't need, and you're simply doing it out of duty. When you don't show any true desire or passion on your own, I start feeling like a little boy depending on Mommy to give me my candy."

Mood should have nothing to do with it. We're called to help out, whether we're in the mood or not. Countless times I've initiated sex with Fred when we both knew I wasn't in the mood.

Every night when Fred comes into the bedroom, he sits in his "talking chair" to make sure he doesn't fall asleep before I have the chance to talk with him. That means so much to me, especially since I know Fred is never in the mood for talking at that time of night. He's a morning person, so he's really tired when we go to bed, but he converses with me because he knows I need it, whether he's in the mood or not.

If your husband is like most guys, he goes to work at his job when he isn't in the mood at least 50 percent of the time. I know that if it weren't for the kids and me, Fred would choose a different path for his life. How often am I tired at the end of the day, and Fred cleans the kitchen so I can sit and read a book? How often does he play Nintendo to draw the kids out of my hair for a break? (He hates Nintendo. He doesn't know what he's doing and always gets slaughtered, even by nine-year-old Michael.)

Can't we do the same for our husbands when we aren't in the mood? Besides, moods are a funny thing. Moods change quickly. Remember, part of our own intimacy is based on hugging and touching. I've found that if I submit and go ahead with things for his sake, more often than not all the touching and caressing changes my mood, and soon I'm enjoying things as much as he is. In fact, this happens so often that I've begun to count on it. I'm usually rewarded, right on the spot!

I have come to the point where I regularly ask Fred about his needs. Last night, for example, when he came into the room, I simply asked, "Would you like to lock the door?" He understood!

I chase after four kids all day. On many of these nights, I'm not really in the mood for sexual intercourse because I'm too tired or because my natural drive is just plain weaker than his. On those occasions, I'll say, "I'm not really interested myself, but I'd love to do something for you." I know I'll at least like the snuggling, even if I don't get all fired up.

And, while a long-term diet of drive-through sex isn't desirable, there's certainly still a place for the quickie since it defuses the power of a man's seventy-two-hour cycle. Sometimes you just don't have the time or energy for the full package, but if you care about him, you can find just enough energy to get by. Regardless, there's something very fulfilling to a man in knowing his wife cares enough to help like this, even if it's not really "her night."

I don't pretend to understand Fred's sexuality. All I know is that sexual purity is not just every man's battle, but every *couple's* battle as well.

As wives, we must always consider this guiding verse in any of our decisions in marriage:

> However, each one of you also must love his wife as he loves himself, and
> the wife must respect her husband. (Ephesians 5:33)

It's easy to cheer that loving sacrifice God expects of our husbands, but it's tougher to get pumped about the sacrifice God expects of us in respecting our husband's sexuality.

Of course, normal sexuality is far more than a service that I regularly and respectfully fulfill among my many conjugal duties. Passionate longings and burning desire are not at all abnormal emotions in the marriage bed. In fact, it is quite normal for a wife to desire her husband passionately. Take a peek at some verses I've condensed from Song of Songs:

> *Husband:* You have stolen my heart, my sister, my bride;
>> you have stolen my heart
> with one glance of your eyes....
> How delightful is your love, my sister, my bride!...
>
> Your head crowns you like Mount Carmel.
>> Your hair is like royal tapestry;
>> the king is held captive by its tresses.
> How beautiful you are and how pleasing,
>> O love, with your delights! (4:9-10; 7:5-6)

Wife: My lover [husband] is radiant and ruddy,
　　outstanding among ten thousand.
His head is purest gold;
　　his hair is wavy
　　and black as a raven....
His mouth is sweetness itself;
　　he is altogether lovely.
This is my lover, this my friend....

I belong to my lover,
　　and his desire is for me....
Let us go early to the vineyards...
　　there I will give you my love.
The mandrakes send out their fragrance,
　　and at our door is every delicacy,
both new and old,
　　that I have stored up for you, my lover. (5:10-11,16; 7:10,12-13)

Does your sex life look anything like this today? It may not, but this is still the point on the compass that you'll want to point your arrow to—normal. And that's the first thing your husband can expect from you as you begin rebuilding your sex life together.

From Fred

What else can God expect from you as you rebuild the marriage bed in your helper role? First of all, you'll have to pick up your iron and grind away, sharpening him toward godliness. Remember, he's likely to have become very blind sexually. He may not even know how to focus on anything but his sexual intensity these days, instead of intimacy with you.

You must firmly guide him toward normal sexuality until his blindness lifts and he understands. You have to insist on having normal sex again, without the porn and the mental fantasies, and you must not be satisfied with anything less. You have God's permission to hold your husband's feet to the fire.

If his sexual selfishness is severe enough, and if your frustration and pain have been devastating enough, it may even require the ultimate, nuclear-tipped solution for a short time, which is a sexual moratorium.

You may be thinking, *My husband would never stand for that—he'd pull out the scripture about the wife not having control over her body:*

> The husband should fulfill his marital duty to his wife, and likewise the wife to her husband. The wife's body does not belong to her alone but also to her husband. In the same way, the husband's body does not belong to him alone but also to his wife. (1 Corinthians 7:3-4)

God commands married couples to provide regular sexual intimacy. And regarding what I said about a sexual moratorium, it would be easy to see why a husband would grab the letter of the law and wave it under your nose, fuming, "If you call a sexual moratorium, that is a sign you don't love me. You have no right to do that!"

But this same husband needs to remember this: the letter of the law in a single verse can never transcend the spirit of the law of love, which is found in Matthew 22:37-39:

> "Love the Lord your God with all your heart and with all your soul and with all your mind." This is the first and greatest commandment. And the second is like it: "Love your neighbor as yourself." All the Law and the Prophets hang on these two commandments.

Any husband ought to know that he is to treat his wife with tenderness as a fellow heir to the kingdom of grace (see 1 Peter 3:7), and doing so makes it far easier for her to desire him. He also ought to know that since God never spoke of sexuality outside of the context of two, He did not give us our sexuality for ourselves. Our sexuality was given to us primarily for our partner's pleasure, not for our own (see 1 Corinthians 7:3-4). That can only mean one thing: a husband is wrong to use this verse in 1 Corinthians to fight for *his* rights, and instead he should be using it to fight for *your* rights.

You have a right to a pure, selfless, pleasurable marriage bed, courtesy of his sexuality, and if you need to turn off his sexuality for a time to get the kinks out of his attitudes and hardwiring, that is a reasonable course of action. You are well within your biblical rights to apply the sharpening iron and to insist on a sexual moratorium if it's in the best interests of making him normal and moving you both toward healing.

It would be unwise, however, to put a sexual moratorium in place without the consent of a third party, such as a spiritual leader or a professional counselor. Your feelings are too raw at the moment to handle that responsibility effectively, and your husband is too blind from his self-inflicted wounds.

Having said all that, you need some insight as to when a moratorium might make sense, so I'll let sexual-addictions counselor Patrick Middleton share what's on his mind when he considers granting his permission for one.

There are several ways I know when it's a good idea to suggest an abstinence contract:

The man admits that sexual sin is a compulsive problem that interferes with his life.

The man reacts with severe anxiety when I suggest he even consider the contract.

The man gets really sad, lonely, or angry when sex is unavailable.

The wife shares with me that after being sexual with her husband, she feels dirty or distant from him.

The wife keeps taking responsibility for the husband's sexuality, saying, *It's my fault, if I were just sexier he would not have this problem.*

Either one of the spouses describes regular sexual sin issues, like porn or adult movies, in the bedroom.

For the purposes of my counseling and even my own marriage, my definition of healthy, normal, biblical sex is utilizing all of my sexual energy to serve my marital bond. In that light, anything I do sexually that is *not* serving my marital bond is abusive in some way. For example, if while having sex with my wife, I imagine some girl I saw in the mall today, that is abusive. I am not available to my wife even while having sex with her. Such abuse must be rooted out.

Men can be out of control with lust even within the marriage relationship. For instance, one of my clients, a wife in this case, had a husband who traveled regularly on business. When he was home, he wanted sex all the time—every couple of hours—and he would get really mad if she was too busy to comply. The question always goes back to this, *How does my sexual activity serve my marital bond?* If I expect lots and lots of sex with my wife because *I* need it, then all that is being served is *me,* not the marital bond. Sometimes we need to take stark measures to break these patterns.

Convincing a man to sign a contract for a sexual moratorium with his wife can be very difficult at first, but it is not uncommon for men to work with me for a month of two and then to suggest on their own that a moratorium contract might be a good idea. Sometimes it takes a while for them to understand the body/brain/chemical aspect of sexual sin, but coming along with that understanding is the awareness of just how high these men have been keeping themselves with sexual lust and porn. The abstinence time allows them to reset the chemical side of the sin, and once they do, they have a better chance of not needing to look for a constant hit of their drug.

While convincing the husband to take on the no-sex mode can be problematic at the beginning, convincing the wife to stick with the contract in the middle presents a much different sort of problem. Of course, the wife happily signs up at first, and she participates in the moratorium and in all the other relational work to be done while the contract is in place.

Surprisingly, while the once-reluctant husband often fulfills the contract, the once gung-ho wife often does not. When that happens, we have surfaced some other issues that would have never been addressed had the husband kept forcing her to be sexual, and the moratorium has helped the husband in a second, unexpected way.

Men fear that their love connection with their wives will disintegrate once sex is eliminated, but it is not all that uncommon for the deal to go the other way. Once sex is taken out of the equation, it is amazing how many wives begin having problems with the relationship. *If we aren't being sexual, then how do I know he will stay with me? If I'm not sexual with him, then he'll get it somewhere else!* That's how some women think.

Lots of such coaddicted fears will surface, and some wives even go into depression. In the end, the moratorium often exposes unhealthy issues about sex and the marriage in the wife as well. She, of course, is usually not happy about that: *What's all this? My husband is the one with the sex problem! Why are we working on my coaddiction?*

But in reality, she should be happy, because the whole point of the contract was to jar them toward normal sexuality as a couple, and the moratorium is accomplishing just that.

There are also positive reasons why wives have a harder time sticking to their contracts than their husbands. When the husband has finally taken responsibility for his sexuality and has started making important changes in his life and relationship, the wife may feel closer to her husband than ever before. That makes him vastly more sexually attractive to her, and sexual intimacy is a natural outcome of that closeness. A wife may have been waiting years for her husband to grow up sexually, and when he finally starts doing so, she may want to sneak him into the marriage bed for an enjoyable evening of intimacy.

FROM BRENDA

Obviously, as a therapist, Patrick's goal is to slowly bring things back to normal for his clients. Your husband, and the Lord, can expect your goal to be the same.

Small steps may be all you can take at first. Even a baby step may look like the Grand Canyon. In time, that will change for you. Nothing feels more foundationally secure to a woman than to have a husband who is faithful, even in his eyes and thoughts. You can't have everything you want right away, but as he changes, you'll desire him again.

Luke once took a sexy, strong, confident Carly and turned her inside out. "After we were married, I soon became abusive in my language, ripping her to pieces and manipulating her words. She withdrew into herself out of fear. Within nine months of our wedding, our sex life fizzled to nothing, so I turned to pornography, spending hours lusting online."

In spite of her pain, Carly chose to sacrifice, as you can see from Luke's letter:

I finally understood that whenever I resented her for her lack of desire for me, I'd use it to justify my habit with porn. After sharing this with Carly, she opened up in return, admitting that my sexual sin makes her feel unloved and homely.

Somehow, on her own she decided to push ahead slowly with me and she's starting to show her love again in the little things. We now sleep close at night like we used to, and we hold hands and kiss. Now when she touches me, I know it is because she loves me and wants my love in return. We're just taking it slow and feeling the intimacy grow.

Sounds like Luke is traveling down the right track for a change, and while it may be a slow train coming for the both of them, he and Carly will arrive at the right destination.

FROM FRED

On a final note, what if it's *your* sexuality that's damaged? Can you expect him to fix his broken sexuality if you aren't working on yours? Jan wrote, "I have had the unfortunate experience of being sexually abused since I was a little girl. As a result, I have many wounds in this area with no resources for counseling. The thought of letting my husband ogle me or that I should be sexually intimate with him every few days repulses me."

This is an extremely tender issue and requires much love from both sides of the table. A couple of our dearest friends were sexually abused. But going back to chapter 15, let's look again at Jesus's clear example: Jesus was wounded plenty but knew that while it's okay to *be* wounded, it's not okay to *stay* wounded. Christ refused to stay wounded, and He didn't dwell on how He'd been mistreated.

If your sexuality has been abused, you bear no guilt, but at the same time, it isn't okay to stay wounded. Your husband is counting on you. You are the only legitimate vessel of sexual satisfaction he has—God's promised stream of mercy and grace on his path to sexual purity (see 1 Corinthians 7:9). When you dam the stream, you have doomed him to the same struggle he so desperately tried to escape through marriage. In fact, he may be even worse off than before marriage. As a single, he could at least flee sexual temptation. Now he has a wife showering in front of him or lying in a silky negligee next to him within his grasp. She ignites his engine in a million ways, and yet she may leave him high and dry with his normal desires.

God's called you to push toward normal as his helpmate. How long are you going to avoid finding healing for your wounds? You have a responsibility to your husband sexually, and though it is rough to face that fact in light of your long-standing pain, with God's help you need to seek resolution of past hurts and move on to Normal—for your own good and joy, too.

If some cold, heartless pervert abused you long ago, I despise his actions with you. But that doesn't change the truth: you are allowing that same heartless pervert to abuse your marriage today by stealing away what God has promised your husband in His Word. Will you stand up to that pervert and stop his abuse in your life and your home?

I do not want to be insensitive. I had to ask those same hard questions myself when I wounded my wife and kids through my harsh temper, which stemmed from abusive wounds I had received from my father. I discovered I had no right to keep those wounds or to allow that old abuse to harm Brenda or to desecrate God's picture of marriage. My father had to be stopped, and by God's grace and revelation, I stopped him.

In every abuse case, someone must stand up to the abuser at some point and stop the cascading pain, or things will never be normal. I pray it will be you. Let it be now.

what if change never comes?

FROM FRED

What do you do if your husband never turns away from sexual sin?

If your husband refuses to turn away from his sin, there are no easy answers. Sin corrupts, and your marriage will remain corrupted as long as he refuses to repent. To maintain your sanity, your focus must migrate to a broader, more macro view of your marriage, and your decisions will distill down to this: *Do I stay or do I go?*

What do I mean by a macro view? Let me explain with a little story about the Iowa State Fair. When our kids were young, a stop at the fair's sand-art booth was a must. A couple of bucks bought a cork, an empty bottle, and free reign to scoop through endless buckets of colored granules. Our kids loved creating their own rainbow masterpieces of layered sand in a bottle.

One October, with visions of sand art still dancing in their heads, Brenda and I shopped for Laura's birthday at Toys "R" Us, where we stumbled over a sand-art-in-a-box toy set. After Laura pealed away the colorful wrapping paper, her beaming face told us that we had hit one out of the park. "My very own sand-art kit!" she squealed, just like in the commercials that run during Saturday morning cartoons.

This awesome kit was comprised of six priceless bottles containing enough sand to create just six fabulous works of art. Unlike a cute, huggable doll, sand art didn't offer endless hours of perpetual joy. Six up and six down and you're done, but that only made each bottle priceless to our little Laura.

Brenda and I applauded when our birthday daughter immediately offered one to Rebecca, a kind, generous thing for a big sister to do. But Laura balked when her older brother, Jasen, asked for a bottle. When Jasen predictably cried foul, Laura dug in her heels, and her brother's antics failed to dislodge her position.

Brenda was not pleased. "Now Laura, you offered one to Rebecca, so it isn't fair to hold one back from Jasen now. How would you feel if you were in Jasen's shoes?"

Her wailing reached the upper levels of heaven. "Mommy, *you* aren't being fair! You gave this gift to me, but now you are taking some of it back. Can't you get Jasen his own box?"

I asked to step in, and peace-loving Brenda was only too happy to turn our strong-willed little girl over to me, but Mom was shocked to silence when I said, "Laura, I am going to let you make whatever decision you want on this one."

"Thanks, Daddy," Laura sniffled as her tear-stained face turned to smiles. The cavalry had arrived, and her precious bottles were safe from poachers.

"You're welcome, sweetheart. I know exactly how you feel about that gift because I once got a special present like that. But before you give me an answer about that bottle, I want you to understand that you are really answering a larger question, and it's this: *Do I want to live in a sharing world or an unsharing world?*"

"What do you mean, Daddy?"

"Well, if you decide not to share, I will have to remember that this is the kind of world you have chosen, and I'll have to keep that in mind the next time you want Jasen to share something with you. On the other hand, if you decide to give him a bottle, I'll know that you've chosen to live in a sharing world, so I'll try to make sure everyone shares with you. Do you understand?"

"I think so, Daddy."

"You're getting to be a big girl, so I tell you what, Peanut. I'll make sure that whatever you decide here will be respected by everyone in this house. So what do you say? Do you think you would like to live in a sharing world or an unsharing world?"

"I don't know," she said cautiously. "What do you think, Daddy?"

"When I make big decisions, I always go to the Bible to check out what Jesus

says. I'm quite sure that He says living in a sharing world is more pleasant than living in an unsharing world."

I could see that the decision was clearly gut-wrenching for Laura as her eyes
bounced between my face and her precious bottles. Her stomach had to be churning, and her little heart had to be beating overtime.

"I tell you what," I said. "If you choose to live in an unsharing world, I'll make
it easier for you. I'll only make you live in that world for three months. Of course,
that will include Christmas and New Year's, so your brothers and sisters won't have
to share anything with you over the holidays, but after that, you can go back to a
sharing world again."

Her eyes went to the bottle, then to Mom's face and to Jasen's and to Rebecca's,
and then she looked at the floor.

"Okay, sweetie, I know this is hard," I offered. "How about this? I'll drop that
time down to two months for you. Your unsharing world will still include Christmas, but it won't last all of Christmas break. You see? Now it won't cost you as
much to choose to live in that unsharing world, will it?"

Her eyes snapped up to mine and peered deeply into my face while she
weighed her decision one last time. "No, Daddy, I think Jesus is right. I think I
want to live in a sharing world."

She reached for one of her sand art bottles. "Jasen, can you come here? I'd like
to give you this."

What Laura did that afternoon was take her focus off the trees (the bottles) so
she could view the forest (her overall web of relationships). How might this relate
to your situation?

FROM BRENDA

It's Wednesday, ten o'clock in the morning—time for a little women's ministry. You
accept a cup of coffee, pick up half a doughnut, and find your seat, but your stomach is unsettled and apprehensive. Why's that? Because today's topic is pornography and how it relates to marriage. You know your husband is hooked like an
Alaskan salmon on the stuff, and he has no clue what he's doing to you. The truth

is, you are in the same gut-wrenching spot as my daughter Laura was—only about a hundred times worse because of the stakes involved. You're thinking, *What kind of world do I want to live in? Should I leave or should I stay?*

Your head is spinning, and it reels even more when you hear your friend Shirley proclaim her story:

My husband, Andy, has battled looking at other women during our entire marriage. We went to Christian counselor after Christian counselor, only to be told that all men do it. One counselor even suggested that I was the one driving my husband to this distraction because of my nagging. The final straw came when Andy announced, "If I have to keep from looking at women to be a Christian, I will serve Satan instead!"

Devastated and terrified, I cried out for the Holy Spirit for help. Instantly, a miracle happened. Andy broke down and confessed his sin and asked God to help him. I gave him *Every Man's Battle,* and I cannot tell you what God has done through this book. Overnight Andy has gone from being a baby Christian to walking as an obedient man. He confessed to our children about his worldliness and lack of commitment to Christ, he canceled cable TV into our home, and he has committed to reading God's Word every day.

Andy prays with me daily, and his head doesn't even flinch at the sight of a well-built, attractive woman. He has committed to rebuilding trust with me, to protect me, and to be the man that God has called him to be. He even calls me during the day from work just to remind me of his commitment to purity, and he asks me to hold him accountable. I tell you, it's a miracle!"

You may be smiling wanly and saying to yourself, *Just great! Shirley's testimony only piles insult on injury.* Then your soul mutters, *Where's my miracle? I've prayed, too, and for a whole lot longer!*

Maybe you've pondered the long, lonely, sexless years lying before you. Maybe you reason, *It's time to pack it in. I've already given him the best years of my life, and heaven knows I'm not getting any younger!*

You've put up with him for twelve years, and your feelings for him are dangling on life support. What are you going to do? Before you can think further, your attention is drawn back to a nearby table where you hear Karen admit, "Quite honestly, my husband is on his third and final try. I caught him lying last week when a charge from an Internet porn site appeared on our credit-card statement. I want to keep our family together, but I will not live with an unfaithful husband."

My sentiments exactly, you think to yourself, cheering her on in your heart. But before long your mind fades back into your own world again. *But divorce is so final! What would my brother say? And my friends? Besides, God hates divorce, doesn't He? Wasn't that in Malachi?*

Flipping your Bible open to Malachi, you find it in no time: " 'I hate divorce,' says the LORD God of Israel" (2:16).

Yep, there it is! And He couldn't have said it any clearer, you concede, and then you flip to the New Testament to read the reference suggested in the footnotes:

Some Pharisees came to him to test him. They asked, "Is it lawful for a man to divorce his wife for any and every reason?"

"Haven't you read," he replied, "that at the beginning the Creator 'made them male and female,' and said, 'For this reason a man will leave his father and mother and be united to his wife, and the two will become one flesh'? So they are no longer two, but one. Therefore, what God has joined together, let man not separate."

"Why then," they asked, "did Moses command that a man give his wife a certificate of divorce and send her away?"

Jesus replied, "Moses permitted you to divorce your wives because your hearts were hard. But it was not this way from the beginning." (Matthew 19:3-8)

Look at that! It's not irreconcilable differences that cause all our divorces after all! God didn't allow divorces because we *couldn't* love our spouses, but because of hardened hearts, we *wouldn't* love our spouses.

You wonder once more how things could have come to this in your marriage.

After all, God implies here that marriage should always work if we have soft, godly hearts.

Then Corrine's words snatch your attention back to the group as she confesses, "I have actually spoken to a Christian lawyer to begin the ground work if I decide to pursue a divorce. He thinks it would be considered an unbiblical divorce since my husband isn't having a physical affair.

"You want to know the sad part? Ever since that day, my level of intimacy with God seems lower than it's ever been before. I have no doubt about God's love for me and or that He understands my pain, but I don't feel worthy to come before His throne and ask for His help anymore. I understand clearly my own hardheartedness in this—I've chosen to purposely live this way while I'm deciding what I'm going to do."

Things then started hopping as Nancy grabs the floor and interjects in frustration, "You've got to be kidding! What kind of a lawyer is that? He's making a silly distinction! I was reading a note from my old college roommate yesterday, and she said that her self-esteem was devastated when her two ex-husbands sank into porn. To be honest, I get really angry at married men who look at pornography. They have no right to crush their wives that way."

You murmur, "You go, girl!" But you soon discover that was only Nancy's warmup before the main event. "These husbands don't *deserve* wives, if that's what they're going to do," she blasted. "They should just go off with their centerfolds and monitors to some filthy hole and live their happy little lives playing with themselves! How's that for my initial response on whether divorce is biblical in situations like this? These men make me sick! They're hitting a wife at her most vulnerable spot and desecrating the intimacy that should have been just between the two of them. These men are stomping all over Scripture, and I think a wife has every right, biblically, to leave a husband who won't get over this problem."

I'll say, you agree. Still, you wonder. For the rest of the morning, your mind keeps coming back to that interchange. *Well, who's right then, Corrine or Nancy? Can I leave or should I stay with my husband for the Lord's sake?*

Before you know it, the closing prayer is over. After some smiles and a few quick hugs, you head out to your car and onto the freeway. Your head is spinning, and you're *still* struggling with what to do.

FROM FRED

What happens if he still doesn't change in spite of your applying the helpmate's iron? I want you to understand that your Father understands both sides of this issue, just like I did with Laura. I also believe He has stepped into your situation through Scripture with a statement very similar to the one I made to my daughter. He's saying, "My little one, I am going to let you make whatever decision you want on this one, and I'm going to support you fully in whatever you decide."

The Christian church has always considered divorce a viable option in cases of adultery, based upon verses like this:

> I tell you that anyone who divorces his wife, except for marital unfaithfulness, and marries another woman commits adultery. (Matthew 19:9)

See? He's given you the choice. While divorce isn't required in the case of adultery, the Father certainly offers it as an option. But that begs an important question: is pornography and masturbation a form of adultery? Let's consider this verse:

> But I tell you that anyone who looks at a woman lustfully has already committed adultery with her in his heart. (Matthew 5:28)

If Jesus defines simply looking lustfully at a woman as adultery for the married man, certainly looking lustfully at a woman *and* masturbating is adultery. This seems indisputable to me.

There are others (mostly men) who would disagree, saying this doesn't reach the same level of viability in terms of divorce because of its addictive nature. I reject that categorically, considering that a rendezvous with your computer monitor is no less a conscious choice than an interlude with your mistress in the hot tub inside the Ritz-Carlton honeymoon suite. That type of behavior is betrayal, and when it goes on and on with no sign of repentance, I believe that divorce becomes a viable option scripturally, although I also believe that the shock of a separation must always precede it as a final effort to jar the prodigal husband to his senses.

Still, I believe that there is a much larger question to consider here, just as there was in my daughter's situation: what kind of world do you choose to live in? In Laura's case, it was pretty cut and dried—did she want to live in a sharing world or a selfish world? Her decision would impact no one but herself.

But your decision will impact many others, including those you love the most: your children (if you have any) and close family members. This decision merits all the adult wisdom you can muster. Before I go any further, you must know that this is your decision alone. I can confidently declare that no one has a right to judge your choice. No one else has walked in your shoes, and your Father has given you the freedom to stay or go.

Having said that, we're right back to our original question again: what kind of world do you choose to live in?

We know that you don't have full control of the kind of world you'll live in. But in your case, your husband has already let you down and stolen a part of your world. Sin corrupts everything, and your husband is still sinning. As long as he is, you will never have what God intended for marriage in terms of oneness, grace, or peace. Even if you stay, you will always struggle with your emotions over that loss.

But still, you must choose. What kind of world do you choose to live in?

- a merciful world?
- a forgiving world?
- a "sharing in Christ's sufferings" world?
- a "loving the unlovely" world?

These worlds are made up of bedrock Christianity, and they all sound noble indeed. They may even sound like the ones you should choose, as opposed to an avoid-all-pain world or even a "dump him, it's my turn" world.

But don't be too hasty to jump on nobility's wagon. Each of these worlds is very, very costly to live in, and each bears a potentially heavy loss for you. I am merely presenting the options, but I wouldn't attempt to manipulate your choice, because if your husband never turns to the Lord in repentance, each of these worlds is bleak in its own right. But it *is* your life and your decision to stay or go, and you must choose a world for better or for worse.

Like Laura, you can't know ahead of time the blessings or stresses that lie ahead of you. No two situations are alike, as each pair of temperaments and personalities is different. Even the depths of the addiction will vary from case to case. We have no simple maps or billowing platitudes to offer.

But also like Laura, your Father will go with you down either path you choose. I actually didn't care which path Laura chose, because I knew that I could teach her and improve her character no matter which way she ran. Your Father will work all things together for your good too.

Only one thing more is certain: no matter which way you choose, there will be a price to pay. In choosing the sharing world, Laura still lost her bottle, a pricey loss indeed. But she was at peace with that loss and far less grumpy than she would have been had Mom forced her hand. You have that same advantage, so be bold, take courage, and choose well. Your Father is kind, and He is with you.

Now we'd like to share the stories of two women, Meredith and Amy, and the worlds they've chosen for their marriages. As you'll see, there are no promises and no guarantees when choices are made. Their stories send a powerful message, and you should think about Meredith and Amy as you seek His face for the world you'll inhabit.

MEREDITH'S WORLD

I wasn't a Christian at first, so Ken and I watched porn together in our early years because I thought that's what everyone did. Sadly, he eventually became less interested in sex, became emotionally distant from me, and began to engage in several fetish activities.

When I realized that he preferred looking at porn and masturbating to having sex with me, I was so deeply hurt that I carry those scars with me to this day. I am a small woman who has kept a good figure in spite of having three children, so I thought it was especially cruel the day I found a porn magazine featuring extra large women. The day that I came home unexpectedly to find Ken wearing my lingerie still ranks very high on the humiliation scale, as well.

He has not admitted that there is anything wrong with his sexual tastes, and he has not fully participated in counseling, but I do not allow him to bring pornography into our home anymore.

Why did I stay with him? I treasure marriage and what it stands for in God's kingdom. I chose to deal with it as my "cross to bear," and I saw it as my sacrifice of love to Jesus. While my marriage can never fully picture Christ's relationship to the church, I can at least do my part to forgive him and be merciful. I want to live in a merciful world.

So, in spite of this secret sin, I worked hard to create a good marriage and raise healthy, happy, and productive children. In order to accomplish this, I allowed my husband to be emotionally absent and focused my energy on volunteer activities and work. However, after twenty-nine years of marriage and after recently being told that he doesn't find me sexually desirable, I am reassessing my situation. I'm now considering a separation or divorce.

I always lived up to the world I'd chosen. I have been extremely merciful to him, and only lately has my mercy begun to wane as I've asked him to do the work to keep the marriage together, to seek the counseling, to make the effort. He is either unwilling or unable to.

For whatever reason, I believed that when the kids were grown, our life together would become more intimate, but instead he's just not interested. I feel angry and cheated of love, warmth, and being cherished.

But if I'm honest, I know I could never have all of what God intended for marriage, so I can live with the emotions for the most part. I didn't exactly predict this ending, but I don't regret my original decision, because some real advantages came along with it.

For instance, I have learned the price and value of commitment to a depth that most people never will. By staying together, we have three adult children unscarred by the divorce of their parents. Ken and I also have a long history together as a couple, so in many ways we are great friends. Surprisingly, we still have a lot of laughs and can get along pretty well outside the bedroom.

That's not to say there weren't heavy costs on many levels, because there were. As an individual, I feel so degraded and unlovely. I lied to myself for years about my attractiveness, appearance, gifts, and sexuality. The wife in me feels extremely beat up, but the real woman inside is wondering whether she should come out and be everything that she was intended to be. It's quite a wrestling match.

As a couple, there've been endless costs. Sexually, all we have is a quiet truce. I am merely a service station, but I'll admit part of that is my fault. Because I have enabled him for so long to have sex without filling any of my needs, intercourse is just something to get through for me.

Why do I keep it up? Sad as it is to say it, if it weren't for those irregular interludes in the bedroom, I would never know any physical touch, sexual or otherwise, and as faulty as that is, it's better than nothing.

There have been other costs outside the bedroom as my minimal trust in Ken has spilled into other areas of our relationship as we age. *Can I trust him to take care of me when I'm ill? When I grow old?* History has proven this to be a no. And what about the newest issue I can't stop thinking about all the time: *Can I trust him to do the right things with our little bit of savings we have for retirement?*

My kids didn't really escape unscathed, either. While they never knew the pain of divorce, I know firsthand how sexual sickness affects an entire family—very painfully. Life seemed to be going peaceably with these incidents behind us until our youngest daughter started counseling for some issues she has. Turns out, her view of herself and her relationship with her father still stems from an incident many years ago when she came across porn in a shared desk. Ken blamed the whole thing on her for snooping.

Ken now understands how wrong that was, but who could have projected that such a little incident would have such a lasting effect on my daughter? She is desperately suffering and will be in counseling for some time because of it.

I want to beat Ken for deeply wounding this dear child so many years ago. As far as I'm concerned, he sacrificed his daughter on the altar of his addiction and the emotional distance that it causes. I also worry about how my husband's sexual sin has hurt our daughters and son in other ways. Will this generational sin continue through my son? My girls have great pain because their father was emotionally unattached and has been reluctant to give them healthy touches. They feel lost and adrift as adult women because of it. Both are in counseling.

I get so angry when people talk about how harmless porn is, and I want to shout the truth from the rooftops, but I also want to hold in my arms and comfort every wife who has felt the emotional distance that I've felt.

And so here we are today. What do I do now that the kids are gone? I guess I'm at another point of decision. Do I want to stay in this merciful world? I could remove myself from my regular disappointment, or I could continue to grow old with this man, become a grandma, and no one will ever be the wiser.

But while I know that Jesus is all about mercy, I've also come to know quite vividly that Jesus is about truth. And through my enabling him to sink deeper into an unhealthy world, Ken was allowed to escape the laws of reaping and sowing and to continue as if everything was all right. Isn't it time to allow those laws to have their effects?

But would Jesus forgive me if I left Ken? How long is the statute of limitations on the infidelity of Ken's mind? Would Jesus look at the pain of a heart neglected for twenty-nine years and feel compassion and mercy for me?

In spite of these twenty-nine long years, I still care deeply about Jesus, and I've learned to lean harder on Him as a result. Of course, I have to admit that sometimes I get mad at God because He doesn't have arms and legs that can caress me. According to the Bible, Jesus is supposed to be my husband, and I understand that He meant that in a spiritual sense, but that doesn't make up for the deprivation of touch that I feel.

Still, all in all, Jesus has been faithful, and I could not have done any of this without Him. I am obviously sad, bitter, and angry, but I also realize that the Christian life is one of struggle, and I'm at peace with that. And in spite of all this, and as surprising as it sounds, I still love my husband dearly. But I still struggle with whether I should leave him.

AMY'S WORLD

I've stayed with my husband for more than twenty years, and I've learned that when sex becomes more important than one's spouse or marriage relationship, then sex is an addiction. The fact that this addiction remains within the confines of the marriage bed doesn't make it less serious or sinful. It only makes it easier to hide.

When my husband and I got married, we used Vaseline to facilitate penetration. Our first time in bed should've gone quite easily—we were in the missionary position—but it proved quite painful for me as I felt something tear. I found myself writhing and scooting up the bed, away from my husband. Finally, I stopped pulling away as my head and back began moving up against the head-board into a partial sitting position. I'd run out of room and was afraid of hurting my husband's back, since he was now being bent backward. When he was done, he asked me why I kept pulling away. I told him why, and he simply stated, "It couldn't have hurt; we used Vaseline."

From then on, he demanded sex every day, even during my periods. He didn't ask again why I crawled away, as I kept doing for a few days. With time, sex became less painful, more along the lines of a paper cut. Finally, I convinced my husband to leave me alone during my periods, which helped me to heal. But his overall lack of tenderness or concern was my first hint of the sexual abuse to come.

Though my husband never hit me, I never was more than the house slave to him and our three children and a sexual slave for him. While I knew that sex had never been good for our relationship, ranging from painful to demanded to demeaning or simply to boring, I didn't realize just how much it meant to my hus-band until we went for marriage counseling.

My husband then made it clear that sex was due him, and that he was entitled to it unconditionally. If I was refusing sex to him, I was refusing love to him, and if I didn't find it enjoyable, it was because I was frigid. It also became clear that he was only willing to work on our relationship as a means to get sex.

My husband was hooked on sex, and when I first realized that, I was shocked, but I could finally understand the despair of the slaves of times past. What choice did I have? He hadn't committed adultery, so there was no Christian way out for me. I couldn't even hope to be "sold to another master" where things might be better.

Eventually, the cumulative anger of sixteen years of verbal, emotional, spir-itual, and sexual abuse took its toll. I would have kicked him out of our home, except I got pregnant with our third child. Obviously, a sexually satisfied husband doesn't automatically yield a thoughtful husband, as so many books claim. To the contrary, too many husbands see a healthy sex life as a sign that there are no prob-lems in their marriage.

Three years ago I gave my husband a choice. He could agree to set sex aside in a moratorium and work on our relationship until we reach the point where sex would be desired by and enjoyable for both of us, or we could keep on having sex under certain conditions that I would define, with the understanding that there would come a point when I wouldn't be able to stand it anymore. Whenever that point would be reached—five years, ten years, I didn't know—sex would be over for good. I was flabbergasted when he chose sex. So I set the conditions: once a week, no rain check, and don't expect me to pretend I'm into it!

One year later I found myself despising and hating him for how he was using me. I can't understand how anyone could choose to use his wife as an inflatable doll rather than having a loving, respectful relationship. That's the last time we had sex. I didn't want that thing to destroy all hopes for our relationship, and I knew that if he kept on using me for sex, there would come a point when I would hate him so much that we could never remain married.

We are now separated. My husband says that Christian couples can abstain from sex solely for the purpose of prayer and for a short while, therefore a sexual separation is intrinsically sinful. When I countered with the verse about a husband loving his wife like Christ loves the church, he replied that he feels love toward me, so therefore he is fulfilling that verse. Then I lowered the boom with this question: "Craig, can you tell me that you would still be a Christian if Christ had loved you in the same way you have loved me in this marriage?" He offered no answer.

Years ago I made a choice to stay with Craig and to live in a merciful world. Why? Because I love Craig, and I still do. I also love the concept of marriage, and I love my kids and didn't want them to face divorce. I meant what I promised on my wedding day, for better or for worse.

Besides, I always believed that God would get through to Craig if I just held out in faith. When we met in college, we were part of the same small-group Bible study during our first year and led one together during our second year. We started dating in our third year, and we were married in our fourth. The Lord and His work were central to everything we were from the beginning.

But after college, that all stopped. Craig said he already knew the Bible well enough. When our relationship was at its worse, I asked him to do a Bible study on love, but he refused. I asked him to pray with me, but he refused. When he finally agreed to pray regularly, that simply meant listening to him pray for twenty minutes on end, either as a lecture to me or as his spectator. Worst of all, good prayer made him think of sex, which was the last thing I needed.

While I don't regret my original decision to stay, and I suppose I would do it again, I have paid a heavy price spiritually. I have a hard time reading the Bible to the children or even praying with them, given my relationship with God. My marriage has taught me not to count on the Lord. While He requires us to risk and sacrifice our lives to help others around us and to bring them to Christ, when it comes to our own desperate plight, He just stands on the wayside with His arms crossed doing nothing, hiding behind His gift of free will. *Amy, I'm sorry if you are being raped by your husband, but I can't intervene, you know. Free will, and all that sort of thing.*

At this point in my life, I find His reasoning deficient and I seriously dislike God for all that He allows. I know He never promised to protect us, but only that all things would come together for good for those who love Him. His principle is simple: sacrifice yourself, get crucified, go through hell, and be resurrected. Still, I am not Jesus, and I don't have the fullness of God in me, just a portion. I only see darkly, and I am tired of going through hell and all the destruction over the years.

We are thrown blindly into situations with only "do right" as our directive. "Turn the other cheek." So we end up with the spiritual equivalent of shaken-baby syndrome after years of having our head slapped one way and then the other, simply because we were trying to do the right thing. How fair is that?

I used to have intimacy with God, but now when I think of Him, I back away. I just can't trust His touch. Oh, I know that He loves me. But it also seems that He loves some more than others and that He blesses some and not others.

God not only allowed my adult life to be destroyed, but He also allowed the seeds of destruction to be planted in my children's lives, with heavy spiritual prices just now coming home to roost. Our oldest is in college and questioning her faith. Our fifteen-year-old boy has decided that there is no God and that praying is useless. "It never helped you and Dad!" He's right. What can I say?

I hope at some point to regain some intimacy with God, and I might even feel the need to get involved in a church. Right now, the church I attend with the kids fits my needs. Nobody asks me anything. It might sound unfriendly, but this is exactly what I need—to be left alone. The worship is a bit boring but honest and sincere, and it leaves me free to worship if I can find it in me.

As to how my relationship with my husband is going, it's all in Craig's hands. Our state law doesn't offer no-fault divorce, and a contested divorce can take years and a lot of money. I am hoping Craig will reach the point where he would rather spend that time and money on counseling and in dealing honestly with his issues, including his sexual addiction. I am not using my separation as a precursor to divorce. I'm using it as a shock to get his attention and hoping that the laws of reaping and sowing will turn his head and his heart back to me.

In spite of it all, I still love my husband. Craig is not a monster—he is simply an unrepentant abuser. His heart is not too far away for God to reach, and I hope for him, for me, and for our children that Craig allows Him to draw near.

From Brenda

Wow! Those were a couple of heavy, heavy stories. As we've said, if your husband won't turn to the Lord, any world you choose will have its costs, and each will bear a potentially heavy loss for you. There is a great danger in suspending the laws of reaping and sowing in your husband's life—it can even backfire and bankrupt your faith in the end. You must be careful not to suspend these laws indefinitely.

Amy chose mercy but suspended these laws too long in her effort to do right by God. She now blames Him, but this was not God's fault, and neither is His Word the least bit faulty. The fault lies with the lopsided, wounding teaching of the Christian church regarding headship and submission in marriage. By obsessing endlessly from the pulpit over the wife's role as "submitter" while largely ignoring her equally vital helper's role as iron sharpening iron, we've falsely inflated the *covenant* aspects of marriage (shut up and take it, no matter what) over the *relational responsibilities* of the husband to deliver oneness and intimacy to his marriage. This leaves wives to endure unspeakable emotional beatings at the hands of narrow, hardhearted husbands, with no recourse at all in the name of Christ.

Yet none of this lopsided "truth" has anything to do with Christ, and it bears no resemblance to His law of love, upon which all of God's truth hangs (see Matthew 22:37-40). Like so many people in our congregations, Amy was led to believe that suspending the laws of reaping and sowing indefinitely in her husband's life by quietly "taking it all" was God's complete truth, but it isn't. Submitting quietly is not a wife's only role in marriage, and it sometimes conflicts with the proper discharge of her helper's role (to lift her husband towards normality in

Christ). While God loves mercy and a wife's submission to her husband's author-ity, He never taught that we are to turn our cheek to any and every behavior in marriage, though insipid feel-good, leave-them-smiling-when-you-go preaching often implies that.

The church let Amy down here, but that can happen. The church sees through a glass darkly too, and will never be perfect. As a wife making your difficult deci-sion on whether to stay or go, you must understand this. All of your decisions must be based upon His full Word, not upon the lopsided teaching of the church alone. Only then will your faith stand through to the end, no matter what your husband does, and only then will you feel free to take any appropriate actions before your husband's unrepentant heart bankrupts your faith and shatters your soul.

Granted, nothing is easy here. All we know is that while each world will be bleak in its own way, each will also have its rewards, so choose well. There are no easy answers and certainly no guaranteed outcomes, but we pray that God will bless you as you choose. May your ear hear His truth, and may His love and grace carry you home.

SUGGESTED READING

If you are thinking about divorce, we counsel you to read the following books on divorce and its effects before you take any serious steps in that direction. Please don't make a decision without a clear understanding of the high costs of divorce. From Fred's point of view as a child of divorce, Jen's book is a masterpiece.

Generation Ex: Adult Children of Divorce and the Healing of Our Pain
    by Jen Abbas

Divorce-Proofing Your Marriage by Gary and Barbara Rosberg

An Affair of the Mind by Laurie Hall: *biography of one woman's battle to cope with her husband's sexual sin*

our parting thoughts

FROM FRED

As we close this final volume of our six-book portion of the Every Man series, Brenda and I are overwhelmed and thankful that we have been able to share what God planted in our hearts.

There have been countless indelible moments, like the times we watched God effortlessly open closed doors to publish *Every Man's Battle*. When that first book hit the shelves, Brenda turned to me, stricken with awe and tears, and said, "It's just like watching the Red Sea open before our eyes."

But we have to tell you that writing *Every Heart Restored* brought incredible spiritual pressures on us. So often I was broken to tears as I read painful e-mail after painful e-mail from crushed wives, with nothing to do but limp away to my prayer room. Time after time I was overcome emotionally by God's presence even before I entered the room.

It was mind-blowing to experience His sustained, tenacious attention to this project, and I only wish you could have been here to feel it. I could scarcely believe my senses. God cares unbelievably about you, His broken daughter. His love for you is intense, passionate, relentless—like a father desperately digging to save his child from a dark, frightening hole.

From here on out as you deal with a difficult situation with your husband, turn to Him fully. His heart is clamoring for yours, and His eyes are ever upon you.

FROM BRENDA

I wish I could sit with each of you right now to reach out and cry and pray with you. That isn't a platitude but rather a concession to the shocking pain that your husband's sexual sin has had upon you and your relationship.

Our prayer is that these pages of *Every Heart Restored* will restore your heart in the coming days. Serve your Father well, my friend. He loves you, and so do we.

start a bible study
and connect with others
who want to be God's man.

Every Man Bible Studies are designed to help you discover, own, and build
on convictions grounded in God's word. Available now in bookstores.

WATERBROOK
PRESS

every man's battle workshops

from New Life Ministries

new Life Ministries receives hundreds of calls every month from Christian men who are struggling to stay pure in the midst of daily challenges to their sexual integrity and from pastors who are looking for guidance in how to keep fragile marriages from falling apart all around them.

As part of our commitment to equip individuals to win these battles, New Life Ministries has developed biblically based workshops directly geared to answer these needs. These workshops are held several times per year around the country.

- Our workshops **for men** are structured to equip men with the tools necessary to maintain sexual integrity and enjoy healthy, productive relationships.

- Our workshops **for church leaders** are targeted to help pastors and men's ministry leaders develop programs to help families being attacked by this destructive addiction.

Some comments from previous workshop attendees:

"An awesome, life-changing experience. Awesome teaching, teacher, content and program." —DAVE

"God has truly worked a great work in me since the EMB workshop. I am fully confident that with God's help, I will be restored in my ministry position. Thank you for your concern. I realize that this is a battle, but I now have the weapons of warfare as mentioned in Ephesians 6:10, and I am using them to gain victory!" —KEN

"It's great to have a workshop you can confidently recommend to anyone without hesitation, knowing that it is truly life changing. Your labors are not in vain!" —DR. BRAD STENBERG, Pasadena, CA

If sexual temptation is threatening your marriage or your church, please call **1-800-NEW-LIFE** to speak with one of our specialists.

guys aren't the only ones fighting a battle for purity

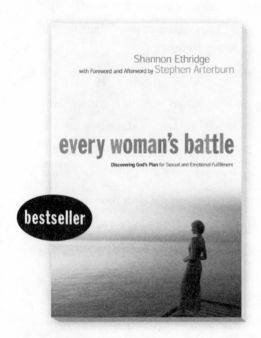